The Forensic Laboratory Handbook

FORENSIC
SCIENCE AND MEDICINE

Steven B. Karch, MD, SERIES EDITOR

THE FORENSIC LABORATORY HANDBOOK

Procedures and Practice

Edited by

Ashraf Mozayani, PharmD, PhD, D-ABFT

Harris County Medical Examiner's Office
Houston, TX

Carla Noziglia, MS

Forensic Scientist
Coral Springs, FL
and
Senior Forensic Advisor
Tanzania, Africa

HUMANA PRESS
TOTOWA, NEW JERSEY

© 2006 Humana Press Inc.
999 Riverview Drive, Suite 208
Totowa, New Jersey 07512
www.humanapress.com

This publication is printed on acid-free paper. ∞

ANSI Z39.48-1984 (American Standards Institute) Permanence of Paper for Printed Library Materials.

Cover Illustration: Cover images (top to bottom): Figures 10 and 18 from Chapter 5, "Explosives and Arson: Boom and Flame," by James B. Crippin; Figure 2 from Chapter 7, "Firearms and Tool Marks," by Edward E. Hueske; Figure 1 from Chapter 11, "Introduction to Forensic Document Examination," by William L. Leaver; and Figure 7D from Chapter 6, "Fingerprints," by Brian E. Dalrymple.

Production Editor: Amy Thau

Cover design by Patricia F. Cleary

For additional copies, pricing for bulk purchases, and/or information about other Humana titles, contact Humana at the above address or at any of the following numbers: Tel: 973-256-1699; Fax: 973-256-8341; E-mail: orders@humanapr.com, or visit our Website at www.humanapress.com

Printed in the United States of America. 10 9 8 7 6 5 4 3 2 1

eISBN: 1-59259-946-X

Library of Congress Cataloging-in-Publication Data

The forensic laboratory handbook : procedures and practice / edited
by Ashraf Mozayani, Carla Noziglia.
   p. cm. -- (Forensic science and medicine)
Includes bibliographical references and index.
   ISBN 1-58829-464-1 (alk. paper)
  1. Crime laboratories. 2. Forensic sciences. I. Mozayani,
Ashraf. II. Noziglia, Carla. III. Series.
  HV8073.F577 2006
   363.25--dc22
                                          2005010942

Preface

"If the law has made you a witness, remain a man of science. You have no victim to avenge, no guilty or innocent person to convict or save— you must bear testimony within the limits of science."

Dr. P. C. H. Brouardel
19th-century French medico-legalist

The media abound with references to and programs about forensic science. No mystery story seems complete without a reference to DNA evidence or a trip to the laboratory for DNA analysis. Sometimes, the main characters are forensic scientists. There are things to be learned from these media happenings and truth does enter into the plots, making them fascinating to watch and read. From such television shows as *Quincy* in the 1970s to *CSI: New York* in 2004, and from the motion picture *The Bone Collector* to the recent television show *Forensic Files*, forensic science has perennially shown the power to entertain.

These media portrayals also educate us, but often, this "education" proves to be more fantasy than reality. *The Forensic Laboratory Handbook: Procedures and Practice* was written for the purpose of separating fiction from reality by demonstrating the real-life practices of forensic laboratories.

The work performed by forensic scientists in the field, forensic laboratories, medical examiners offices, and private companies is often critical to the proper functioning of the justice system and regulatory bodies. Forensic analysis has provided fresh information in "cold cases," served to identify the last descendants of the Russian imperial family, and exonerated the wrongfully convicted. This is not to say that the original analyses were flawed, but rather that new technology provides more and better information.

Where would society be without the analysis and comparison of fingerprints, bullets, DNA, and handwriting? The identification of drugs, flammables, bones, and explosives is often central to a case. Newer applications of technologies are used in investigating cyber crime, bite marks, and the reconstruction of a crime scene or a face from a skull.

With such an important place in the justice system, the integrity of scientific information is crucial. The ethical analysis of evidence must be a given constant. The exchange of new technology and open access to scientific information assists others in understanding, and possibly implementing, new procedures.

Although the job of a forensic scientist is important and one of the most satisfying of career choices, as with every other profession, the work can sometimes seem mundane and repetitious. Although many media programs may portray some aspects of the profession correctly, they also tend to glamorize the jobs. In the media, many separate jobs are rolled into one so that the story flows better and the crime is solved in the time allowed. Cases that in reality would take months or even years to solve are wrapped up in 42 minutes on television. Not mentioned is the time needed to describe and prepare the evidence for analysis, the expertise needed to interpret the results, the time spent writing the scientific report, and the time spent in court giving expert testimony. Add the time spent educating law enforcement, attorneys, and judges, and the time spent in training to ensure that the scientist is on the cutting edge with specialized skills and you can well appreciate the demands placed on forensic professionals.

The forensic scientists who wrote the chapters in *The Forensic Laboratory Handbook: Procedures and Practice* are real—they actually do what they write about. Each is an unsung hero, a seeker of truth, a dedicated scientist. They will tell you how it is in a real forensic laboratory, and it will be a fascinating story.

Ashraf Mozayani, PharmD, PhD, D-ABFT
Carla Noziglia, MS

Contents

Contributors

ROBERT P. BIANCHI, BS • Bianchi Consulting, Fairfax, VA

RICHARD E. BISBING, BS • Vice President and Director of Research, McCrone Associates Inc., Westmont, IL

JOYE M. CARTER, MD • Forensic Pathologist, Consultant, Author, and Lecturer, J & M Forensic Consulting, Memphis, TN

W. JERRY CHISUM, BS • Independent Consultant, Elk Grove, CA

DONNELL CHRISTIAN, BS • CEO and Senior Forensic Advisor, Criminalist.us, Professional Business Solutions Inc., St. Louis, MO

JAMES B. CRIPPIN, BS • Director, Western Forensic Law Enforcement Training Center; Department of Chemistry, Colorado State University, Pueblo, CO

BRIAN E. DALRYMPLE, AOCA • President, Brian Dalrymple and Associates, Orillia, Ontario, Canada

LISA A. GEFRIDES, MS • Forensic DNA Analyst, Harris County Medical Examiner's Office, Houston, TX

EDWARD E. HUESKE, MA • Criminalistics Coordinator, University of North Texas, Denton, TX

WILLIAM L. LEAVER, BS, D-ABFDE • Forensic Document Examiner, Los Angeles County Sheriff's Department, Scientific Services Bureau, Downey, CA

ASHRAF MOZAYANI, PharmD, PhD, D-ABFT • Harris County Medical Examiner's Office, Houston, TX

CARLA M. NOZIGLIA, MS, FAAFS • Forensic Scientist, Coral Springs, FL; Senior Forensic Advisor, Tanzania, Africa

MARK POLLITT, MS • President, Digital Evidence Professional Services, Inc., Ellicott City, MD

HELENA SOOMER, DDS, PhD • Forensic Odontologist, Estonian Disaster Victim Identification Team, Tallinn, Estonia

WILLIAM J. TILSTONE, PhD • Executive Director, National Forensic Technology Science Center, Largo, FL

KATHERINE E. WELCH, MS • Harris County Medical Examiner's Office, Houston, TX

List of Color Plates

Color Plate to follow p. 182.

Chapter 1

Serology and DNA

Lisa A. Gefrides, MS and Katherine E. Welch, MS

1. INTRODUCTION

In the forensic community, serology and DNA analyses are closely related. In fact, in many laboratories they are included within the same personnel section. In the forensic crime laboratory, "serology analysis" refers to the screening of evidence for bodily fluids, whereas "DNA analysis" refers to the efforts to individualize bodily fluids to a specific person. In most cases, bodily fluid identification is performed on evidentiary items before DNA analysis is attempted. Depending on the qualifications of laboratory personnel, analysts can be trained to perform either serology or DNA analysis or can be trained in both disciplines. Although serology procedures have been employed for most of the 20th century and the techniques have essentially remained unchanged, DNA has emerged in the forensic realm within the last two decades and its applications and technology are continuously developing.

2. TYPES OF EVIDENCE EXAMINED

The types of evidence submitted to crime laboratories for serology/DNA analysis are those items on which bodily fluids are thought to be present. A large majority of DNA/serology cases involve sexual assaults. Evidence from these types of cases commonly includes sexual assault kits, complainant clothing, bedding, and sometimes suspect clothing. Other common case submissions include potential blood evidence from homicides, aggravated assaults, and burglaries. Items commonly submitted for blood testing include swabbings from crime scenes, clothing, weapons, or any number of other items that may

From: *The Forensic Laboratory Handbook: Procedures and Practice*
Edited by: A. Mozayani and C. Noziglia © Humana Press Inc., Totowa, NJ

possess bloodstains. If an item is small it can be submitted to the laboratory in its entirety. For larger items, stains can either be collected onto a sterile cotton swab or a cutting from the item can be taken for submission.

It is also possible to collect items that have been in contact with an individual's mouth, e.g., cigarette butts, drinking cans, cups, bottles, gum, candy, toothbrushes, or ski masks. These items usually provide enough DNA for a profile to be established. Objects that have been touched or handled, e.g., a steering wheel, gun, phone, or even a fingerprint may also contain biological evidence that can be collected for analysis, but may not always produce a DNA profile. Generally, all these pieces of evidence do not contain a substantial amount of biological material and are processed for DNA without going through any type of serological screening to maximize the amount of sample available for DNA testing.

Cases involving kinship determination do not require serology screening and can also be sent immediately for DNA analysis. Most often, DNA profile comparisons to determine kinship are used in cases of criminal paternity, child abandonment, or identification of remains. All of these cases rely on the comparison of known DNA profiles from individuals to determine whether two people are related, as opposed to the comparison of evidence to a known profile to determine the source of the biological fluid on a piece of evidence.

Reference samples from known individuals are used for kinship determination and also for comparison to evidentiary samples. Typically, blood or saliva is collected from a living individual to serve as a reference sample. Blood is collected intravenously and stored in a purple or lavender top blood tube, which contains an additive to prevent DNA from becoming degraded. The blood is then placed onto a filter paper card, dried, and stored. Blood samples dried in this manner are stable for many years even at room temperature. Saliva can be collected either by chewing sterile gauze, by depositing saliva onto a collection card, or by swabbing the inside of a person's cheeks (buccal swabs) to collect epithelial cells. Pulled hairs can also be used as a reference sample, but are not as abundant a source of DNA and, therefore, are not preferred. Reference samples can also be collected from deceased individuals in the form of blood, tissue samples, or bone samples depending on the state of decomposition of the remains.

3. PLANNING THE EXAMINATION

The real challenge in evidence screening is determining which items of evidence should be processed and the most effective way in which to process them. In general, probative samples are those in which a transfer of bodily fluids, and therefore DNA, has occurred. A suspect's bodily fluid on a complainant's body or clothing, or a complainant's bodily fluid present on clothing or items belonging to a suspect are the objects that hold the most evidentiary, or probative, value. For some cases, the most logical course of evidence examination is rather obvious. For example, in most cases of sexual assault the identification of semen is central to supporting a claim of sexual assault. Furthermore, semen found on swabs in a sexual assault kit may have more probative value than semen found on clothing or bedding because, along with demonstrating the presence of semen on the complainant, semen can only survive inside a victim for a finite amount of time whereas semen stains on clothing or bedding can have a much longer duration depending on whether the evidence is washed. For these cases, a determination can be readily made for the type of testing to perform and for the most efficient order in which to process the items. Other cases are less obvious. If a sexual assault is oral, digital, or utilizing a foreign object, then it is useful to determine the details associated with the alleged assault to process the evidence most effectively. In sexual assault cases where semen is not alleged, examining an item for the presence of semen may have no evidentiary value. All cases may be affected by any post-assault activity by the victim, such as washing, wiping, eating, drinking, etc. The time between the assault and the examination can be a critical factor in the successful identification of bodily fluids because the longer the time span, the more evidence that may be lost.

Homicide cases are more time-consuming to process than other types of cases because the victim cannot verbally relate any details of the assault. Homicides generally involve many items of evidence that must be analyzed because a determination cannot always be made on which evidence is the most probative. Thorough crime scene investigation is essential to ensure that probative items in a case are collected and submitted to the laboratory. In addition, important case details should be communicated to the laboratory analysts to ensure that evidentiary items are processed in the most logical manner.

When evidence is submitted, a determination must be made as to whether that evidence must go through serology screening or whether the evidence can be sent directly for DNA analysis. Generally, all evidence goes through serology screening first. However, cases involving samples with trace amounts of DNA may not benefit from serology screening. Paternity and remains identification cases also do not require any type of serology screening because only reference samples are processed.

Criminal paternity cases involve a sexual assault in which conception occurs. For these sexual assault cases, serology analysis is rarely performed. Instead, DNA analysis can be performed on the conceptus (living or aborted) and on the alleged father in order to establish or disprove parentage (paternity testing). Although it is not necessary to have a reference sample from the mother/complainant for paternity testing, having the DNA profiles of the off-spring and both parents facilitates the DNA interpretation. Maternity/paternity testing can also be used in cases of child abandonment to establish whether a suspected individual is a parent by comparing the profiles obtained from the child and alleged parent(s).

Comparing DNA profiles to test for kinship is also useful for remains identification and missing person cases. DNA can be collected from the blood or tissue of a decedent or from skeletal remains and compared to the blood or saliva from a potential relative. In cases where there is a suspected identity for a set of remains, the profile of the deceased can be directly compared to a family member for confirmation. In some cases, investigators may have no idea of the identity of the deceased individual. Unidentified remains can be analyzed and DNA profiles placed into a database of missing persons. Relatives of individuals who are missing can also be placed into this database to be searched against unidentified remains with the hope of establishing a relationship. Depending on the type of DNA analysis performed, kinship can be established from immediate family members to aunts, uncles, cousins, or, possibly, even more distant relatives.

4. EVIDENCE PROCESSING, NOTE TAKING, AND REPORT WRITING

Most of the evidence processing and note taking occurs during serology analysis because this is usually the first time evidence is opened in the laboratory. Serologists are responsible for documenting the type, quantity, and packaging of the evidence received. In addition, a description of the evidence with notes and diagrams or pictures regarding the types of stains present and their location on each item is placed into the case file. Serologists also take detailed notes of their testing and outcomes. This documentation is referenced during an analyst's testimony during criminal proceedings. Thorough and precise note taking is essential because there may be a substantial amount of time between the completion of case analysis and an analyst's testimony in court. It is also important in circumstances where a different analyst must interpret the case notes.

Reports are written copies of an analyst's findings and should be an accurate representation of the results as they would be testified to during criminal proceedings. Results should be conservatively stated and should take into account guidelines established by the forensic community and accrediting agencies. Reporting statements should also take into account the individuals who will be receiving the results. Police officers, attorneys for both parties, and jurors may find the scientific principles behind serology and DNA analyses difficult to interpret. For this reason, reporting statements should be clearly written and in layman's terms whenever possible.

5. SEROLOGY TESTING

Serology methods are relatively simple and straightforward. Forensic serology is not to be confused with conventional serology, which deals solely with serum and its properties. Instead, forensic serology involves the identification of many different types of bodily fluids. The identification of biological fluids during serology analysis is accomplished through presumptive and confirmatory testing. Presumptive testing refers to testing that is sensitive, fairly specific to the bodily fluid in question, and can be performed quickly. It allows an analyst to narrow down the number of items or areas of an item to focus on for further testing. Presumptive testing can only indicate that a bodily fluid *might* be present on an item. It is not considered specific enough to state that a particular bodily fluid is unequivocally present on an item because other substances may also produce a positive test result, known as a "false-positive." The limitations and types of false-positive reactions will be discussed for each particular presumptive test in the subsequent sections.

Confirmatory testing is specific to the bodily fluid in question and sometimes also to a particular species. Confirmatory testing is still sensitive, but the time required for the testing can be much longer than that required for presumptive testing. In some instances, DNA analysis can be considered a type of confirmatory test because it is species, although not bodily fluid, specific for human DNA. Confirmatory testing is discussed in more detail under Subheadings 5.1.3, 5.1.4, and 5.2.2.

5.1. Identification of Semen

The identification of semen is important in many cases of alleged sexual assault. Semen is a bodily fluid produced by male individuals for fertilization. For forensic purposes, the composition of semen can be simplified into two components: seminal fluid and spermatozoa. Seminal fluid is a protein rich bodily fluid originating primarily from the prostate and seminal vesicles. Spermatozoa, commonly referred to as "sperm," are the male gametes, or sex cells, produced in the testis. Not all men produce spermatozoa. In men who have had a vasectomy, certain birth defects, or as the result of some diseases, seminal fluid will either not contain spermatozoa or contain very few. Therefore, it is useful to be able to forensically test for the presence of both seminal fluid and spermatozoa.

5.1.1. Acid Phosphatase Screening

The most commonly used presumptive test for the detection of seminal fluid relies on the identification of an enzyme known as acid phosphatase (AP). The AP that is present in seminal fluid originates in the prostate. Bodily fluids, such as blood, saliva, urine, vaginal secretions, and others also contain AP. However, the amount of AP in seminal fluid is greater than that found in other tissues. It is this property that makes AP important for the screening of seminal fluid. The detection of AP is only considered a presumptive identification of seminal fluid because other bodily fluids might also give a positive reaction; therefore, a positive test result indicates the possible presence of seminal fluid, but its actual presence must be confirmed by other testing methods.

AP is identified in most forensic laboratories by using the Brentamine spot test, which commonly employs the chemicals α-napthyl phosphate and diazo blue dye in a buffered solution. When these chemicals are placed onto an item where seminal fluid is present, the tested area quickly changes to a purple color. It is not advisable to test evidentiary items directly because of the possibility of contamination and also because the chemicals used in AP detection may interfere with subsequent analysis. Instead, a small portion of the stain is either cut from the item or some of the stain is transferred to sterile filter paper or a sterile cotton swab for testing. The speed and intensity of the color change reaction can be used to determine if the stain in question is seminal fluid. A rapid color change with intense coloration strongly indicates that a stain is seminal fluid. A slow and weak color change may either indicate a small amount of seminal fluid or the presence of a different bodily fluid containing AP. Because the test for AP is very sensitive, a lack of color change may indicate that no seminal fluid is present; however, it may also indicate that the level of AP is below the detection limit of the test. There have been instances in which spermatozoa were found from a stain negative for AP. For this reason, both negative and positive results must be interpreted with caution. Further testing may be required to confirm the presence or absence of semen.

5.1.2. Alternate Light Source or Ultraviolet Light

It would be time consuming, costly, and tedious to test large items in their entirety for the presence of AP using the Brentamine test. Instead, large items are visually examined and stained areas are identified and tested. Unfortunately, not all semen stains are visible to the naked eye depending on the amount of semen deposited and the fabric on which the deposition was made. To enable the laboratory analyst to identify these nonvisible stained areas, a method utilizing an alternate light source is applied to prescreen evidence in an effort to identify discrete areas for AP testing. Many bodily fluids fluoresce when

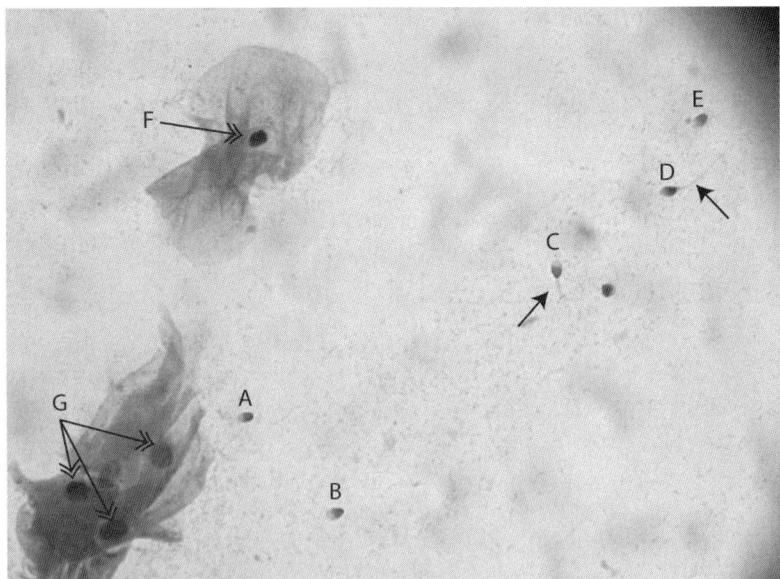

Fig. 1. A laboratory analyst can identify spermatozoa (A–E) to confirm the presence of semen on an item. The presence of spermatozoa (C–D) with tails (arrows) indicates that the semen may be of relatively recent deposition. Nuclear DNA resides in the spermatozoa heads (A–E) and the nuclei of the epithelial cells (F and G). Leica DM LS2 Microscope at ×400.

excited with ultraviolet (UV) light. Semen stains have the tendency to fluoresce more intensely than most other bodily fluids. In this way, fluorescing areas of an item can be identified and AP tested. Alternate light screening works well on light colored fabrics, but dark and coarse fabrics are notoriously difficult to examine under visible or UV light.

5.1.3. Microscopic Identification of Spermatozoa

Items that have tested presumptively positive for seminal fluid using the AP test can be confirmed either by microscopic detection of spermatozoa or chemical detection of a semen specific protein (Subheading 5.1.4). Positive swabs or a small cutting from a positive stain can be smeared onto a microscope slide and then stained for visualization. Two common stains used for visualization of semen are Nuclear Fast Red (red stain) and Picroindigocarmine (green stain) and are sometimes referred to as the "Christmas Tree" stain because of the red-green color combination. Once stained, epithelial cells (a group of cells such as skin cells and cells that line body orifices) and spermatozoa have a specific appearance (*see* Fig. 1; color image appears in e-book). The nucleus of an epithelial cell will turn red while the cytoplasm takes on a light green or blue appearance. The heads of spermatozoa will turn red with a lighter or white tip, whereas the tail, if present, will turn blue-green.

Microscopically identifying spermatozoa is an absolute indicator that semen is present on an item. It is also useful because the relative quantity of spermatozoa and epithelial cells can be assessed. This determination becomes important during subsequent DNA analysis because spermatozoa contain male DNA, whereas most epithelial cells in a male–female sexual assault will contain female DNA from the complainant. The drawbacks to using microscopy for spermatozoa identification are that it can be more time consuming than the protein confirmation method described next and that it is not necessarily specific to human spermatozoa.

5.1.4. Protein Confirmation of Semen

Not all cases where seminal fluid is identified can be confirmed with microscopy. If the semen belongs to a male who is vasectomized, or a male with a congenital or other defect of the male reproductive system, spermatozoa may not be present in the semen. In cases such as these it is useful to have another method to confirm the presence of seminal fluid. It is possible to test for the presence of a protein specific to semen known as prostate-specific antigen (PSA), also referred to as "p30" in forensic terminology.

There are several different methods that can be used to confirm the presence of p30 on an item. Traditional p30 detection tests utilize electrophoretic methods, such as crossover electrophoresis or diffusion methods, such as Ouchterlony double diffusion. More recently, a commercial test known as the OneStep ABAcard® p30 test (Abacus Diagnostics, West Hills, CA) has become prevalent in forensic laboratories because of its sensitivity and ease of use. All of these methods require a small cutting of an AP positive stain to be incubated in water or saline until rehydrated. Afterwards, the liquid is separated from the cutting by centrifugation so that the stain will be retained in a liquid form instead of dried to the cutting. At this point, a portion of the stain can be used to test for the presence of p30.

All of the methods that detect p30 rely on the formation of an antibody–antigen complex. If semen is present in an extract, a band will be formed during crossover electrophoresis and Ouchterlony double diffusion. In the OneStep ABAcard p30 test, a pink band is formed in the sample area; the test and results are similar to those of an over-the-counter pregnancy test. The lack of a band in any of the tests would indicate that the stain does not contain semen or that there is not enough present to facilitate a visible reaction. This test can be used alone to confirm semen or it can be used in conjunction with the microscopic method described in the previous section. If no spermatozoa are seen during microscopic examination, it is preferable to also perform the p30 protein test before the absence of seminal fluid is reported. Although the crossover electrophoresis and Ouchterlony double diffusion methods are effective for the confirmation of semen and still used in some laboratories today, these methods are more time consuming and less sensitive than the newer OneStep ABAcard p30 commercial test.

5.2. Identification of Blood

The identification of blood is important in many of the cases submitted to the crime laboratory for analysis. Blood identification is central to many homicide investigations and is also useful in cases involving aggravated assault, sexual assault, and burglary. The evaluation of blood evidence can be crucial to substantiate a complainant's or suspect's account of alleged events. The presence of blood on evidentiary items can be critical in establishing guilt or innocence during criminal proceedings. The analysis of blood evidence can be important not only in establishing which individual might have been bleeding, but also the manner in which blood was deposited. Blood spatter interpretation can be valuable in determining how blood was deposited on an item or at a scene thus making it useful in crime scene reconstruction. All of these factors can be taken into account during the investigation and prosecution of a crime and may corroborate or refute an individual's account of an assault.

5.2.1. Presumptive Testing for Blood

The presumptive identification of blood relies on the peroxidase activity of the heme group in hemoglobin. Phenolphthalein (PH), tetramethylbenzidine (TMB), leuchomalachite green (LMG), and other indicators work by oxidation of the test sample in the presence of hemoglobin to produce a color change reaction. PH is the most commonly used presumptive test for blood and may be used by itself or in conjunction with other presumptive tests. A positive PH result is indicated by a bright pink color that appears typically within 10–15 s after the test chemicals are added. This test is very sensitive and positive results can be obtained from stains that are barely visible or invisible to the naked eye. One drawback to this presumptive test is the number of substances that can produce false-positive results. Rust, copper and metal salts, salt-treated lumber, potatoes, and horseradish may all cause a positive result with PH. Usually, if one of these substances is present, the reaction time is slower and the color change takes longer to appear. Some laboratories use PH together with TMB in a double presumptive test. TMB, which works in the same manner as PH, turns a blue-green color in the presence of blood. Although TMB is more specific than PH, meaning less false-positives are indicated, it is less sensitive than PH and does not work as well on highly diluted blood stains.

In any case where blood is suspected, the analyst must first determine what areas of an item of evidence may possibly contain blood. Although the color change presumptive tests are good indicators for the presence of blood, they are not practical for testing whole items on which no stains are visible. Porous materials that have been stained with blood may absorb some of the blood even if the object has been washed and appears clean. For this reason, the luminol and fluorescein tests are used to indicate nonvisible blood stains. Luminol is a chemical presumptive test that, instead of producing a color change reaction, causes stained areas to emit light. Fluorescein also causes a light reaction but the fluorescence must be observed using an UV light source. Either luminol or fluorescein can be sprayed onto large surfaces such as walls or floors and the positive areas marked for further testing. Both tests are very sensitive and will indicate bloodstains that may not be visible. Positive areas should be marked and photographed immediately because the light reaction is not permanent and will fade. One disadvantage to these tests is that both can have false positive reactions. Luminol and fluorescein will react with the same false positives as PH and also with bleach and other cleaning fluids, which may interfere with blood detection on surfaces that have been cleaned. For this reason, fluorescein or luminol positive areas should be retested with one of the color change presumptive tests. Another problem with the light-based tests is that they are typically used on very faint stains. Spraying a chemical onto an already weak stain may dilute the stain even further, which could then lessen the chances of obtaining DNA from the sample.

5.2.2. Species Testing of Blood

Species testing of blood may be accomplished through a number of methods, the most popular of which are the Ouchterlony and the OneStep ABAcard® Hematrace™ (Abacus Diagnostics, West Hills, CA) methods. Similar to the test for semen confirmation, the Ouchterlony method works by diffusion except that an extract of the suspected blood stain, as opposed to semen stain, and the antibody are placed opposite each other in a gel medium. As they migrate toward each other, the blood antigens and antibodies attach together to form a precipitate band that is visualized in the gel. The OneStep ABAcard Hematrace test works in the same manner as the OneStep ABAcard p30 test (*see* Subheading 5.1.4.); the stain extract is placed on a test card and the result is indicated by a pink band in the test area. Hematrace is less time consuming than the Ouchterlony test, but may show cross reactivity with other species besides human and upper primate blood. Ouchterlony can be more widely applied because it can be used to determine whether a stain may have come from a variety of different species, as long as an antiserum has been made to that species. Typically it is only necessary to determine whether a stain is of probable human origin, unless there are indications that animal blood may be present on a sample.

5.2.3. ABO Blood Typing

Prior to the advent of DNA analysis for forensic science, other methods were developed for the comparison of biological fluid stains to individuals. The most common of these is ABO blood group typing. ABO blood typing identifies specific antigens present on the surface of blood cells. Within the population, individuals may have different forms of these antigens producing what is commonly referred to as a person's blood type. Comparing the blood type obtained from an evidence stain to that of a known individual allows for the determination of whether the individual could have contributed to the stain. A proportion of individuals known as "secretors" produces similar substances in other bodily fluids in addition to blood, which enables ABO typing to be performed on all bodily fluids in such individuals. The main drawback to ABO blood typing is that there are relatively few different ABO blood types throughout the population, making it difficult to individualize crime stains. Nearly 40% of the population has blood type A and another 40% type O. In addition to being much less informative than DNA analysis, ABO typing requires a fairly large amount of sample for accurate testing, much more than is required for current DNA testing procedures. Some laboratories still use ABO blood typing as an exclusionary tool in cases where a large amount of sample is available. However, with the development of faster and more accurate DNA methods, most forensic laboratories have given up ABO testing.

5.2.4. Blood Spatter Interpretation

Blood spatter interpretation can be a useful tool during the investigation of a crime. Interpreting bloodstain patterns can yield information on the manner in which a bloodstain was deposited. The distance from the impact origin, the object that may have been responsible for the impact, the direction of the impact, the number of impacts (e.g., shots, blows, etc.), or the movement of an individual after injury may be determined by studying blood deposition (1). All of this information can help investigators establish events that may have occurred at a crime scene and also whether an individual's account of an offense can be corroborated.

5.3. Identification of Saliva

The detection of saliva can be a useful tool in many types of criminal cases, although saliva testing is not requested as often as testing for semen or blood. Although there is a presumptive test that can be used to indicate saliva, it has many limitations. Of the forensic laboratories that still perform presumptive testing for saliva, the detection of amylase, an enzyme found at high levels in saliva, is currently the most widely utilized method.

Amylase is found in a variety of bodily fluids—saliva, blood, urine, sweat, tears, semen, breast milk, feces, and vaginal secretions *(2,3)*—but is more concentrated in saliva than in other bodily fluids. In the body, amylase functions to break down starch into smaller molecules. In the forensic laboratory, amylase function is examined by dissolving a portion of a stain in water or saline and incubating it at body temperature in the presence of starch. If amylase is present, the starch will be broken down into smaller byproducts and will not be able to react with an iodine-based test solution to produce a purple-blue color. For this presumptive test, an absence of color change denotes amylase activity. Unfortunately, this test is not particularly sensitive or specific to saliva; as a result, many laboratories forego screening of evidence for saliva in this manner because there is no confirmatory test for its presence. Instead, depending on the circumstances surrounding a case, some laboratories opt to save these samples for DNA testing where a more conclusive determination might be made.

UV light can also be used to prescreen clothing and other evidence to identify possible saliva stains. Like seminal fluid, saliva will fluoresce when excited with UV light. In these instances, it is important for a laboratory analyst to know the details of an alleged assault so that a determination can be made on the most likely area where saliva might be present. Because many bodily fluids and other substances can fluoresce, this screening method only identifies areas for further examination.

DNA testing can be thought of as a type of confirmatory test for the presence of saliva and other bodily fluids on an item because DNA testing is specific to human DNA. However, DNA analysis without initial presumptive or confirmatory testing only indicates that human DNA is present on an item, not from which bodily fluid the DNA came. Nevertheless, on items that are suspected of having been in contact with a person's mouth (e.g., drink containers, bitemark swabbings, cigarettes, envelopes, toothbrushes, partially ingested food) it is logical to expect that saliva might be present on these items and that any DNA obtained from these items might be from that saliva.

6. DNA TESTING

After evidentiary items have been screened and positive samples identified, DNA analysis can begin. DNA is the inherited cellular material that is the blueprint for human development. DNA molecules are found in almost every cell in a person's body, inside each cell's nucleus where it is packaged into 23 pairs of chromosomes. One chromosome from each pair is contributed by an individual's mother and the other by an individual's father. Each person's DNA is unique, except in the case of identical twins. Identical twins will have exactly the same DNA sequence. Fraternal twins' DNA, on the other hand, will not be any more similar than that of regular siblings. Another property of DNA that is important to forensic analysis is that a person's DNA is the same in every cell in that person's body throughout life. Although there are rare instances related to cancer, aging, and other cellular events when this statement might not be true, these occurrences rarely affect forensic examinations.

Although each person's DNA is unique, most of the sequence of the DNA molecule is the same for all individuals. Forensic DNA analysis is interested in the small percentage of the DNA sequence that is different between people. Because forensic DNA analysis attempts to individualize DNA to a specific person, it would not be useful to look at segments of DNA that are the same across the population. Instead, polymorphic, or highly variable, regions of DNA are targeted for analysis. The various methods by which this is accomplished are discussed in Subheadings 6.3. to 6.7.

6.1. DNA Extraction

The first step in any forensic DNA analysis is the purification of DNA from an item, also called a substrate, on which the DNA is deposited. This process is commonly referred to as DNA extraction. There are a wide variety of DNA extraction techniques, all of which function to (1) separate the cells containing DNA away from the substrate on which they are embedded; (2) lyse, or break open, the cells to release DNA and other cellular material; and (3) separate the DNA from these cellular components and any inhibitors that might be present in a sample. (Inhibitors are chemicals or other compounds in a sample that might interfere with subsequent DNA analysis.) The goal of DNA extraction is to yield purified DNA in an aqueous, or liquid, solution that can be used in other applications.

Some of the methods used for DNA extraction are better at purifying DNA, increasing maximum DNA yield, decreasing processing times, or a combination of these depending on which method is used. Different extraction techniques may work better for different types of samples. It is the forensic laboratory's responsibility to find the best DNA extraction technique for each sample type. New techniques are being developed all the time in attempt to make DNA extraction more streamlined with a higher DNA yield (quantity).

Regardless of which type of DNA extraction is being performed, or which type of chemicals are used, all DNA extractions attempted in forensic laboratories must be processed concurrently with an extraction negative control, also known as a reagent blank. A reagent blank is a sample that goes through the extraction process without the addition of a substrate. Its purpose is to monitor for contamination. In this sense, "contamination" refers to the presence of foreign DNA in a sample. Ideally, reagent blanks should never give any DNA result. If DNA is detected in a reagent blank, it can either mean that DNA contamination is present in the chemicals used for the extraction process or that an event occurred during the extraction process to introduce foreign DNA into the extracts. If this happens, the DNA extraction for all the samples processed with that reagent blank should be repeated from the beginning. It is very important that reagent blanks are treated just like every other sample in the reaction process so that they can monitor for contamination most effectively.

In forensic casework, it is not good laboratory practice to consume an entire sample during DNA extraction. Typically, only half of a sample should be processed for each extraction in order to leave enough specimen for retesting. Retesting is important for several reasons. First, if the original extraction becomes compromised, either by contamination of the extraction reagents or another event, or the results are inconclusive, then the extraction may need to be repeated by the laboratory. For items for which no DNA profile is obtained, saving a portion of the sample can be important so it can be processed in the future when new technology becomes available. Finally, a portion of each sample should be saved so that the evidence can be retested by another laboratory to confirm findings if requested by the court.

6.1.1. Differential DNA Extraction

One distinct type of DNA extraction used in forensic laboratories is commonly referred to as "differential extraction." Semen-positive sexual assault samples are usually swabs from a sexual assault kit, sometimes referred to as intimate samples, or cuttings from a complainant's clothing or bedding. These types of samples generally involve a mixture of DNA from the perpetrator, in the form of spermatozoa, and the complainant, in the form of epithelial cells. Because these samples contain DNA from more than one source, it is useful to attempt to separate DNA derived from spermatozoa from all other sources of DNA.

Differential extraction relies on the distinction in the physical properties of spermatozoa from other, usually epithelial, cells. Spermatozoa are more robust than other cell types when it comes to the process of DNA extraction. They can withstand higher incubation temperatures for longer periods and remain intact. Using this property, it is possible to perform a two-step incubation in an attempt to separate epithelial DNA from spermatozoa DNA. In the first step, the entire sample is incubated for a short period of time under less stringent conditions. Afterwards, the sample is centrifuged to separate lysed cells (epithelial), which remain in the aqueous solution, from unlysed cells (spermatozoa), which pellet at the bottom of the tube. The aqueous solution, now called the nonsperm cell fraction, can then be removed to another tube for further processing while the spermatozoa pellet can be resuspended and digested under more stringent conditions to release the spermatozoa's DNA.

Differential extractions are by no means exact. In a perfect world, differential extraction results in a pure nonsperm (epithelial) cell fraction and a pure sperm cell fraction. Ideally, during subsequent DNA analysis, the nonsperm cell fraction would yield a single DNA profile consistent with the complainant, whereas the sperm cell fraction would yield a single DNA profile consistent with a male. Although this sometimes happens, it is not always the case. One of the variables that influences the success of a differential extrac-tion is the amount of spermatozoa in relation to other cells. This distinction is usually made during the microscopic examination of spermatozoa either during semen confirmation or by preparing a slide from the differential extraction products themselves (*see* Fig. 1). This determination can produce valuable information on the best way to process the sample during DNA extraction. Large quantities of the complainant's epithelial DNA may not all be lysed in the first incubation step and the unlysed cells may pellet with the spermatozoa to introduce complainant DNA into the sperm cell fraction. Another factor that may influence a differential extraction is the presence of perpetrator DNA in a form other than spermatozoa. It is possible for a perpetrator's blood cells or epithelial cells (from skin, saliva, or seminal fluid) to be present in a sample. These cells would become a part of the epithelial cell fraction and may cause the perpetrator's profile to be observed in the nonsperm cell fraction.

Even though differential extraction is not always precise, it is still worth performing because it allows at least a partial separation of spermatozoa from other cells. Researchers are currently working on other methods to more reliably separate spermatozoa from other cells. Some of these techniques involve passing the DNA through a filter to separate spermatozoa from other cells based on cell size (epithelial cells are very large, whereas spermatozoa are small), or binding the spermatozoa to a membrane using antibodies. Also, a new method of DNA analysis has been developed in the last few years that is specific to male DNA, called Y-short tandem repeat (Y-STR) analysis (*see* Subheading 6.6.) that can give additional information on samples with small amounts of male DNA or samples that are a mixture of male and female DNA.

6.2. DNA Quantification

After evidentiary samples and comparison reference samples have been extracted, the amount of DNA in each sample must be measured in a process known as DNA quantification. It is important for subsequent steps to determine the amount of DNA in each sample. The DNA analysis techniques currently being used in most laboratories, such as short tandem repeat (STR) analysis, mitochondrial DNA (mtDNA) sequencing, and Y-STR, all require very precise amounts of DNA for processing. There are several different methods that can be used to quantify DNA. The newer methods have greater sensitivity and can more accurately identify the amount of human DNA in a specimen than traditional methods.

6.2.1. Agarose Gel Electrophoresis

The most widespread method of DNA quantification used in many research laboratories and still in use in some forensic laboratories is agarose gel electrophoresis. Agarose is a chemical that forms a gel-like solid when melted and allowed to cool to room temperature. An agarose gel functions like a sieve to separate DNA fragments based on their size when an electrical current is applied to the gel. The smaller the DNA fragment, the quicker it can pass through a gel. Ethidium bromide, another chemical, is commonly added to each agarose gel during the solidification process. Ethidium bromide incorporates itself into DNA fragments and will fluoresce when excited by UV light, providing a way to visualize DNA in the agarose gel. The DNA from each sample is compared to standards of known DNA quantity to determine the size and concentration of sample DNA. Agarose gel electrophoresis provides a "quick and dirty" method to calculate the amount of DNA in a sample but is not as sensitive as other methods of DNA quantification. It is also not specific to human DNA as are the other quantification methods that will be discussed (*see* Subheadings 6.2.2. and 6.2.3.). Instead, all of the DNA in a sample (human, animal, bacterial, mitochondrial) will be quantified together, making it difficult to establish an accurate concentration of DNA to be used for subsequent applications. For both of these reasons, agarose gel electrophoresis is no longer commonly used in forensic laboratories and should not be used to quantify evidentiary sample DNA, which is usually present in low enough quantity to be under the level of detection of this method.

6.2.2. Human-Specific DNA Quantification

Currently, the most commonly used method for quantification in forensic laboratories is to hybridize (adhere) a labeled probe to the DNA in a sample. These probes are specific to human DNA, but may also react with upper-primate DNA if it is present in a sample. Except in cases where a biological fluid of an upper-primate may be present in a sample, these quantification methods can be considered a reliable estimate of the amount of human DNA in a sample. Once the probe attaches to the DNA, a chemical reaction produces either color or light, depending upon the method used. The intensity of the color/light that is produced is measured to determine DNA concentration. The amount of DNA in a sample is directly proportional to the amount of color/light detected. Similar to agarose gel electrophoresis, DNA standards of known concentration are run concurrently with the samples to be quantified and the relative intensities between the DNA samples and the known standards are used to determine concentration. These methods offer improved sensitivity over agarose gel electrophoresis. In addition, because of their specificity, they will not detect any bacterial, animal (nonprimate), or other DNA that may be present in a sample.

6.2.3. Real-Time Polymerase Chain Reaction Quantification

The newest technique available in DNA quantification involves a process known as real-time polymerase chain reaction (PCR). The PCR is a way to amplify (copy) specific regions on the DNA strand. Real-time PCR is a way to monitor the amplification process as it occurs. A commercially available kit, the Quantifiler™ Human DNA Quantification Kit (Applied Biosystems, Foster City, CA), uses real-time PCR to quantify the *amplifiable* human DNA in a sample. Similarly to the quantification techniques discussed in Subheading 6.2.2., the probes for the real-time procedure are human specific, but may also react to upper-primate DNA if present in a sample.

Real-time PCR, when applied to DNA quantification, is different than any of the other quantification methods previously discussed because, instead of only determining the amount of DNA in a sample, this method can also predict how the DNA will respond during subsequent analysis conditions (amplification). In this way, the real-time PCR technique identifies potential inhibitors (substances in the DNA extract that prevent amplification). The Quantifiler kit also offers improved sensitivity over any of the other quantification methods and is still specific to human nuclear DNA. The Quantifiler™ Y Human Male DNA Quantification Kit (Applied Biosystems, Foster City, CA) is another real-time PCR based quantification method, but this kit quantifies the amount of *male* human nuclear DNA in a sample. This quantification method is useful for Y-STR analysis (*see* Subheading 6.6.).

6.3. Restriction Fragment Length Polymorphism and Early PCR-Based Methods

In the mid to late 1980s, the technique known as restriction fragment length polymorphism (RFLP) was introduced to forensic science and became the first assay used for forensic DNA analysis. The DNA molecule contains sequences known as variable number of tandem repeat (VNTR) sequences which are pieces of DNA whose sequence repeats over and over a different number of times in different individuals. These repeating sequences, each up to several hundred bases in length, can be cut out of the DNA strand using restriction enzymes and then isolated and their size determined using the Southern blotting technique. The VNTR sequences were shown to be highly variable in the population and revolutionized DNA typing in forensic science. RFLP was eventually supplanted by STR analysis as the leading DNA technology in forensic crime laboratories because RFLP requires a very large amount of sample to obtain enough DNA for detection and is not suitable for processing very small or degraded samples. It is also very time consuming to perform. A typical case from start to finish could take as long as 8 wk to complete. In contrast, current STR-DNA analysis can be completed in days.

The PCR-based methods for DNA typing were developed to handle the many crime scene stains that are of limited DNA quantity. PCR is a process that amplifies, or copies, specific regions on the DNA strand to produce enough DNA to examine. This process is accomplished by combining the sample DNA with Taq polymerase (an enzyme) and human-specific primers (short segments of DNA that indicate which area of the DNA should be copied) in a buffered chemical solution. Each sample, including reagent blanks, is placed into a separate tube for analysis. In addition, for each set of amplification reactions, a positive and negative amplification control should be processed. A positive control is a DNA sample for which a profile is already established. A negative control is set up just like any other sample but does not contain DNA; instead, the water or buffer used for sample dilutions is added to the amplification reaction. Once all the samples and controls are prepared, they are placed into a machine known as a thermal cycler. The thermal cycler facilitates PCR by incubating the samples in repetitive cycles of denaturation (unwinding and separating the DNA strands at high temperature), annealing (laying down primers in the target region at the primer specific temperature), and elongation (addition of bases to create a copy at the enzyme specific temperature). Each cycle increases the amount of target DNA inside the sample tube. The amplification process generally continues for 25–40 amplification cycles depending on the manufacturer's established procedure and internal laboratory validation.

The AmpliType™ HLA DQα Forensic DNA and the AmpliType® PM PCR Amplification and Typing Kits (formerly supplied by Perkin-Elmer, Foster City, CA) used sequence based polymorphisms at specific DNA locations instead of the size based polymorphisms used in RFLP analysis. These PCR-based methods were preferable to RFLP because DNA from very limited sources could be amplified to detectable levels and the time required for processing was greatly reduced. The biggest disadvantage to these PCR-based methods was that the sequential differences at DQα and the Polymarker loci showed less variability in populations than the repeating sequences in RFLP, making statistical analysis less discriminating.

6.4. STR Analysis

The most widespread method of DNA analysis currently used in crime laboratories is STR analysis. STRs are repetitive sequences of DNA, usually two to five base pairs in length. Forensic STR analysis determines the number of tetranucleotide (four base) or pentanucleotide (five base) repeats at specific locations (loci) on the DNA strand. The numbers of repeats observed at these locations are compiled into what is known as a DNA profile. Profiles from evidence can be compared to profiles from known individuals and conclusions can be drawn regarding whether specific individuals may have contributed to the DNA on evidentiary items.

The STR procedure is similar to RFLP in that it examines repetitive units on the DNA strand, although the repeat units in STR are significantly smaller in size than the VNTR units analyzed in RFLP. STR analysis is also a PCR-based procedure, making it much more sensitive than RFLP. STR analysis became popular in crime laboratories because of its sensitivity, reduced processing time, and increased statistical discrimination over previous forensic DNA methods. Although each location examined for STR shows less variability than those examined in RFLP typing, the increased number of DNA sites examined during the STR procedure makes it more discerning than RFLP.

After DNA samples have been extracted and quantified, a small amount, usually less than two nanograms of DNA, is used for the PCR portion of the STR procedure. The PCR procedure is the same as described in Subheading 6.3. except that during each cycle of amplification a fluorescent tag is attached to each new copy of DNA. After the DNA is amplified, the amount and size of the DNA must be determined. This process is accomplished by detecting the fluorescently labeled tags attached to the amplified DNA. First, the DNA is separated by size using electrical current. The amplified DNA is either applied to a polyacrylamide slab gel (gel media sandwiched between two large glass plates) or a polymer-filled capillary (gel-like medium contained in a long, thin glass capillary). When electrical current is applied to either the slab gel or capillary, the shorter DNA fragments migrate through the gel medium faster than the longer fragments. In this way, DNA fragments can be resolved down to a one base difference in size. After the amplified DNA has been separated by size, each fragment is detected by its fluorescent label. Detection is either accomplished by the electrophoretic instrument's laser and charge-coupled

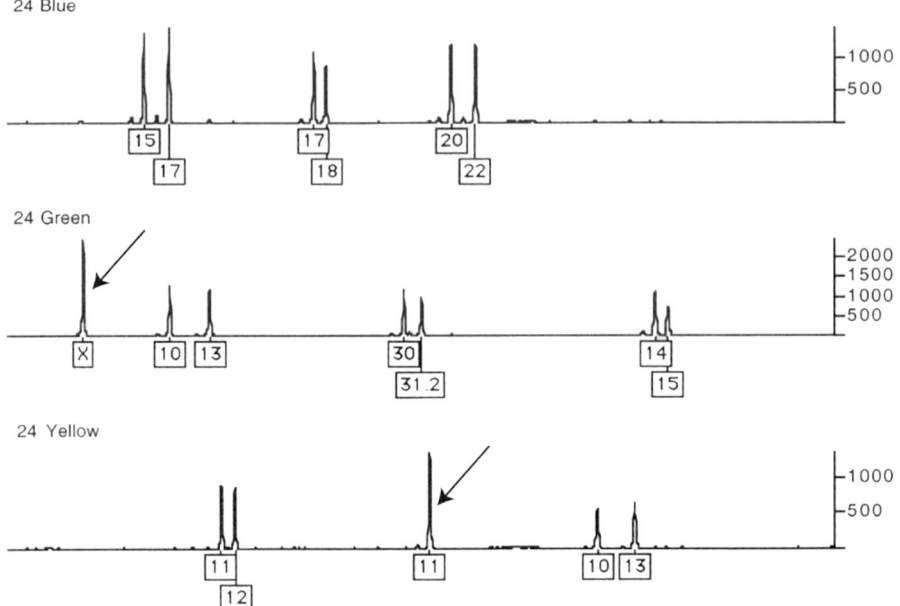

Fig. 2. A DNA profile from a single female individual. Loci where only one peak is present are homozygous (arrows). Loci where two peaks are present are heterozygous. The presence of an "X" allele without a "Y" allele indicates that this profile is from a female individual. The numbers indicated below the peaks are the number of repetitive fragments observed at each locus. These numbers are listed as a person's DNA profile. Figure was generated with the AmpFLSTR Profiler Plus Amplification Kit (Applied Biosystems, Foster City, CA).

device (CCD) camera or by using a flat bed scanner with fluorescent detection capability. After the fluorescence has been read, computer software converts the fluorescent information into a format that can be analyzed.

STR systems detect DNA at several different locations on the DNA strand. At each of these locations (loci) a person will have up to two different fragment sizes (alleles; *see* Fig. 2). Because DNA is packaged into pairs of chromosomes, the occurrence of two alleles is caused when the fragment size at one locus on one chromosome differs from the fragment size of that same locus on the other chromosome (heterozygous). If the sizes of the detected fragments are the same on both chromosomes, then a person will only have one allele at that locus (homozygous).

Once fragment sizes are determined for all of the loci under examination, then a DNA profile can be generated. A DNA profile is a listing of all observed allele sizes at each locus (*see* Tables 1 and 2). The DNA profile of an evidentiary sample can then be compared to the DNA profile of a known

Table 1
CODIS Case Data

Locus	White styrofoam cup	Plastic drinking straw
D3S1358	16	15, 16
VWA	15, 16	15, 16, 18
FGA	22, 23	20, 25
Amelogenin	X, Y	X, Y
D8S1179	11, 12	11, 14, 15
D21S11	27, 28	28, 29
D18S51	14, 20	16, 19
D5S818	11, 12	11
D13S317	12, 13	11, 13
D7S820	8, 11	8, 11
D16S539	10, 13	9, 12
THO1	6, 9	7, 9
TPOX	8, 10	10, 11
CSF1PO	10, 12	8, 11

Table 2
Aggravated Sexual Assault Data

Locus	C	S1	S2	V-SP	A-SP
D3S1358	15, 18	16	15	15	15
VWA	18	15, 16	16, 18	16, 18	16, 18
FGA	24, 25	22, 23	20, 25	20, 25	20, 24, 25
Amelogenin	X	X, Y	X, Y	X, Y	X, Y
D8S1179	12, 13	11, 12	14, 15	14, 15	12, 13, 14, 15
D21S11	29, 33.2	27, 28	28, 29	28, 29	28, 29, 33.2
D18S51	15	14, 20	16, 19	16, 19	15, 16, 19
D5S818	10, 13	11, 12	11	11	10, 11, 13
D13S317	11, 14	12, 13	11, 13	11, 13	11, 13, 14
D7S820	8, 10	8, 11	8, 11	8, 11	8, 10, 11
D16S539	11	10, 13	9,12	9,12	9, 11, 12
THO1	9.3	6, 9	7, 9	7, 9	7, 9, 9.3
TPOX	8	8, 10	10, 11	10, 11	8, 10, 11
CSF1PO	10, 11	10, 12	8, 11	8, 11	8, 10, 11

C, complainant; S1, suspect 1; S2, suspect 2; V, vaginal; A, anal; SP, sperm fraction.

reference sample (complainant, suspect, witness, or relative). If the evidentiary sample is from a single source and the DNA profiles are the same between an evidence sample and a reference sample, then that individual cannot be excluded as the individual to whom the bodily fluid belongs.

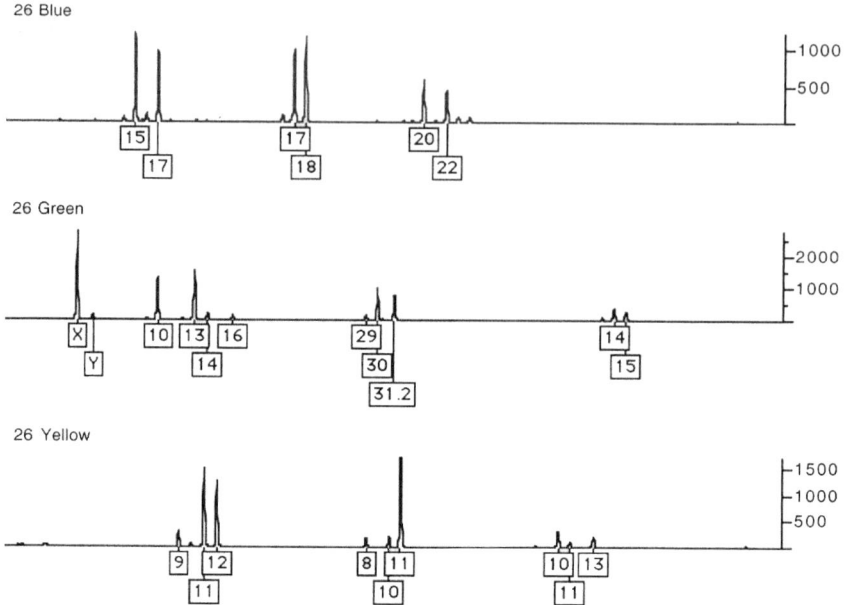

Fig. 3. A mixture of DNA from the individuals from Figs. 2 and 4. The taller peaks at each locus are consistent with the female individual from Fig. 2 indicating that more of her DNA is present in the mixture. Not all of the alleles from the male individual from Fig. 4 are observed in this profile above the threshold. When not all of the alleles from an individual are evident in a mixture, it makes interpreting the mixture difficult. Figure was generated with the AmpFLSTR Profiler Plus Amplification Kit (Applied Biosystems, Foster City, CA).

In forensic science, reporting statements for profiles that are the same between a piece of evidence and an individual rarely use the word "match." Because only representative areas of the DNA molecule are tested in STR analysis, the possibility still exists that if other locations on the DNA strand were tested, the results might be different between the DNA profiles of the evidence and of the individual. Statistics can be calculated to determine how common the DNA profile of the evidence is in a given population. There are databases for the frequency of alleles at each locus in different populations. The statistical rarity of a profile will be influenced by the number of loci tested and the rarity of the observed alleles at those loci *(4)*. If the statistics generated for a certain profile meet a specified threshold, then some laboratories may make a reporting statement indicating that a certain individual is the source of an evidentiary stain or bodily fluid *(5)*.

More than two alleles observed at one or more loci are indicative of a mixture of DNA from more than one individual (Fig. 3). Mixtures can arise if bodily fluids from more than one person are present on a sample or when more than

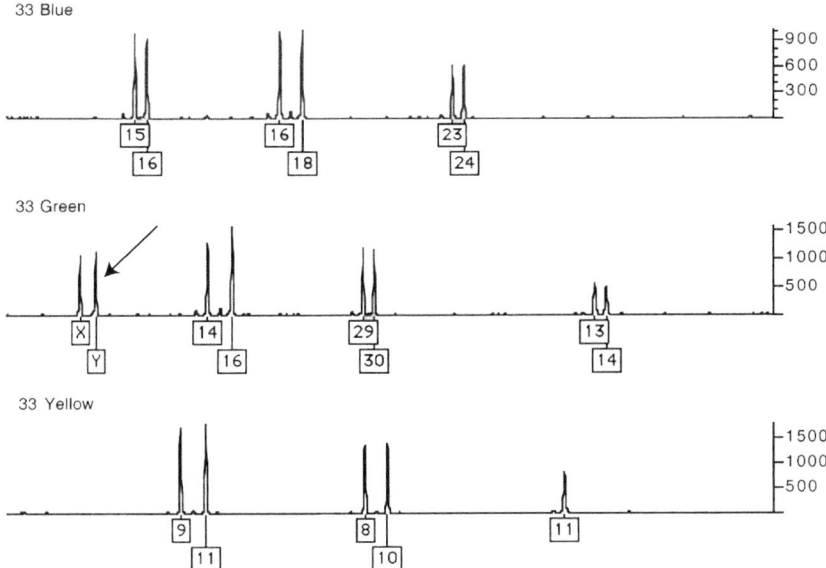

Fig. 4. The DNA profile of a male individual. The presence of an "X" allele and a "Y" allele at the amelogenin locus (arrow) indicates that this profile is from a male. Each locus has no more than two alleles, each with similar height, indicating that the source of this profile is from a single individual. This individual contributed to the mixture profile from Fig. 3. Figure was generated with the AmpFLSTR Profiler Plus Amplification Kit (Applied Biosystems, Foster City, CA).

one individual contributes the same type of bodily fluid to a stain. Mixtures are observed frequently on sexual assault evidence because the DNA of the complainant in the form of skin cells, sweat, or vaginal secretions and DNA from semen may be present on the same item. Likewise, during homicides or assaults it is possible for more than one person to deposit blood on an item. A profile with more than two alleles at only one locus must be interpreted with caution. In rare instances, it is possible for an individual to have more than two alleles at a single locus but this exception is identified when a profile is established from an individual's known saliva or blood. When this tri-allelic pattern does occur, it is typically only observed at one locus where a true mixture will be observed at two or more loci.

Mixture profiles can be difficult to interpret. If there are only two contributors to a DNA mixture and all of their alleles are present at equal intensity with no additional alleles observed, then the interpretation is fairly straightforward. However, if a mixture is from more than two individuals or if the amounts of DNA from different individuals vary in intensity so that not all of the alleles are observed (Figs. 3 and 4), mixture interpretation becomes very difficult. In any event, it is not possible to determine with absolute certainty that

DNA from a specific individual is present in a mixture; instead, it is only possible to conclude that a specific individual might be a contributor. Because mixtures are a combination of alleles from more than one person, it is possible to have more than one combination of profiles that would explain the mixture on an item. As a result, it is difficult to state that a person is represented in a mixture absolutely. Using allelic frequencies, mixture statistics can be calculated to determine the number of unrelated individuals in the population who might be able to contribute to a certain mixture profile.

While it is helpful to have a reference sample from a developed suspect to be used for DNA comparison, it is not always necessary. The advent of the Combined DNA Index System (CODIS) database (*see* Subheading 6.8.) makes it possible to process cases without a known suspect. If a presumed perpetrator profile is developed, the profile can be entered into the CODIS database and compared with evidentiary samples from other cases and to convicted offender samples. In some cases, even mixture profiles can be entered into the CODIS database. Success in using the CODIS database to help resolve crimes has produced an incentive to work old, unprocessed, or cold cases. Cases that were not processed for DNA because the technology was not available at the time or the available technology was not sensitive enough or a suspect sample was not available for comparison can now be worked in an attempt to identify a suspect using the CODIS database.

6.5. Mitochondrial DNA Sequencing

Many people do not realize that there is more than one type of DNA in a cell. All of the discussion to this point in this chapter of text has been in reference to "nuclear DNA," which is specific to an individual (refer to Section 6). The second and less commonly discussed type of DNA in a cell is mtDNA. Mitochondria are very small organelles found outside the cell nucleus within a cell's cytoplasm. Each mitochondrion has its own DNA. mtDNA is only inherited maternally; therefore, mtDNA is not unique to any one person. Each individual will share the same mtDNA sequence with their mother, siblings, and other maternal relatives. Because of the shared mtDNA profile between maternal family members, mtDNA is not as discriminating as nuclear DNA analysis. However, mtDNA has several properties that make it useful in forensic science.

mtDNA is circular in shape in contrast to nuclear DNA, which has a long, linear configuration that is packaged into chromosomes. mtDNA's circular shape enables it to be more stable over time because it is less susceptible to degradation. This stability allows mtDNA to be utilized in cases involving skeletonized remains or old biological samples that are not able to yield a nuclear DNA profile. mtDNA is also useful in cases of mass disaster where remains may be subjected to harsh conditions, such as salt water, charring, or other elemental conditions that degrade DNA. As a consequence of the maternal inheritance of mtDNA, mtDNA analysis also allows for the comparison of remains to more distantly related individuals than nuclear comparisons allow. This aspect is helpful in cases where no immediate family members are available to supply a reference sample.

One of the most famous remains identification cases in which mtDNA sequencing was utilized involved the identification of the Romanov family *(6)*. STR analysis established that the remains from a mass grave in Ekaterinburg, Russia were of a family unit (both parents and three daughters) and four unrelated individuals. Because the Romanov family disappeared in 1918, no immediate living relatives were available to confirm the identity of the remains by STR testing. Instead, Tsarina Alexandra was identified through an mtDNA sequencing comparison between her remains and that of Prince Philip, Duke of Edinburg, a maternal grand-nephew. Tsar Nicolas II was identified using an mtDNA comparison to two separate individuals: his sister's great granddaughter and his maternal grandmother's great-great grandson.

In addition to remains identification cases, mtDNA analysis is routinely used to compare DNA derived from single hairs to known reference samples. Hairs with intact roots can yield enough nuclear DNA for STR analysis, but hairs without available roots will typically be unable to produce any analyzable nuclear DNA. Even very small cut hairs are capable of generating an mtDNA profile for comparison. Because mtDNA analysis is time consuming and not as statistically discriminating as nuclear analyses, mtDNA analysis is usually only performed on hair or other evidence when there is no other probative physical evidence available in an investigation.

Unlike STR analysis, which looks at repetitive segments of DNA, mtDNA analysis actually compares the DNA sequence between individuals. DNA sequencing breaks down the DNA fragment by order into its respective bases (A, C, T, or G). To facilitate interpretation, the sequence is then compared to a reference sequence and any difference from the reference sequence is noted. This annotation becomes a mtDNA profile or haplotype. mtDNA haplotypes can be compared between evidence and reference samples and conclusions can be drawn as to whether a certain individual may have contributed to the mtDNA on an item. If the profiles are consistent between a reference sample and an evidentiary sample, statistics can be generated to indicate how many times that mtDNA haplotype has been observed in a given population.

More recently, a method using sequence specific oliconucleotide (SSO) probes, similar to DQα and Polymarker for nuclear DNA (*see* Subheading 6.3.), has been developed in an attempt to circumvent the need for actual sequence determination thereby decreasing the time necessary for mtDNA analysis *(7)*. These probes have been used in some instances, but may require sequencing for confirmation *(8)*. The SSO probe approach to mtDNA analysis may be helpful to laboratories who would like to begin mtDNA analysis but do not want to have to purchase costly equipment. One drawback is that SSO probes do not provide as much genetic information as actual sequencing of the mtDNA molecule.

Like STR analysis, reagent blanks and amplification positive and negative controls must be processed through sequencing to determine if there is any underlying DNA present in any of the chemicals used during analysis. Because mtDNA amplification is so sensitive, evidentiary samples are usually processed individually, each with their own reagent blank to closely monitor for contamination. Because of the necessity of processing evidentiary items singly and because of the time involved in the sequencing analysis, mtDNA casework takes much longer to complete than STR casework. Generally, laboratories that perform mtDNA sequencing can only process one or two mtDNA cases per analyst per month *(9)*.

mtDNA analysis for criminal cases can only be performed when a reference sample is available for comparison. Unlike nuclear DNA analysis, a database does not exist for the comparison of unknown mtDNA profiles from criminal cases. mtDNA profiles are not unique to individuals, so any database match would not necessarily aid an investigation. On the other hand, an mtDNA database does exist for searching profiles obtained from unidentified remains against relatives of missing persons. Databases similar to a missing person database are also useful in mass disaster identifications and identifying remains from mass graves, human right violations, or war.

6.6. Y-Chromosome STR Analysis

Because many sexual assault cases involve the DNA typing of a semen donor and most case samples are a mixture of complainant and semen donor sources, a new technology focusing on the Y-chromosome, which is only present in males, has been developed. Currently, Y-chromosome testing is an STR-based assay; however, single nucleotide polymorphisms (SNPs) specific to the Y-chromosome are under development (*see* Subheading 6.7.).

Y-STRs are useful in forensic testing because they are specific to the Y-chromosome, and therefore to male DNA. Y-STR analysis is able to simplify interpretation in cases where there is a mixture of male and female DNA by focusing on the male portion of DNA only. Y-STR is also applicable to cases where there is a mixture of more than two people. In complex mixtures such as these, Y-STR analysis can provide information on how many male donors have contributed to a sample. Y-STR is also instructive in cases where semen is present on a sample but no sperm type is detected because the ratio of complainant to sperm DNA is too large. In cases where the complainant is female, the complainant's contribution to the DNA in a sample is ignored and a Y-STR profile can be identified for the semen donor. Using Y-STR analysis on a sample may also preclude the need for performing a differential extraction in cases of male–female sexual assaults since separation of male and female DNA becomes unnecessary.

Although Y-STR is practical for many sexual assault cases, it is not without limitations. Similar to mtDNA, the Y-chromosome is inherited uniparentally, meaning it is passed from father to son. Therefore, male relatives will have the same Y-profile as other male members of their family. For this reason, Y-STR testing is not as statistically discriminating as nuclear DNA. Consequently, Y-STR analysis is usually employed as an extension of nuclear DNA testing to provide additional information and does not stand on its own, unless a male profile is not identified during nuclear DNA testing.

Y-STR analysis is essentially the same as STR analysis. The only real difference is that the primers for Y-STR analysis are specific to male, human DNA instead of only being human specific. One caveat of Y-STR analysis is that it is sometimes difficult to determine how much DNA to amplify because the DNA concentration of a sample is usually reported as the total amount of human DNA. In this case, the amount of male DNA present must be inferred. To address this shortcoming, a Y-specific quantification system has recently emerged using real-time PCR in order to remove guess work from determining the amount of male DNA present in a sample (*see* Subheading 6.2.3.). Precise amounts of starting DNA are required for STR procedures to process samples most efficiently.

6.7. SNP Analysis

SNPs are scattered throughout the genome. A SNP is one base pair of DNA that is variable between people. SNP technology for forensic science applications is currently under development for nuclear DNA, mtDNA, and Y-chromosome testing. It is already being used to a limited extent to help identify victims of the World Trade Center collapse in New York.

Research into SNP technology is aimed at the identification of meaningful markers and grouping as many probes as possible for these informative sites onto a microchip or similar technology so that many sites can be screened at once with very low quantities of DNA. This new technology should be better able to produce a profile from degraded DNA because the probes utilized are very short sequences. Each SNP site on its own is less informative than a single STR locus, so more SNPs will have to be processed to achieve the level of discrimination of current STR analysis. However, using microchip technology, hundreds of SNPs or more can be analyzed at the same time, offering a much higher level of discrimination than current STR analysis. The more SNP sites assayed, the more discriminating the testing ability to be able to individualize evidentiary stains.

6.8. CODIS Database

CODIS is a database of DNA profiles maintained at the local, state, and national levels. Its purpose is to aid criminal investigations by linking perpetrators to biological evidence. In order for a laboratory to participate in the CODIS system within the United States, the laboratory must follow the Quality Assurance Standards for DNA Laboratories *(10,11)*. Locally, laboratories participating in CODIS may enter DNA profiles obtained from forensic evidence. These profiles are then uploaded to a designated state laboratory and searched against forensic DNA profiles from other cases within the state and also against the DNA profiles of convicted offenders from that state. In this way, the investigation of crimes for which there is no known suspect may be aided by linking the biological evidence to either another case perpetrated by the same individual or to an individual who has been previously convicted of a felony. Each state participating in CODIS can upload their forensic unknown and convicted offender profiles to the national CODIS database, administered by the Federal Bureau of Investigation (FBI). Searches at the national level can link cases and offenders from across the country.

Internationally, there are more than 15 countries outside the United States that have their own CODIS databases, including countries in Europe, Asia, and North and South America. Because many countries use some of the same loci for DNA analysis, it is possible for profiles to be sent to these countries to be searched against their CODIS databases if warranted by the investigation.

6.9. DNA in Criminal Proceedings

Typically, DNA evidence does not stand alone in a criminal investigation. DNA evidence must be used in conjunction with the other case evidence to provide a whole scenario to allow jurors to make the best decision on the alleged course of events. The most important thing to remember when dealing with DNA during criminal proceedings is that the presence of an individual's DNA on an item does not prove their guilt; conversely, a lack of DNA does not necessarily prove their innocence. DNA evidence, in and of itself, is only as probative as the piece of evidence on which the DNA is found. DNA from semen in a sexual assault case that is consistent with the defendant's DNA would only have evidentiary value if the defendant denies knowing or having sexual contact with the victim. This same DNA would not be probative if both parties admit that a sexual encounter occurred but the question is one of consent. If the DNA profile of a semen sample in a case of sexual assault does not match the defendant, it could either mean that he was not the perpetrator, or that he did not ejaculate and the semen may belong to a sexual partner of the victim. Similarly, if semen is not present on samples from a sexual assault case, it does not necessarily mean that a sexual assault did not occur.

7. CASE STUDIES

7.1. Case Study: Probable Saliva for CODIS

In June of 2002 a woman's car was reported stolen. The car was later recovered and a white Styrofoam cup, a straw, and white plastic spoon were collected from the interior of the vehicle and submitted to the laboratory for analysis. Serology testing was not performed on these items to save as much sample as possible for DNA testing. Instead, swabbings were collected from areas that were suspected to contain saliva—the lip of the cup, the entire straw, and the spoon—and all were extracted and processed for DNA.

A DNA profile was obtained from the white cup that was consistent with a single male individual (Table 1). A DNA profile was also obtained from the straw consisting of a mixture of DNA from more than one person; the major portion of the DNA was different from the male type from the white cup (Table 1). A DNA profile was not obtained from the white plastic spoon. Because no suspects had been developed for this case, the profiles from the white cup and straw were both submitted to the CODIS database.

7.2. Case Study: Aggravated Sexual Assault

Also in June 2002, a woman was abducted and sexually assaulted by two men. A sexual assault kit was collected at a local hospital and submitted to the laboratory for analysis. Serology testing was performed on the items from the kit and seminal fluid (AP-positive reaction) was detected on the vaginal and anal swabs. Spermatozoa were visualized on the vaginal and anal smears (microscope slides). These items were saved for DNA analysis.

A differential DNA extraction was performed on the vaginal and anal swabs and the profiles that were obtained were compared to the profiles obtained from the complainant and two suspects (Table 2). The sperm fraction of the vaginal swabs was consistent with one of the two suspects identified in the case (suspect 2). The sperm fraction of the anal swabs was consistent with a mixture of DNA from more than one individual; both the complainant and the same suspect (suspect 2) were included as possible contributors to the mixture.

Because of the DNA evidence, other evidence from the case, and extenuating circumstances, both suspects pled guilty to a considerable jail sentence. The profile from the sperm fraction of the vaginal swabs was entered into the CODIS database, as was the profile from the other suspect (suspect 1). These profiles later produced a high stringency match at the local level with the profile from the straw (to the sperm fraction of the vaginal swabs) and the Styrofoam cup (to suspect 1) from the case study in Subheading 7.1. Because both suspects were already serving an extended sentence, the investigation into the stolen car case (Subheading 7.1.) was able to be closed.

USEFUL WEBSITES

1. http://www.cstl.nist.gov/biotech/strbase/
2. http://www.ascld-lab.org
3. http://ystr.charite.de/
4. http://www.mitomap.org/

GLOSSARY

Acid phosphatase:	An enzyme present in high concentrations in seminal fluid.
Allele:	Alternate forms of DNA that occur at any one locus.
Amylase:	An enzyme highly concentrated in saliva.
CODIS database:	A repository of DNA profiles from forensic evidence and convicted offenders.
Conceptus:	Child or offsping; in criminal paternity testing may be tissue from an aborted fetus.
Confirmatory testing:	In serology analysis, testing that confirms the presence of a bodily fluid on an item.
Contamination:	The presence of foreign DNA in a sample.
Criminal paternity testing:	A comparison of the DNA profiles of a conceptus, an alleged father, and a mother/complainant (if available) to establish or disprove parentage.
Cytoplasm:	The portion of a cell outside the nucleus.
Differential extraction:	A DNA extraction that attempts to separate spermatozoa DNA from all other DNA in a sample.
DNA profile:	A listing of all observed alleles at each locus of a sample.
Electrophoresis:	A method to separate proteins or DNA, usually by size, using an electrical current.

Epithelial cells:	Cells lining the skin surface and body orifices.
False-positive:	In serology analysis, a substance other than the specific bodily fluid in question that may produce a positive reaction during presumptive testing.
Heterozygous:	Having two alleles at one locus.
Homozygous:	Having a single allele at one locus.
Inhibitors:	Chemicals or other compounds in a sample that interfere with DNA analysis.
Loci:	Plural of "locus".
Locus:	A location on the DNA strand.
Lyse:	In DNA extraction, to break open cells in order to release their components.
Mitochondrial DNA:	DNA that is found outside a cell's nucleus, in a cell's cytoplasm that is contained within mitochondria.
Mixture:	In DNA analysis, the presence of more than one individual's DNA on a sample.
Negative control:	In DNA analysis, PCR (amplification) reagents without the addition of sample DNA to monitor for contamination of the amplification reagents.
Nuclear DNA:	DNA that is found inside a cell's nucleus; unique to an individual.
Nucleus:	A portion of a cell that contains (nuclear) DNA.
p30:	Also known as PSA (prostate-specific antigen), a protein found in seminal fluid.
Paternity testing:	Comparing DNA profiles from a child/offspring and an alleged father to establish or disprove paternity.
Presumptive testing:	In serology analysis, testing that indicates that a bodily fluid might be present on an item.
Phenolphthalein (PH):	A chemical used for the presumptive testing of blood.
Probative:	Referring to items that have evidentiary value, or that are substantiating, especially when presented at court.
Polymorphic regions:	Sections of the DNA strand that are highly variable between individuals.
Positive control:	In DNA analysis, a sample for which a DNA profile is established.
Primers:	Short segments of DNA that are used to target portions of the DNA strand for amplification by PCR.
Reagent blank:	All the reagents in the extraction process without any sample added; used to detect contamination of the extraction reagents.
Reagents:	Chemicals used in laboratory processes.
Remains identification or body identification:	Comparing DNA profiles from a body or set of remains to a family member to determine whether the two are related.

Semen:	A bodily fluid produced by male individuals for fertilization containing seminal fluid and spermatozoa.
Seminal fluid:	A protein rich bodily fluid originating primarily from the prostate and seminal vesicles.
Sequencing:	A process that breaks down the DNA strand by order into its respective bases (A, C, T, or G).
Spermatozoa:	Male sex cells produced in the testis, also known as "sperm."
Tetramethylbenzidine (TMB):	A chemical used for the presumptive testing of blood.

REFERENCES

1. James SH. Bloodstain pattern interpretation. In: Eckert WG and James SH, eds. Interpretation of Bloodstain Evidence at Crime Scenes. New York: Elsevier Science Publishing, 1989, p.11–67.
2. Gaensslen, RE, ed. Sourcebook in Forensic Serology, Immunology, and Biochemistry. National Institute of Justice, Washington, D.C., 1983.
3. Quarino L, Hess J, Shenouda M, Ristenbatt RR, Gold J, Shaler RC. Differentiation of α-amylase from various sources: an approach using selective inhibitors. J Forensic Sci Soc 1993;33:87–94.
4. National Research Council. The Evaluation of Forensic DNA Evidence. National Academy Press, Washington, D.C., 1996.
5. Budowle B, Chakraborty R, Carmody G, Monson KL. Source attribution of a forensic DNA profile. Forensic Sci Communications 2000;2(3): www.fbi.gov/hq/ lab/ fsc/backissu/july2000/source.htm.
6. Gill P, Ivanov PL, Kimpton C, et al. Identification of the remains of the Romanov family by DNA analysis. Nat Genet 1994;6:130–135.
7. Reynolds R, Walker K, Valaro J, et al. Detection of sequence variation in the HVII region of the human mitochondrial genome in 689 individuals using immobilized sequence-specific oligonucleotide probes. J Forensic Sci 2000;45:1210–31.
8. Gabriel MN, Calloway CD, Reynolds FL, Primorac D. Identification of human remains by immobilized sequence-specific oligonucleotide probe analysis of mtDNA hypervariable regions I and II. Croat Med J 2003;44:293–8.
9. Melton T, Nelson K. Forensic mitochondrial DNA analysis: two years of commercial casework experience in the United States. Croat Med J 2001;42:298–303.
10. Federal Bureau of Investigation, Quality Assurance Standards for Forensic DNA Testing Laboratories, 1998.
11. Federal Bureau of Investigation, Quality Assurance Standards for Convicted Offender DNA Databasing Laboratories, 1999.

SUGGESTED READING

Butler J. Forensic DNA Typing: Biology and Technology Behind STR Markers. San Diego, CA: Academic Press, 2001.

National Research Council. The Evaluation of Forensic DNA Evidence. National Academy Press, 1996.

Baechtel FS. The identification and individualization of semen stains. In: Saferstein R, ed. The Forensic Science Handbook, Vol. 2. Englewood Cliffs, NJ: Prentice Hall, 1988.

Gaensslen, RE, ed. Sourcebook in Forensic Serology, Immunology, and Biochemistry. National Institute of Justice, 1983.

American Society of Crime Laboratory Directors-Laboratory Accreditation Board (ASCLD-LAB), ASCLD-LAB Accreditation Manual, 1999.

Technical Working Group on DNA Analysis Methods. Guidelines for a Quality Assurance Program for DNA Analysis. Crime Laboratory Digest, 1995;22:21–43.

Federal Bureau of Investigation, Quality Assurance Standards for Forensic DNA Testing Laboratories, 1998.

Federal Bureau of Investigation, Quality Assurance Standards for Convicted Offender DNA Databasing Laboratories, 1999.

Chapter 2

Forensic Chemistry

Donnell Christian, BS

1. INTRODUCTION

"Forensic chemistry" is a broad term that, if taken literally, would encompass most of the functions within a crime laboratory. Techniques used in forensic chemistry are also used by the toxicology and trace analysis sections. However, forensic chemistry generally refers to controlled substance or drug analysis.

Traditionally, an examiner enters a crime laboratory career through the forensic chemistry door. Working in this area provides the opportunity for the new examiner to develop the tools required to move on to more complex and subjective examinations. He has the opportunity to learn and master the fundamentals of evidence handling, note taking, and report writing by processing the large volume of cases that pass through this section. Similarly, the examiner also has the opportunity to learn and hone testimony skills.

Generic educational requirements for an examiner/forensic chemist are the same in most US forensic laboratories. A degree in a natural science with a minimum number of hours of chemistry is generally accepted as the baseline educational standard. This standard is reflected in the recommendations of the Scientific Working Group for the Analysis of Seized Drugs (SWGDRUG). This basic education serves as the necessary foundation for the balance of the examiner's career. To paraphrase a former colleague, "We can teach you forensic applications. We don't have time to teach you chemistry."

Developing a trained thought process is also taught during an examiner's early years in the forensic chemistry section. His deductive reasoning skills

From: *The Forensic Laboratory Handbook: Procedures and Practice*
Edited by: A. Mozayani and C. Noziglia © Humana Press Inc., Totowa, NJ

are cultivated. He is taught how to utilize his education and training to identify and defend the identification of controlled substances in an exhibit using information from a series of nonspecific tests. The examiner then supports his findings with a specific test, confirming the presence of the controlled substance.

The analysis of controlled substance exhibits is pretty straightforward. The examiner uses a series of nonspecific tests and deductive reasoning to form an opinion concerning the contents of the exhibit under examination. He supports his opinion using modern instrumentation that provides documentable confirmation. The thought process learned and developed performing these black and white examinations will be invaluable experience to the examiner as he moves onto types of examinations whose results are, at best, seen as shades of gray.

2. EXAMINATION PROCESS

The controlled substances section of forensic chemistry receives a variety of evidence types ranging from botanicals to pharmaceuticals and can be in any physical state (i.e., solid, liquid, or gas). Controlled substance examinations can be simply divided into two basic forms: botanical and chemical. Botanical examinations identify physical characteristics of plants that are considered controlled substances. Chemical examinations use wet chemical or instrumental examination techniques to identify specific substances that are controlled by statute.

2.1. Planning

The examination planning process begins before the examiner ever encounters the evidence. It begins as he reviews the "request for analysis" form. Every laboratory has its own version of this document. However, they all contain a section listing who requested the analysis, the type of examination, a description of the exhibits submitted for analysis, and chain of custody sections.

During the initial review, the examiner compares the type of evidence that has been submitted to the information the submitter wants from the examination. He or she evaluates whether the available technology will provide the information the submitter desires, compares the submitter's request to the applicable statutes and laboratory policy, and evaluates other examination requests for the same exhibits to ensure that his or her analysis will not affect the results of the other examinations.

Local laws and criminal procedure codes influence the examiner's analysis. For example, criminal procedures in the United States provide examiners more latitude in planning their examination than laboratories in former Soviet Republics. The request for analysis document in the former Soviet Republics is actually a request from the Court to perform a specific examination that will answer a specific question. In the United States the examination of physical evidence is a fact-finding exercise used to identify the contents of the exhibit. Once the presence or absence of a controlled substance is determined the appropriate criminal charge can be applied or dismissed.

The right of the examiner to perform the tests he feels appropriate may be both a blessing and a curse. On the positive side, it provides for the examiner the ability to identify and report the presence of any controlled substances detected during his examination. On the other hand, the examiner may have to justify why the examinations he performed may have been outside the scope of the requests listed on the submission form.

As the examiner reviews the analysis request concerning what information the investigator desires and what information is required by statute, he formulates a list of questions that must be answered. The questions that need to be addressed in controlled substance examinations are the same in most cases:

- "How much does the exhibit weigh?"
- "What controlled substance does the exhibit contain?"
- "What is the statutory classification of the controlled substance?"

Auxiliary questions that may need to also be asked and answered are:

- "What percentage of the exhibit contained a controlled substance?"
- "What adulterants and diluents were identified?"

Below are two examples of an examiner working outside the parameters listed on the request form:

1. A sample from a clandestine laboratory was submitted with a request to examine for the presence of methamphetamine. The analysis did not detect methamphetamine. However, the sample did contain a controlled hallucinogen, diethyltryptamine. As a result of the examination the charges against the suspect were amended to reflect the controlled substance that was present.
2. A narcotics officer requested a qualitative and quantitative examination of an exhibit suspected to contain cocaine. When the examiner was asked why he did not perform the quantitative portion of the exam, he replied that neither the statute nor laboratory policy required quantitative examination.

In the first case, the examiner went beyond the scope of the request; his standard analytical scheme screened for all controlled substances. If a controlled substance was detected, he confirmed its presence. This method allowed the charges to be modified to include the identity of the controlled substance that was detected.

The second examiner's decision not to quantitate the exhibit did not affect the legal proceedings. The governing statutes and sentencing structure did not contain language that required quantitation. Additionally, laboratory policy did not require quantitation as part of the analytical scheme.

The legal system in the United States is adversarial. The examiner must be able to articulate the rationale behind each step of the examination process to the satisfaction of both the prosecution and the defense. He must keep this in mind as he draws his analytical road map. For every step of the process, the examiner must ask himself, "Can I explain how and why I performed this examination on this exhibit?"

Once the examiner receives the exhibit he goes through the same decision-making process for each item. Like a computer, he routinely goes through a series of yes/no or if/then questions during the examination. This analytical approach should be the same with each piece of evidence to avoid a perception of bias on the part of the examiner. If accused of preconception, the examiner can success-fully defend his process by responding that the same analytical scheme was always used and that the test results themselves dictated the direction of the analysis.

2.2. Documentation

Documentation is the life blood of the legal system. It has been said that "if it is not written down, it does not exist." Therefore, it is essential that each step of the examination process be documented.

This adage has become more important since the O. J. Simpson defense team implemented the "call you a liar" defense. Investigators and forensic personnel were required to prove that tests were performed and that the results presented in court represented the results observed in the laboratory or at the crime scene. This defense strategy forces the forensic examiner out of the shadows of the "trust me: I am from the government and here to help" mentality to an objective seeker of scientific truth.

Documentation provides a mechanism for peer review, which is a mark of good science and a cornerstone of a quality assurance program. An examiner's notes and analytical data must justify the conclusion articulated in the final report. More importantly, a reviewer in the same area of expertise should agree with the report's conclusion after reviewing the original examiner's notes and analytical data. The reviewer may have a different opinion. However, he agrees that the examiner's data supports his conclusion.

Documentation of physical evidence has three critical components: chain of custody, working notes, and final report. Each component has its own documentation requirements. Although every laboratory and laboratory section may have its own format in addressing these documentation requirements, each component must still be addressed.

2.2.1. Chain of Custody

The chain of custody is the list of procedures and documents that account for the integrity of a sample by tracking its handling and storage from its point of collection to its final disposition. Simply put, the chain of custody is a document (or series of documents) that tracks the location of an exhibit from crime scene to courtroom and beyond.

Forensic chemistry section chain of custody issues are simple for the most part. The examiner documents when and from whom he initially received the exhibit(s) and when and to whom he returned the exhibits after the examination was completed. It is generally accepted that the exhibit is in the examiner's sole care and custody during this time frame. The documentation is usually accomplished through the use of an official form and supplemented by notations in the examiner's working notes.

What happens to the exhibit once it has been received by the examiner are issues that are rarely addressed, but equally require documentation. The date and time an examination is performed have become issues. The identity of the person who actually performed one or more of the tests is another issue that must be documented, as well as the time and date the exhibit or test sample was transferred to a different examiner for specific testing.

Intralaboratory transfers of exhibits or samples from an exhibit should be treated the same as an interlaboratory transfer. The examiner transfers control of the exhibit or sample to another individual for a specific examination. The time of the transfer and the identity of the second examiner are just as relevant in a legal proceeding as the transfer into and out of the laboratory. Therefore, they should be documented in a similar manner.

The early use of mass spectrometry is an example of when this transfer should be documented. The mass spectrometer was an expensive, highly specialized piece of instrumentation when it was first introduced into the forensic laboratory. The primary examiner had to rely on the mass spectroscopist to perform examinations specific to the mass spectrometer. Often the primary examiner had no direct knowledge of how the sample was handled once it was transferred to the mass spectroscopist. Even though the primary examiner interpreted the resulting data and possessed theoretical knowledge of the instrument's operation and the sample preparation techniques used, he could not provide direct knowledge that every procedure was followed. This is a chain of custody issue that therefore demands documentation.

2.2.2. Working Notes

The examiner's working notes are the second component of the documentation process. Consisting of a compilation of handwritten notes, worksheets, and instrumental data, these notes have two functions: (1) they document that the examination actually occurred and (2) they are used to refresh the examiner's memory during the report-writing phase or before and during trial testimony.

Handwritten notes have two formats. Notes can either be a series of notations on a blank sheet of paper or preprinted worksheets used to streamline the documentation of the repetitive testing procedures used in drug analysis. No matter which form the notes take, each page should contain the examiner's initials, the date the examination occurred, the case number, the exhibit number, the page number, and the total number of pages (including pages of instrumental data).

Legibility is a key component of handwritten notes. Not only are notes used to refresh the examiner's memory, but they are also a part of the peer review process. If the examiner uses shorthand, it must be decipherable for the peer review process to be effective. If the shorthand is confusing, then its meaning may be misinterpreted leading to ambiguity rather than clarity.

2.2.3. Final Report

The official report is the final component of the documentation procedure. This report summarizes the examination of the evidence into a single concise document. All of the information in the case notes and analytical data, as well as the examiner's professional opinions should be reflected in this report. The final report should provide the reader a road map of the trip the exhibit took through the forensic examination process. Ideally, this report should be able to stand on its own and not require courtroom explanations from the examiner.

Every laboratory has its own examination report format. Most of these formats are based on the criteria set forth by the American Society of Testing Materials, the American Society of Crime Laboratory Directors/Laboratory Accreditation Board, or one of the various scientific working groups. Although visual layout may vary, every report should include:

- Examining laboratory identity.
- Case file number.
- Name of the individual requesting the examination(s).
- Examiner's name.
- A list and description of the exhibit(s) submitted for examination.
- Description of the examination(s) performed.
- Results of the examination.
- Chain of custody information.

As stated above, there should be sufficient information in the final report to make the testimony of the examiner unnecessary. Simple one and two word answers in the administrative sections are usually adequate. The examination descriptions and results sections do, however, require more detail. Some formats have already separated these sections. Other formats include a description of the testing process in the results narrative. In either case, the report's reader should be able to discern what controlled substance was identified and the testing process used to make that determination.

Two examples of styles of reporting examination results are provided:

Example 1

Items	1. White powder
	2. Plant material
Exam	Drugs
Results	1. Contained cocaine, a narcotic drug. Substance weight 1.32 g. A usable quantity.
	2. Contained marijuana. Substance weight 6.29 g. A usable quantity.

Example 2

Items	1. Item 1 contained a paper packet containing a white powder.
	2. Item 2 contained a plastic bag containing green leafy plant material.
Results	1. The examination of Item 1 using wet chemical tests, microcrystal tests, gas chromatography and infrared spectroscopy concludes that Item 1 contained a usable quantity of cocaine. The total substance weighing was 1.32 g, which is considered a usable quantity. Cocaine is defined as a narcotic drug under ARS 13-3401.20.
	2. The examination of Item 2 using microscopic and wet chemical techniques concludes that Item 2 contained marijuana. The total substance weighing was 6.29 g, which is considered a usable quantity. Marijuana is defined as a narcotic drug under ARS 13-3401.20

Example 1 provides the basic information in a no-nonsense format. The reader can quickly identify what each exhibit contained, the quantity of the substance, its classification under the governing statutes, and a case law required opinion concerning the amount of substance seized. However, information concerning how the examiner reached his conclusions is not presented. This omission may lead to an unnecessary and time-consuming court appearance.

Example 2, by contrast, includes information concerning how the examiner reached his conclusions. The key pieces of information, i.e., the identity, weight, and classification of the controlled substance, are not as readily discernable as in Example 1. However, the information concerning the basis for the examiner's conclusions is included. This addition may lead to more stipulations by the opposing attorney, thus reducing the number of court appearances required by the examiner.

3. ANALYSIS

In October 2000, the SWGDRUG met in Vienna, Austria to finalize its recommendations concerning the examination and identification of controlled substances. Some of these contained suggestions for the minimum examination requirements for the identification of controlled substances. Although these recommendations do not hold any statutory authority, they do represent the accepted analytical standards established by a consensus of the scientific community engaged in the analysis of drugs of abuse.

3.1. Botanical Examinations

Botanical examinations are the most common analysis performed in the controlled substance section. It is not unusual for marijuana examinations to exceed 50% of the caseload. Programs utilized by some agencies allowing trained law enforcement personnel to provide preliminary cannabis identifications have dramatically reduced the number of laboratory examinations.

The forensic chemist walks a tightrope when performing botanical examinations. Generally he is a chemist by education and training, not a biologist or a botanist. However, he is identifying plants and plant material, not the specific psychoactive ingredient. He must remember he is trained in the identification of specific types of plants or plant parts. He can only identify whether plant material is or is not marijuana, peyote, or opium. Beyond that, he should not render an opinion as to the identity of the substance.

The plants that require botanical examinations by the forensic chemistry section include marijuana, peyote, mushrooms, and opium. Marijuana is by far the most common botanical examination. The examination of mushrooms, peyote, and opium poppies samples is rare in the United States. However, the examiner must know the physical characteristics of these plants in order to be able to recognize them when they are presented in case samples.

The examination techniques used for botanical examinations are subjective and cannot be documented in a manner that can be objectively reviewed. The peer reviewer only has the comments in the working notes to evaluate, unless some form of photography is used to document the visual and wet chemical examinations. Therefore, the examiner's working notes should contain as much detail as possible when describing visual examination.

There are documentable instrumental techniques that can be employed to identify specific chemical components within the botanical sample. However, the presence or absence of the component in question may or may not be an element of the identification criteria. The four legal definitions of plants that are considered controlled substances demonstrate the variation of need to identify specific chemical compounds.

1. The term "marihuana" means all parts of the plant *Cannabis sativa L.*, whether growing or not; the seeds thereof; the resin extracted from any part of such plant; and every compound, manufacture, salt, derivative, mixture, or preparation of such plant, its seeds or resin. Such term does not include the mature stalks of such plant, fiber produced from such stalks, oil, or cake made from the seeds of such plant, any other compound, manufacture, salt, derivative, mixture, or preparation of such mature stalks (except the resin extracted there from), fiber, oil, or cake, or the sterilized seed of such plant which is incapable of germination *(1)*.

2. "Marijuana" means all parts of any plant of the genus *cannabis*, from which the resin has not been extracted, whether growing or not, and the seeds of such plant. Marijuana does not include the mature stalks of such plant or the sterilized seed of such plant which is incapable of germination *(2)*.

3. "Coca leaves," except coca leaves and extracts of coca leaves from which cocaine, ecgonine, and derivatives of ecgonine or their salts have been removed *(3)*.

4. "Coca leaves" means cocaine, its optical isomers and any compound, manufacture, salt, derivative, mixture or preparation of coca leaves, except derivatives of coca leaves which do not contain cocaine, ecgonine or substances from which cocaine or ecgonine may be synthesized or made *(4)*.

These legal definitions establish the baseline from which the analytical process is derived. Examples 1 and 2 each present an instance in which identifying the presence of the psychoactive component of the plant is not a requisite element of the definition. However, some laboratories do require the chemical identification of the psychoactive component to enhance the level of the examination's specificity. Examples 3 and 4 are instances in which the presence or absence of specific psychoactive component(s) determine the botanical's legal status.

3.2. Chemical Examinations

The balance of the samples encountered by the controlled substances section require the identification of specific compounds within a mixture. Composition of the samples may vary, but the identifying procedure remains the same. Each sample requires a screening step, an extraction or sample preparation step, and a confirmatory step to be performed.

The SWGDRUG recommendations divide chemical tests into three categories based upon specificity and documentability. Category A tests are specific and documentable, Category B examinations are documentable and characteristic in nature, and Category C tests are characteristic examinations with less specificity, which may or may not be documentable. Ideally, one or more Category B and C tests are used to screen for the presence of a controlled substance within a sample. Category A tests are used to positively identify the controlled substance present.

Chemical examinations can be simply subdivided into wet chemical and instrumental procedures. Wet chemical procedures are used as a screening method or for sample preparation. Instrumental procedures are used for screening or as a confirmation tool.

Wet chemical procedures are used during the initial stages of the identification process. They consist of chemical color tests, microcrystalline tests, thin layer chromatography and liquid extraction techniques. These nonspecific tests provide a method to quickly determine whether a controlled substance may be present within a sample. Some procedures can be used to isolate controlled substances for confirmatory testing using instrumental techniques. A series of these tests can be used to deductively identify a controlled substance.

Instrumental examinations are documentable testing methods. This point is a key element of the confirmation and peer review process. It is not enough for the examiner to be able to claim the compound has the same chemical fingerprint as a controlled substance. In a criminal proceeding he has to be able to prove it beyond a reasonable doubt, which includes subjecting the examination to peer review. Instrumental examinations provide the vehicle for this review.

3.2.1. SWGDRUG Examination Categories

As previously stated, SWGDRUG has established three categories of analytical techniques that can be used for the identification of controlled substances. The groupings are based on the technique's discriminating power. Listed here are the categories and associated analytical techniques:

Category C

Nonspecific techniques

Chemical color tests	A nondocumentable technique that uses the colors produced by chemical reactions to provide information regarding the structure of the substance being tested.
Fluorescence spectroscopy	A documentable analytical technique that uses the release characteristic wavelengths of radiation following the absorption of electromagnetic radiation (fluorescence) to establish a compound's potential identity.
Immunoassay	A documentable laboratory technique that uses the binding between an antigen and its homologous antibody to identify and quantify the specific antigen or antibody in a sample.

Melting point	The temperature at which a solid becomes a liquid at standard atmospheric pressure. The documentability of this technique depends upon the instrument used.
Ultraviolet spectroscopy (UV)	A documentable technique that uses of the absorption of ultraviolet radiation to classify a substance.

Category B

Moderately Specific Techniques

Capillary electrophoresis (CE)	A documentable separation technique using the differential movement or migration of ions by attraction or repulsion in an electric field through buffer-filled narrow-bore capillary columns as an identification tool.
Gas chromatography (GC)	A documentable separation technique that uses gas flowing through a coated tube to separate compounds by their size, weight and chemical reactivity with the column coating.
Liquid chromatography (LC)	A documentable separation technique that uses liquid flowing through a coated tube to separate compounds by their size, weight and chemical reactivity with the column coating.
Microcrystalline tests	A technique that uses the microscopic crystals produced by chemical reactions to provide information regarding the identity of the substance being tested. A series of positive microcrystalline tests can be considered to be a conclusive test. This technique can be considered documentable if photomicrographs of the crystals used for identification are taken at the time of the examination.
Pharmaceutical identifiers	Comparing the physical characteristics of a commercially produced pharmaceutical product to known reference material to tentatively establish the composition of the preparation.
Thin layer chromatography	A traditionally nondocumentable technique that uses solvent(s) traveling through a porous medium to separate compounds by their chemical reactivity. This technique can be documented through photographing or photocopying the developed thin layer plate.

Category A

Specific Examinations

Infrared spectroscopy (IR)	A specific documentable technique that uses the absorption of infrared radiation to produce a chemical fingerprint of a substance. This technique can be used in conjunction with GC.
Mass spectroscopy (MS)	A specific documentable technique that uses molecular fragment (ion) patterns to produce a chemical fingerprint of a

	substance. This technique can be used in conjunction with GC and liquid chromatography.
Nuclear magnetic resonance spectroscopy (NMR)	A specific documentable technique that monitors the splitting of nuclear energy levels within a molecule when it is exposed to oscillating magnetic fields.
Raman spectroscopy	A specific documentable technique that uses the inelastic scattering of light by matter to produce a chemical fingerprint of a substance.

3.3. Scope of Analysis

Local laws and criminal procedures will be the driving force behind the scope of the analytical process. The laboratory's mission within its agency will also weigh heavily into the depth of analysis each exhibit will receive. For example, the amount of analytical effort involved in the identification of a controlled substance for criminal prosecution purposes is significantly less than that required for intelligence gathering and investigative purposes. The only information required in a criminal prosecution is the identity and amount of controlled substance contained in an exhibit. Laboratories responsible for intelligence gathering will also identify the types and quantity of the exhibit's diluents and adulterants.

The level of analytical detail required not only affects the time involved, but also the type of instrumentation required. Most forensic chemistry sections can provide a complete range of analytical service wet chemical techniques and a basic MS or IR. As the level of information detail increases, so does the type and sensitivity of the instrumentation required. For example, the equipment and procedures required to confirm the presence of heroin in a street sample is far less sophisticated than the one needed to identify the region of the world in which the opium used to produce the heroin was grown.

The final issue that determines the depth of analysis is laboratory policy. The laboratory's policy is generally developed through collaboration between the laboratory's management and a peer group consisting of the examiners who perform the examinations on a daily basis. This represents a balance between the need to produce timely results that meet the applicable legal criteria while at the same time not compromising the scientific integrity of the examination.

An example of this collaboration is the need for quantitative analysis. Unless mandated by statute, the amount of a controlled substance in an exhibit is not an element of the crime. However, this information may have investigative significance and can also be used as part of an internal quality control (QC) procedure. It may not be realistic to quantitate every exhibit submitted for analysis. Therefore, laboratory and investigators work together to establish a quantitation policy that satisfies the needs of both parties.

3.4. Data Interpretation

Over time, a forensic chemist develops an intuition that can identify the controlled substance in an exhibit by simply observing the consistency of the powder, the texture of the plant material, or the odor of the liquid. Observations and intuition are not documentable objective tests that can be subject to peer review. Documentable data that can be interpreted and reviewed is required to support the examiner's sixth sense.

The analysis of controlled substances can be considered a black and white type of examination. The exhibit under examination either contains a controlled substance, or it does not. The comparison of the chemical "fingerprint" of the unknown to the fingerprint of a known reference standard is more complicated than laying one on top of another. Spectra can and do vary for a number of reasons. The lack of superimposability of two spectra does not preclude identification.

The term *chemical fingerprint* can be misleading. It implies a given chemical will produce one unique spectrum using a given technique without regard to sampling technique or the instrumental conditions at the time of analysis. Conceptually, the term is correct in that a given chemical will produce a unique spectrum using a given technique. However, the resulting spectrum can have slight variations as a result of the sampling technique used to prepare the sample for examination and the operating conditions of the instrument at the time of analysis.

Library spectra should never be used for conclusive identification purposes because of spectral variations. Library spectra present a wonderful tool for preliminary identification purposes. Conclusive identifications should only be made after the comparison of spectrum of the unknown to one of a traceable primary reference standard produced on the same instrument. A new reference spectrum must be produced each time a suspected controlled substance produces an unfamiliar spectral variation. This demonstrates the reproducibility of the substance's spectrum on the instrument being used.

3.5. SWGDRUG Recommendations

The SWGDRUG guidelines provide recommendations for the types and minimum number of tests required to identify seized drugs. A validated Category A technique with documentable data, supported by one Category A, B, or C technique is the suggested minimum examination criteria. A combination of three different Category B and C techniques can be used if a Category A technique is unavailable. The Category B techniques must produce reviewable data.

3.6. Quality Assurance/Quality Control

A documented quality assurance (QA) and quality control (QC) program is just as important as documenting the results of individual examinations. The examination

results may not be accepted by the court if the reliability of the instruments, protocols, and chemicals used to perform the examinations cannot be established.
Individual QC protocols demonstrate the reliability of the examination process. It is
the combination of both which displays the reliability of the whole process (QA).

QA is a documented system of protocols used to assure the accuracy and
reliability of analytical results and consists of a variety of components.
Proficiency testing and employee qualifications and training standards are
directed at the forensic chemist's performing the examinations. Documented
evidence collection and handling procedures as well as documented, standardized,
and validated analytical protocols are used to ensure that the analytical methods used meet an accepted scientific standard. Instrument maintenance logs,
reagent preparation records, and the use of traceable chemicals used in the
preparation of testing reagents document the reliability of the chemicals and
equipment used in the examination process. The use of traceable reference
material ensures that the material being used to generate the data being used for
identification purposes is from a known source.

A QA program produces intangible effects that may be difficult to assess.
Service is improved through a streamlined operation. The numbers of challenges to
the analytical results are reduced because of the documented reliability of the
equipment, chemicals, and protocols used. The need for re-analysis is reduced, saving
the laboratory time and money. The laboratory's image and credibility is improved,
which leads to fewer court appearances resulting from testimony stipulation. Each of
these effects enhances those of the others. Quality work leads to credibility, which
enhances staff morale and ultimately produces a more productive work environment.

4. CLANDESTINE DRUG LABORATORIESS

Clandestine drug laboratories (herein referred to as "clan labs" as they are
called by law enforcement officers) are illicit facilities that manufacture
controlled substances. The types and numbers of laboratories seized reflect
national and regional trends concerning the types and amounts of illicit substances that are being manufactured, trafficked, and abused. Clan labs have been
found in remote locations, in urban and suburban neighborhoods, hotels and
motels, industrial complexes, as well as academic and industrial laboratories.
Each location may produce toxic and explosive fumes that can pose a significant
threat to the health and safety of local residents, as well as respondents such as
police, fire, and hazardous materials officers.

The sophistication of clandestine labs varies widely. The production of
substances such as methamphetamine, phencyclidine, methylenedioxymetham-
phetamine (more commonly known as "ecstasy"), and methcathinone requires

little sophisticated equipment or knowledge of chemistry. The synthesis of drugs, such as fentanyl and lysergic acid diethylamide, requires much higher levels of expertise and equipment.

The investigation of clan labs is one of the most challenging efforts of law enforcement. No other law enforcement activity relies on forensic science as heavily. The controlled substances section's involvement commences with the drafting of the affidavit used to obtain the search warrant. Their expertise is needed to process the crime scene as they analyze the evidence in a laboratory and render opinions in a written report or in courtroom testimony. Occasionally, they are called on to testify on auxiliary issues concerning the clan lab investigation that occur after the case has been adjudicated.

The controlled substance section addresses the what, where, why, and how questions of investigation: what controlled substance were the operators making? What are the chemicals and equipment that were purchased by the operators used for? Where were the operators manufacturing the controlled substances? Why did the operators use a certain chemical or type of equipment? How did the operator manufacture a controlled substance using chemicals and equipment commonly found in kitchens or bathrooms? Investigators must use other investigative techniques to fill in the "who" and "when" questions.

4.1. Crime Scene Support

The amount and type of crime scene support provided to clan lab seizures varies between forensic laboratories. Some laboratories provide a full range of support, with a group of chemists dedicated to providing crime scene and analytical support for clan lab investigations. Other laboratories provide support by sending to crime scenes chemists who may or may not have specialized training in clan labs.

The on-scene chemist provides a wide range of technical support. He identifies the chemicals and equipment that can potentially be used in the manufacture of illicit drugs. He assists in the sampling process. He can also provide preliminary opinions as to the proposed final product and the manufacturing method used by the operation. His scene report is used by the laboratory examiner as a guide to assist in devising the analytical scheme used to identify the controlled substance being manufactured, as well as establishing the manufacturing method used.

4.2. Laboratory Analysis

The laboratory analysis of samples taken from the scene of a clan lab is the link between the investigation and the opinions. It provides the scientific foundation that corroborates the investigator's theories and is used to support the opinions rendered in reports, legal depositions, and court testimony. Without complete and thorough laboratory analysis the case may remain unresolved.

The analysis of exhibits from clan labs involves the use of a variety of scientific techniques. Some examinations use techniques outside of those normally associated with drug identification. These techniques range from simple chemical color tests to the use of X-ray and infrared energy to elicit the compound's chemical fingerprint. The type of test used depends on the information desired from the sample and the burden of proof required to establish its identity.

The forensic laboratory analysis of clan lab exhibits is more involved than the simple identification of a controlled substance. The identification of the components of the sample matrix may be just as important. A complete analysis is essential to establish the manufacturing method. Yet in some instances it may not be absolutely necessary.

Ramifications outside the laboratory should be considered when the examiner maps out his analysis. The lack of a complete analysis may affect aspects of the investigation or prosecution of which the examiner is not aware. If the examiner is asked to render opinions concerning the manufacturing operation, he must have documentation to support his opinion. A complete laboratory analysis is one source of the information he needs to support his opinions.

It is not sufficient to say that the clan lab operator was using a particular method simply because some or all of the ingredients appear to be found at the site. The presence or absence of a particular precursor or reagent chemical cannot be established beyond a reasonable doubt without laboratory examination. The relabeling of ingredients by the laboratory operator or lack of labels on the containers at the scene often makes the actual identity of the chemicals at the location questionable.

Presented here is an excerpt of an analytical chemist's testimony. The defense contended that the lack of the presence of hydriodic acid precluded the operator from manufacturing the controlled substance that the state contended. The cross examination of the analytical chemist charged with analysis of the evidence proceeded as follows:

Defense Attorney:	You stated exhibit 12 contained hydrochloric acid?
Chemist:	Yes sir.
Defense Attorney:	So there was no hydriodic acid found at the scene?
Chemist:	No Sir, I cannot say that.
Defense Attorney:	But your report states that you found hydrochloric acid, not HI. How can you say that there was hydriodic acid present?
Chemist:	The items in exhibit 24 and exhibit 31 were not sampled. The packaging and the color of the liquid are consistent with hydriodic acid.

Defense Attorney:	But your report states that hydrochloric acid was the only acid identified.
Chemist:	That is correct. However, the items in exhibit 24 and 31 were not sampled so I could not analyze the contents. Without laboratory analysis I cannot comment on the contents.
Defense Attorney:	So you are saying you did not find any hydriodic acid?
Chemist:	What I am saying is that I cannot say that there was no hydriodic acid at the scene. The packaging and color of the liquid of items 24 and 31 is consistent with commercially packaged hydriodic acid.

From ref. 5.

This whole exchange could have been avoided if the items at the scene were sampled properly. This would have provided the analytical chemist the opportunity to identify the contents of each container.

The same holds true with reaction mixtures. The chemist should identify the ingredients within the reaction mixture. The fact that a chemical or chemical container was located at the scene does not establish its presence in a reaction mixture. It only provides the chemist information he can utilize in developing his analytical scheme.

4.3. The Chemist

The chemist performing the laboratory examinations should specialize in clan lab analysis. In bookkeeping, all CPAs are accountants but not all accountants are CPAs. The same is true with forensic chemists. All clan lab chemists are forensic chemists, but not all forensic chemists are clan lab chemists. The cland lab chemist has additional training in clandestine manufacturing techniques, as well as in inorganic analysis. This allows him to expand his analytical scheme to identify all the chemicals used in the manufacturing process. His analytical scheme is geared to identifying the manufacturing process, not just the controlled substance involved.

The clan lab chemist's role in a clan lab investigation requires a different thought process when approaching his analysis. His examination reaches beyond the basic identification of a controlled substance in an exhibit. He approaches each sample as if he has to explain to a jury what components are in the sample and how they fit into the manufacturing process. From an investigative standpoint, his analytical approach is geared toward profiling the sample to provide the investigators information concerning the sample's composition so the investigators know what components to look for.

4.4. Expert Opinions

A clan lab is a Pandora's Box of illegal activities. Controlled substances are produced using household chemicals mixed in ordinary utensils in what some have called a "kitchen of death." What appears at first glance to be simply atrocious housekeeping or even just a hobby gone awry may actually be the final step in the production of many of the drugs sold on the street or the explosives used in various forms of domestic terrorism.

The clan lab chemist provides the expert opinions that draw calm from the chaos. He couples his clan lab training and experience with his deductive reasoning ability and laboratory examination results to develop a plausible scenario concerning the clandestine manufacturing operation in question. The clan lab chemist combines the black and white answers of the laboratory analysis with the crime scene information to provide answers to the investigation's and prosecution's who, what, when, where, why, and how questions.

Many types of opinions can only be generated from the laboratory analysis of evidentiary samples. Some opinions are a result of generalities that do not require the support of analytical data. For example, just because a red powder is found at the scene of a suspected ephedrine reduction laboratory does not make the powder the critical red phosphorus. It is absolutely essential for an analytical chemist who is going to render an opinion concerning a clan lab to have the analytical data ready to support that opinion.

As with laboratory analysis, opinions concerning clan lab operations should be able to withstand peer review. A component chemist or other forensic expert should be able to review the facts of the case or the laboratory data and draw the same conclusion the original expert did. Alternative opinions can and do exist, as is evidenced by prosecution and defense differences. But the information must support the opinion or the opinion is worthless.

5. SUMMARY

The forensic chemistry section of a traditional crime laboratory generally refers to the drug analysis or controlled substance identification section. Many forensic examiners begin their career in this section. Here they learn the tools of their trade by performing a wide variety of examinations using a plethora of analytical methods. They learn and develop the deductive reasoning skills to move from straightforward identification of controlled substances to examinations that require professional opinions to questions that just do not have black and white answers. The skills and knowledge the examiners cultivate here will serve them well if they transfer to other sections of the forensic laboratory.

GLOSSARY

Accreditation:	Procedure by which an accreditation body formally recognizes that a laboratory or person is competent to carry out specific tasks.
Accreditation Body:	Independent science-based organization that has the authority to grant accreditation.
Accuracy:	The ability of a measurement to match the actual value of the quantity being measured. Correctness
Adulterant:	A substance used to increase the mass of a controlled substance. These substances produce a physiological effect on the body and are used to give the illusion that there is more controlled substance present than actually is present.
Alkaloid:	A class of substances occurring readily formed in the tissues of plants and the bodies of animals. E.g. morphine and codeine are alkaloids of opium.
Analysis:	Technical operation to determine one or more characteristics of, or to evaluate the performance of, a given product, material, equipment, physical phenomenon, process, or service according to a specified procedure.
Analyst:	A designated person who:

- Examines and analyses seized drugs or related materials, or directs such examinations to be done.
- Independently has access to "open" (unsealed) evidence in order to remove samples from the evidence for examination.
- As a consequence of such examinations, signs reports for court or other purposes.

Aqueous:	Made from, or by means of, water.
Audit:	A review conducted to compare the various aspects of the laboratory's performance with a standard for that performance.
Blank:	Specimen or sample not containing the analyte.
Calibration:	Set of operations that establishes. under specified conditions, the relationship between values indicated by a measuring instrument or measuring system, or values represented by a material measure, and the corresponding known values of a measurand.
Certified reference material (CRM):	A reference material, one or more of whose property values have been certified by a technical procedure, accompanied by or traceable to a certificate

or other documentation that has been issued by a certifying body.

Certifying body:	Independent science-based organization that has the competence to grant certification.
Chain of custody:	Procedures and documents that account for the integrity of a sample by tracking its handling and storage from its point of collection to its final disposition.
Class characteristic:	A feature of an item that is unique to a group of items.
Control sample:	A standard of comparison for verifying or checking the finding of an experiment.
Controlled substance:	Any substance, commonly drugs, whose possession or use is regulated.
Controls:	Samples used to determine the validity of the calibration, that is, the linearity and stability of a quantitative test or determination over time. Controls are either prepared from the reference material (separately from the calibrators, that is, weighed or measured separately), purchased, or obtained from a pool of previously analyzed samples. Where possible, controls should be matrix-matched to samples and calibrators.
Deductive reasoning:	Using nonspecific details to infer a specific fact.
Depressant:	A drug that reduces excitability and calms a person.
Deficiency of analysis:	Any erroneous analytical result or interpretation, or any unapproved deviation from an established policy or procedure in an analysis.
Diluent:	An inert substance used to increase the mass of the controlled substance. These substances have no physiological effect on the body and are used to give the illusion that there is more controlled substance present than actually is present.
Drug:	A substance other than food intended to affect the structure or function of the body.
False-positive:	Test result that states that a drug is present when, in fact, such a drug is not present in an amount less than a threshold or designated cut-off concentration.
Gas chromatography:	The use of gas flowing through a coated tube to separate compounds by their size, weight and chemical reactivity with the column coating.
Gravametric quantitation:	Using the ratio of pre and post extraction weights to determine concentration.
Hallucinogen:	A psychoactive drug that induces hallucinations or alters sensory experiences.
Health and safety manager:	A designated person who is responsible for maintaining the laboratory health and safety program (including an annual

	review of the program) and who monitors compliance with the program.
Independent test result:	Result obtained in a manner not influenced by any previous results on the same or similar material.
Individual characteristic:	A feature that is unique to a specific item.
Inductive reasoning:	Using specific facts to infer a general conclusion.
Infrared spectroscopy:	The use of the absorption of infrared radiation to produce a chemical fingerprint of a substance.
Laboratory:	Facilities where analyses are performed by qualified personnel using adequate equipment.
Limit of detection:	Smallest measured content from which it is possible to deduce the presence of the analyte with reasonable statistical certainty.
Macroscopic examination:	Visual examination, generally performed with the unaided eye, used to identify class characteristics.
Method:	Detailed, defined procedure for performing an analysis.
Microscopic examination:	Visual examination, performed utilizing some type of magnification, used to identify individual characteristics.
Mass spectroscopy:	The use of molecular fragment (ion) patterns to produce a chemical fingerprint of a substance.
Narcotic:	An addictive substance that reduces pain, alters mood and behavior, and usually induces sleep or stupor.
Organic:	The class of chemical compounds having a carbon basis; "hydrocarbons are organic compounds."
Polymorphism:	Crystallization of a compound in at least two distinct forms.
Precision:	The ability to achieve the same result. Reproducibility
Procedure:	Specified, documented way to perform an activity.
Proficiency testing:	Ongoing process in which a series of proficiency samples, the characteristics of which are not known to the participants, are sent to laboratories on a regular basis. Each laboratory is tested for its accuracy in identifying the presence (or concentration) of the drug using its usual procedures.
Qualitative analysis:	Analytical technique used to determine the composition of a substance or mixture.
Quality assurance (QA):	System of activities whose purpose is to provide, to the producer or user of a product or a service, the assurance that it meets defined standards of quality with a stated level of confidence.
Quality assurance manager:	A designated person who is responsible for maintaining the quality management system and who monitors compliance with the program.

Quality management: That aspect of the overall management function that determines and implements the quality policy.

Quality manual: Document stating the general quality policies, procedures and practices of an organization.

Quantitative analysis: Analytical technique used to determine the concentration of one or more of the components of a mixture.

Racemic mixture: A combination of the different types of stereoisomers of the same compound.

Reference material: Material or substance one or more properties of which are sufficiently well established to be used for calibrating an apparatus, assessing a measurement method, or assigning values to materials.

Retention time: The time require for a substance to travel from the injection port to the detector.

Relative retention time: The ratio of the retention time of the substance of interest divided by the retention time of an internal standard run on the same instrument at the same time.

Report: Document containing a formal statement of results of tests carried out by a laboratory.

Representative sample: Statistically, a sample that is similar to the population from which it was drawn. When a sample is representative, it can be used to make inferences about the population. The most effective way to get a representative sample is to use random methods to draw it. Analytically, it is a sample that is a portion of the original material selected in such a way that is possible to relate the analytical results obtained from it to the properties of the original material.

Reproducibility: Closeness of agreement between the results of successive measurements of the same analyte in identical material made by the same method under different conditions, e.g., different operators and different laboratories and considerably separated in time.

Sample: A portion of the whole material to be tested. Statistically, it is a set of data obtained from a population.

Sampling: Analytically, the whole set of operations needed to obtain a sample, including planning, collecting, recording, labeling, sealing, shipping, etc. Statistically, it is the process of determining properties of the whole population by collecting and analyzing data from a representative segment of it.

Selectivity: Extent to which a method can determine particular analyte(s) in a mixture without interference from the other components

	in the mixture. A method that is perfectly selective for an analyte or group of analytes is said to be specific.
Standard operating procedures (SOPs):	A written document which details the method of an operation, analysis, or action whose techniques and procedures are thoroughly prescribed and which is accepted as the method for performing certain routine or repetitive tasks.
Stereo isomers:	Compounds with identical structural formulas whose differences are in the way the molecule is arranged in space.
Stimulant:	A drug that produces a temporary increase of the functional activity or efficiency of an organism or any of its parts.
Structural isomers:	Compounds that contain the same number and type of atoms but differ in the order in which the atoms are arranged. The types of structural isomers include chain, positional and functional group.
Supervisory chemist:	A designated person who has the overall responsibility and authority for the technical operations of the drug analysis section.
Technical/assistant analyst:	A person who analyses evidence, but does not issue reports for court purposes.
Technical support personnel:	A person who performs basic laboratory duties, but does not analyze evidence.
Thin layer chromatography:	The use of a solvent(s) traveling through a porous medium to separate compounds by their chemical reactivity with the solvent(s).
Traceable:	Ability to trace the history, application, or location of an entity by means of recorded identification. *See also* Chain of custody.
Traceability:	The property of a result of a measurement whereby it can be related to appropriate standards, generally international or national standards, through an unbroken chain of comparisons.
Ultraviolet spectroscopy:	The use of the absorption of ultraviolet radiation to classify a substance.
Validation:	Confirmation by examination and provision of objective evidence that the particular requirements for a specific intended use are fulfilled.
Verification:	Confirmation by examination and provision of objective evidence that specified requirements have been fulfilled (method works in your lab as well as where it was validated.)

REFERENCES

1. Title 21 of the United States Code (21 USC) Chapter 13, Subchapter I, Part A, Section 802.16.
2. Arizona Revised Statutes, Title 13, Chapter 34, 13-3401.19.
3. Title 21 of the United States Code (21 USC) Chapter 13, Subchapter I, Part A, Section 802.17c.
4. Arizona Revised Statutes, Title 13, Chapter 34, 13-3401.5.
5. Christian DR. Forensic Investigation of Clandestine Laboratories. Boca Raton, FL: CRC Press, 2004, p. 204.

SUGGESTED READING

Alm S, Jonson S, Karlsson H, Sundholm EG. Simultaneous gas chromatographic analysis of drugs of abuse on two fused silica columns of different polarity. J Chromatogr 1983;254:179–186.

Bailey MA. The value of the Duquenois test for cannabis: a survey. J Forensic Sci 1979;24:817–841.

Baker PB, Phillips CF. The forensic analysis of drugs of Abuse. Analyst, 1983; 108:777–807.

Balinger JT, Shugar GJ. Chemical Technician's Ready Reference Handbook, 3rd ed., 1990.

Bartle KD, Lee ML, Yang FJ. Open Tubular Column Gas Chromatography. John Wiley and Sons, 1984.

Boke NH, Anderson EF. Structure, development and taxonomy in the genus lophophora. Amer J Bot 1970;57:569–578.

Brenner JC. Forensic Science, An Illustrated Dictionary. Boca Raton, FL: CRC Press, 2004.

Brown JK, Shapazian L, Griffin GD. A rapid screening procedure for some street drugs by thin-layer chromatography. J Chromatogr 1972;64:129–133.

Butler WP. Methods of Analysis. Internal Revenue Service, publication number 341, 1967.

Budavari S, ed. The Merck Index, 11th ed. Merck and Company, Inc., 1989.

Christian DR. Deviation of cast film heroin spectra. Southwestern Association of Forensic Scientist Journal 1986;7:59.

Christian DR. Cast films as an alternative to pellets for solid sample IR. Southwestern Association of Forensic Scientist Journal 1987;9:14.

Christian DR. Clandestine drug laboratories. The DRE 1991;3:3.

Christian DR. Field Guide to Clandestine Laboratory Identification and Investigation. Boca Raton, FL: CRC Press, 2004.

Christian DR. Forensic Investigation of Clandestine Laboratories. Boca Raton, FL: CRC Press, 2003.

Clarke, EGC, ed. Isolation and Identification of Drugs, Vol. I. The Pharmaceutical Press, 1969.

Clarke EGC, ed. Isolation and Identification of Drugs, Vol. II. The Pharmaceutical Press, 1986.

Clandestine Laboratory Investigating Chemists Association Journal.

Churchill KT. Synthetic Tetrahydrocannabinol. J Forensic Sci 1983;24:762.

Cole MD. The Analysis Of Drugs Of Abuse: An Instruction Manual. Boca Raton, FL: CRC Press, 1994.

Concise Encyclopedia of Chemical Technology, 3rd ed. Wiley-Interscience, Inc., 1985.

Engel RG, Kriz GS, Lampman GM, Pavia DL. Introduction to Organic Laboratory Techniques, A Microscale Approach. Saunders College Publishing, 1990.

Fiegl F. Spot Tests For Inorganic Compounds, 2nd ed., Elsevier Science, 1987.

Fiegl F. Spot Tests For Organic Compounds, 7th ed., Elsevier Science, 1989.

Fisher BA. Techniques of Crime Scene Investigation, 7th ed. Boca Raton, FL: CRC Press, 2003.

Fulton CC. Modern Microcrystal Tests for Drugs. Wiley-Interscience, 1969.

Gill R, Bal TS, Moffat AC. The application of derivative uv-visible spectroscopy in forensic toxicology. J Forensic Sci 1982;22:165.

Gough TA, Baker PB. Identification of major drugs of abuse using chromatography. an update. J Chromatogr Sci 1983;21:145.

Gough TA, Baker PB. Identification of major drugs of abuse using chromatography. J Chromatogr Sci 1982;20:289.

Hughes RB, Kessler RR. Increased safety and specificity in the thin-layer chromatographic identification of marihuana. J Forensic Sci 1983;24:842.

Griffiths PD, de Haseth JA. Fourier Transform Infrared Spectrometry. John Wiley and Sons, 1986.

Heagy JA. Infrared method for distinguishing optical isomers of amphetamine. Anal Chem 1970;42:1459.

Hughes RB, Warner Jr VJ. A study of false positives in the chemical identification of marihuana. J Forensic Sci 1978;23:304.

Inman K, Rudin N. Principles and Practices of Criminalistics, The Profession of Forensic Science. Boca Raton, FL: CRC Press, 2001.

James SH, Norby JJ. Forensic Science, An Introduction to Scientific and Investigative Techniques. Boca Raton, FL: CRC Press, 2002.

Johns SH, Wist AA, Najam AR. Spot tests: a color chart reference for forensic chemists. J Forensic Sci 1979;24:631.

Kriz GS, Lampman GM, Pavia DL. Introduction to Spectroscopy. Saunders College Publishing, 1979.

Liu JH, et al. Approaches to drug sample differentiation. iii : a comparative study of the use of chiral and achiral capillary column gas chromatography/mass spectrometry for the determination of methamphetamine enantiomers and possible impurities. J Forensic Sci 1982;27:39.

McLafferty FW. Interpretation of Mass Spectra, 3rd ed. University Science Books, 1980.

Mahmoud AE, Holley JH, Lewis GS, Russell M H, Turner CE. Constituents of cannabis sativa l. xxiv: the potency of confiscated marijuana, hashish and hash oil over a ten year period. J Forensic Sci 1984;29:500.

Maher JT. Narcotics and Other Substances Subject to the Controlled Substance Act of 1970. Drug Enforcement Administration, Public Law 91-513.

Marihuana Its Identification US Treasury Department, 1948.

Marnell T. Drug Identification Bible, 2nd ed. Amera-Chem. Inc., 1997.

McLinden VJ, Stenhouse AM. A chromatography system for drug identification. Forensic Sci Int 1979;13:71.

Microgram, Drug Enforcement Administration, US Department of Justice.

Mills III T, Roberson JC. Instrumental Data for Drug Analysis, Vol. 1–7. CRC Press, 1996–1999.

Moss WW, Posey FT, Peterson PC. A multivariate analysis of the infrared spectra of drugs of abuse. J Forensic Sci 1980;25:304.

Nakamura GR. Forensic aspects of cystolith hairs of cannabis and other plants. J Assoc Off Anal Chem 1989;52:5.

Nakamura GR, Thornton JI. The forensic identification of marijuana: some questions and answers. J Police Sci Admin 1977;1:102.

Perrigo BJ, Peel HW. The use of retention indices and temperature-programmed gas chromatography in analytical toxicology. J Chromatogr Sci 1981;19:219.

Petraco N, Kubic T. Color Atlas and Manual of Microscopy for Criminalistics, Chemists and Conservators. Boca Raton, FL: CRC Press, 2004.

Pettitt BC. Rapid screening for drugs of abuse with short glass capillaries and a nitrogen selective detector. HRC CC J High Resolut Chromatogr Chromatogr Commun 1982;5:45.

Plotczyk LL. Application of fused-silica capillary gas chromatography to the analysis of underivatized drugs. J Chromatogr 1982;240:349.

Physician's Desk Reference, 52nd ed. Medical Economics Company, Inc., 1998.

Ravreby MD, Gorski A. Effects of Crystal Habits in Heroin on the Infrared Spectra. Proceedings of the International Symposium on the Forensic Aspects of Controlled Substances, 1988.

Saferstein R. Criminalistics: An Introduction to Forensic Science, 7th ed. Prentice Hall, 2000.

Schepers P, et al. Applicability of capillary gas chromatography to substance identification in toxicology by means of retention indices. J Forensic Sci 1982;27:49.

Shugar GJ, Ballinger JT. Chemical Technician's Ready Reference Handbook 4th ed. McGraw-Hill, Inc., 1996.

Smith F, Siegel J. Handbook of Forensic Drug Analysis. Academic Press, 2004.

Stead AH, Gill R, Wright T, Gibbs JP, Moffat AC. Standardized thin-layer chromatographic systems for the identification of drugs and poisons. Analyst 1982;107:1106.

Sundholm EG. More economical use of high performance thin-layer plates for chromatographic screening of illicit drug samples. J Chromatogry 1983;265:293.

Sunshine, I, ed. Handbook of Analytical Therapeutic Drug Monitoring and Toxicology. CRC Press, 1996.

Thornton JI, Nakamura GR. The identification of marihuana. J Forensic Sci 1972;12:461.

Velapoldi RA, Wicks SA. The use of chemical spot test kits for the presumptive identification of narcotics and drugs of abuse. J Forensic Sci 1974;19:636.

Vinson JA, Hooyman JE, Ward CE. Identification of street drugs by thin-layer chromatography and a single visualization reagent. J Forensic Sci 1975;20:552.

Chapter 3

Crime Reconstruction

W. Jerry Chisum, BS

1. INTRODUCTION

Have you ever wondered how the great fictional detectives of literature, such as Hercules Pierot, Sherlock Holmes, Mrs. Marple, etc., were able to "solve" crimes quickly, yet it takes so long for the police to do the same? The authors, of course, can write and shape things as they want, whereas the police have to work under specific rules. The authors can create "clues" that are used by the sharp minds of their detectives to eliminate the innocent and identify the guilty and to reconstruct what happened. Law enforcement must find and recognize clues. The authors have studied human behavior and the environments in which they live so they are able to point out those things that are out of the ordinary. They use the logical extension of the clues that they have created to develop the story. Similarly, law enforcement has studied the behavior of criminals and the environment in which they work. They use the same logical extension of the clues to develop a theory (or a story) about the crime. This is crime reconstruction.

Not all law enforcement personnel can do crime reconstruction. It must be someone who is a keen observer, understands science, recognizes evidence, and can apply critical thinking* and logic. The criminalist, forensic scientist, or

---

*Critical thinking is a purposeful, reflective, and goal-directed activity that aims to make judgments based on evidence rather than conjecture. It is based on the principles of science and the scientific method. Critical thinking is a reasoned, interactive process that requires the development of strategies that maximize human potential. (Old Dominion University, School of Nursing faculty minutes, 1997).

From: *The Forensic Laboratory Handbook: Procedures and Practice*
Edited by: A. Mozayani and C. Noziglia © Humana Press Inc., Totowa, NJ

scientific investigator uses "clues," critical thinking, and logic in the process of crime reconstruction. Crime reconstruction can be defined as the logical analysis of the physical evidence and other facts into the formulation of a theory regarding the actions that took place in the commission of a crime. Henry Lee[*] pointed out that it is not just the physical evidence that is incorporated into forming a theory. "Reconstruction not only involves the scientific scene analysis, interpretation of scene pattern evidence, and laboratory examination of physical evidence, but also involves systematic study of related information and the logical formulation of a theory" (1).

The process of crime reconstruction is not an easy one because we are dealing with human action and are trying to tell details of what happened at a particular time in the past. There may not be a full picture: we can sequence events, but we cannot tell what happened in between those events. As Dr. John Thornton[†] stated, "Recognize that the physical evidence may not tell the whole story of what happened, but only isolated bits of the whole story. The entire landscape provided by the physical evidence may in fact be akin to looking at a tapestry from the back side" (Thornton, J., personal communication, May 1998).

Whoever approaches the crime scene, either in person or through documentation, must be able to understand that the entire story may not be revealed.

Reconstructionists must have an understanding of how things work. They must be able to use both inductive and deductive logic in their analysis of the crime. Inductive logic is used to formulate a theory. If the theory is true, then deductions can be made regarding what happened. However, one must be careful in making deductions, because the theory must prove to be true. The testing of the theory is done by the "scientific method." Usually, after more than one theory is postulated, the scientific method is then applied to eliminate the impossible.

2. THE SCIENTIFIC METHOD

Crime reconstruction is the observation of the results of an act or action then postulation of the cause of those results. In the scientific world this is not unusual. Phenomena are observed. The scientist postulates or forms a hypothesis about what caused the phenomena, then designs experiments to test the

---

*Dr. Henry Lee was the Director of the Connecticut State Police Crime Laboratory, Commissioner of the State Police, and Professor of Criminalistics at the University of New Haven. He is now the director of the Lee Institute for Forensic Science in West Haven, CT.

†Dr. John Thornton is a retired Professor of Criminalistics at the University of California, Berkeley.

hypothesis. If the experiments fail, a new hypothesis is formed and more testing is done until the experiments work thereby supporting the hypothesis with data. Therefore, this hypothesis is only as valid as the experiments. Another experiment along a different approach could prove this to be an inaccurate hypothesis.

This same scientific method approach is used in crime reconstruction. We form a theory about the crime and then test that theory or hypothesis against the physical evidence found at the scene or developed through laboratory experiments. If an item of physical evidence is contrary to the theory, then that theory must be abandoned and a new theory is formulated. Again, a hypothesis may prove not to be valid, but it needs to be presented so that it may be tested.

In everyday life, an effect is frequently observed from which we can conclude or surmise what happened. For example, a broken vase on the floor with cat footprints in the dust on the table near where the vase was previously sitting may be observed. The obvious conclusion is that the cat pushed the vase off the table. This is putting the clues together to explain an event. If, however, the dog's teeth marks are in the tablecloth on which the vase had been sitting, a different conclusion would be reached and the cat exonerated.

The following is an example of an observation and the application of scientific methodology: we see a ball of clay sitting on the floor and we observe that the clay is flat on one side. We hypothesize that the clay ball was dropped onto the floor because there is nothing above the ball from which it could have fallen. Therefore, our hypothesis appears to be true.

We can now also determine more about the incident. We can measure the flattened area and weigh the clay. Then we make balls out of the same type of clay and the same weight. We drop them from various heights and compare the size of the flattened areas until we find one that matches. We then theorize about how far the clay fell. That is a simple experiment to determine a cause from the effect.

To complicate this experiment, we see a second ball of clay sitting near the wall. We see a "greasy" spot* on the wall above it with two flattened sides. We form the hypothesis that one was side was flattened by throwing the ball against the wall, and the other side was flattened by falling to the floor. We can tell which side was flattened first by application of logic. If the ball is on the floor then it must have fallen there after it hit the wall. We note which flattened area is touching the floor, then we can compare our previously collected measurements with our measurements to the height of the greasy spot. We have

---

*Hypothesis: the greasy spot was caused by the clay. The reader is encouraged to design an experiment that would test this hypothesis.

sequenced the events. Now we measure the flattened area that was not on the floor. This flattened area may have been changed or altered when the ball fell to the floor. Therefore, our measurement may be of an area of flattening *plus an area that should have existed.*

To test the hypothesis, we project clay against the wall until we produce a flattened side of the same size as the second measured area. By measuring the velocity at which each ball struck the wall we can now say how fast the original ball was traveling when it hit the wall. We must consider any other factors that might affect the results. For example, if the temperature was considerably different between the time of the events and the experiments, then the conclusions we reached are not valid because the physical properties of the clay are changed by temperature.

These experiments sound simple; however, as illustrated, many factors must be considered in even these simple experiments. The reconstructionist must be able to design and conduct the same types of experiments with blood drops, bullets, and other types of physical evidence. In the above experiment, data was available after the first set of experiments that could be used to determine the cause in subsequent events without having to redo the experiments. "Crime reconstruction requires a broad base of knowledge regarding forensic science and an ability to determine the cause from the effect" *(2).*

In the scientific method we cannot establish absolutes. The array of solutions we start with are eliminated to the most logical. Alternative solutions involving aliens, ghosts, and other outlandish creatures or events are not even considered. The alternatives can be considered falsehoods. "Falsification is the central concept behind the scientific method. Consequently, when developing a reconstructive analysis the reconstructionist develops an hypothesis that he or she will attempt to disprove. If the hypothesis is falsified the reconstructionist can opine that this hypothesis (or theory of the crime) is not conceivable or compatible with the evidence submitted and analyzed. The scientific method appears very similar to the writings of Sir Arthur Conan Doyle when he stated, 'You eliminate the impossible, then whatever is left, however improbable, is the truth'" *(3,4).**

3. TYPES OF EVIDENCE EXAMINED

In the past few years, there has been a great emphasis on training law enforcement personnel to recognize and interpret bloodstain evidence. At this time, bloodstains are probably the most common type of evidence examined for

---

*The quote from AC Doyle in *The Adventure of the Beryl Coronet* reads: "Eliminate the impossible, then whatever is left, however improbable, is the truth."

a reconstruction. However, the entire crime scene must be examined and all the evidence taken into account. Errors in reconstruction occur when only one evidence type is examined. A "holistic" approach must be followed, accounting for all the evidence in the case. Nothing can be ignored or "sorted out" as is done in some departments for efficiency and expediency.

Everything is evidence of something; the hard part is deciding whether or not that evidence is part of the crime. Some things are predictable, like the flattening of the clay in the earlier examples, whereas other things are unpredictable, such as damage done by insects or animals. Evidence can be transitory, such as the odor of cologne in a room, ice cubes in a glass, or footprints in sand on a windy day, or destroyed or altered by improper procedures in the investigation.

Blood drops (and raindrops) are almost perfect spheres. When the drop strikes a surface at an angle it will leave a teardrop shape, with the tail pointing in the direction of forward movement. (This phenomenon can be seen by observing the stains left by vehicles dripping oil or paint while traveling. The tail of the oil or paint points in the direction of traffic.) Reconstruction experts must conduct experiments to determine the striking angle that causes the particular shape of the drop. This is just one of several experiments that must be performed; they must have a good understanding of how various bloodstain patterns are produced and the role of bloodstains in crimes.

The same is true with firearms evidence. The reconstructionist must conduct or witness experiments that show how various evidence is produced. This includes, but is not limited to the following:

- Distance determinations from powder or lead residues at various angles and with different types of cartridges (calibers and manufacturers).
- The deflections of bullet paths caused by penetrating or perforating various materials.
- The shape and size of the holes made in various materials.
- Ricochet marks on various surfaces.
- The damage to the bullet from ricocheting.
- The path change by ricocheting, including left vs right twist.

The list could go on for a number of pages; reconstructionists should consult the literature for experiments performed by others for ideas on how to approach special problems.

The role of trace evidence in reconstruction is often overlooked. Hairs and fibers can show that a particular person was present. Trace evidence can show contact between the victim and suspect or the suspect and the environment of the crime including the path taken and some of the actions. These clues need to be incorporated into the reconstructive analysis. The problem in using this type of evidence is that it requires a crime laboratory analysis before it becomes useful. The information is available for court purposes but is not present during the investigative phase.

The position of an item may be extremely important in determining its role in a crime. This is information that cannot be determined by looking at the object in the laboratory. This information must be documented and processed at the scene. Without information regarding the location of the item it may be of no value for reconstructive purposes. This information is true not only for crime reconstruction, but also for the reconstruction of human behavior by the archeologist as well.

> *The patterning of human behavior is key to the concept that the study of the spatial arrangement of artifacts can be used to infer the behavior from which they result. Because of this, the spatial context of artifacts, including their relationship with the natural environment, is more important than the artifact itself. Removing an artifact from its context destroys much of its potential to help reconstruct human behavior. (5)*

The "tag and bag" approach to the crime scene will destroy the potential that the crime reconstructionist uses to reconstruct recent human behavior. According to Ogle, "It is important to remember that crime scene reconstruction begins with a systematic, meticulous, and competent endeavor by the crime scene processing team" *(6)*. The reconstructionist must rely on documentation of the scene to establish these relationships. For example, the location of a gun may yield information regarding whether a death is a suicide, homicide, or an accident. Firing the weapon and comparing the test bullets with the fatal bullet can only show that the gun in question was the one responsible.

4. WHAT CAN BE DETERMINED

The position and/or actions of the people involved in the incident can also be established through the physical evidence left behind or altered. The functional condition of an item also gives information. A bullet through a clock may stop its functioning at a specific time establishing when the shooting occurred.*

A reconstructionist was able to determine from the physical evidence left behind at the scene that an elderly man was lying when he called to say his wife had committed suicide with a shotgun. She was lying in front of the TV with a coat hanger bent to push the trigger. However, the shotgun was fully loaded.

---

*The Far Side cartoon by Gary Larson showing several bullet holes in the clocks at a clock shop while the detective states he wishes there was some way to establish the time of death comes to mind.

The husband always reloaded after shooting and it did not occur to him that the gun's functionality would be checked.

Many of these items of evidence cannot be packaged and brought to the laboratory for examination. That is, you could not package the relationship of the bloodstain above a kitchen drawer to the knife drawer or the footprint impression in the carpet or the location of blood streaks on the wall. This information must be carefully documented and recorded in sketches and photographs and the items must be accurately measured so their positions can be reflected in the sketches.

The evidence clues can tell us information about the sequence of events and establish direction. For example, the bloody footprints on the floor of a prison hallway establishes the direction the victim was going and the direction from which he was coming. The sequence of events is simple logic: he was stabbed, then he staggered down the corridor. This is a simple example of establishing sequence and directions; most crime scenes will have some evidence that will provide information regarding the sequence of events, but it may not always be this simple.

The position of a shooter can be established by tracing back the bullet paths and/or by the location of the cartridge casings. This technique was used in a crime scene where a driver of a car was shot by his jealous girlfriend. She said she accidentally fired the gun about 3 ft from the car. The gun she used was a .25 automatic. The ejection of the cartridge casing from this gun is to the right rear. The cartridge casing was found in the passenger's seat. Therefore, it can be concluded that she reached inside the vehicle through the passenger window to fire the weapon. Her position was established through the analysis of the physical evidence, i.e., the location of the casing and the trajectory of the bullet.

Reconstruction evidence may not necessarily be present at the scene, but may take the form of inferred or derived conclusions. This inferred evidence is frequently used to establish the apparent motive. The empty wallet lying beside the body, the jewelry removed from the open drawer, the photo missing from a frame all are motive evidence. Their absence is the clue; we infer that they existed. Shadow patterns are another example of inferred evidence. The lack of a portion of the blood spray behind the victim of a shotgun blast shows that something was removed after the shot. The shape of this void may also yield information. We also expect a blood spray to be present on the item if it is located.

5. TYING IT ALL TOGETHER

Simply utilizing the scientific method to determine certain activities or facts from the clues is not reconstruction. Logic and critical thinking must be applied to the separate events or facts that have been determined. At this point the alternatives must be considered. The theories of the detectives, the attorneys, the witnesses, the suspect, and, if living, the victim must be tested against the established events or facts.

The reconstructionist must take facts from different areas to determine if there is a connection. One fact will affect the way in which another could have happened. Critical thinking is applied to these facts. However, one must be cautious in this approach to reconstruction. It is easy to go too far and say things that cannot be supported. This may be acceptable in the investigative phase, but not in court where each and every point must be explained and supported by the evidence. The following shows how extensive the reconstruction can be:

On Christmas night two women were found shot in a bloody scene in a suburban neighborhood. The scene had several types of physical evidence, including shoeprints, blood, and clothing. The male suspect had a bloodstain pattern and a bullet hole with gunpowder residue surrounding only one half of the hole. He also had makeup under this hole and on his forearm and near the bloodstain. The autopsies showed both victims had been shot, one of them three times, the other only once.

Based on examination of the evidence it was determined that one of the women had taken a bath, and was getting dressed when the suspect entered the bedroom and hit her with a baseball bat. She was incapacitated, but, because of a three-quarter-in. skull thickness, she was not killed. The suspect then grabbed the other woman, held her in a headlock and put the gun to her temple catching a fold of his coat when he shot her. He let her fall to the floor and caught the first woman approaching the door. He shot her in the neck; as she fell he shot her in the cheek and in the eye.

He then removed his coat and proceeded to arrange the bodies into a "crucifixion" pose. The arms outstretched and the feet crossed. He then went to the bathroom, relieved himself, and washed. He put on his coat and left the house. He disposed of the weapon before his mother told him to go to the police because he had blood on his coat. The case did not go to trial as the defendant pled guilty.

6. WHY RECONSTRUCT THE CRIME?

Ogle, a criminalist, wrote in a book on evidence collection, "Crime scene reconstruction is one of the major purposes for the collection of physical evidence" *(6)*. The question is: Why is this so important?

Crimes are reconstructed for several reasons depending on the phase of the case. The investigation, the trial preparation, the defense preparation, the trial itself all can benefit from reconstruction. Knowing what happened makes the task of finding justice easier.

The first step is to determine if there is a crime or what crime has been committed. Because the edge of a piece of glass will indicate the direction of the force applied to it to break it out, this can be used to determine if a person broke the window from outside as in a burglary or from the inside for insurance fraud or just for attention. The discovery of bear hair on a cloth found on an elderly woman's porch showed it came from inside the house where there was a bearskin. It was not a "death threat" or an "alien invasion" as she suspected.

After a crime is established, crime reconstruction is used to aid in determining the what, who, when, how, and why of the crime. The reconstructionist becomes part of a team of persons involved in the investigation. The information developed in reconstruction is used by the following:

- Investigators conducting interviews to test the veracity of the statements.
- Criminal profilers in making a "profile" of the perpetrator.
- District Attorneys or Defense Attorneys to determine how to prepare and argue their cases in court.
- The Court in determining sentences.

The following case illustrates how the use of reconstruction would have saved the city and county from prosecuting the wrong person. Betty was in jail for 8 mo awaiting trial before the evidence was examined for reconstruction purposes.

Sue and Betty were competing for the same man's attention. Sue had been living with him, but now he had moved in with Betty. Sue claimed she was walking home from work when Betty and three other women came on her in their car. She was thrown to the sidewalk on her back, then flipped over and held by three of the women while Betty cut her shirt and back. She said she could feel the blood running down her back so she struggled until she could finally get up and get away.

Sue called the police with a report. It was 1.5 h before an officer arrived. He said she had about 20 cuts on her back that were still "dripping blood." Betty was charged with assault.

The photos showed very superficial cuts, more like scratches that could be self-inflicted. The shirt was cut only part way up the back, with jagged cuts at the top where the shirt was bunched up. Examination of the shirt revealed no blood on the inside back.

This case shows how physical evidence is used to determine the veracity of a statement. This is one of the more common uses of reconstruction. The stories told by the victim (if living), the suspect, and the witnesses should all be tested because, in some cases, there are fabricated stories that sound good but are false. The statement was made in this case by the alleged victim. The story does not agree with the physical evidence. The "victim" should be charged with filing a false report.

This case involves what is called a "staged crime scene." A staged crime scene is one in which the evidence is altered or created to shift the direction of the investigation *(7)*. When physical evidence is changed or created to direct the investigation toward a specific individual, as in this case, this type of staged crime scene is called a "frame." Usually, the evidence in a staged scene is altered to cover up the crime. The removal of a body from the house and dumping it in a remote area and cleaning the house is one of the most common cover-ups. This is almost always the act of someone living with the decedent.

If there is an idea how the crime was committed then the evidence can be easier to locate and identify. The reconstructionist at the crime scene will see relationships that can quickly lead to other evidence. For example, multiple blows to the head of a body indicate there should be blood cast off on the weapon. If there is no cast off blood nearby, then the beating did not occur at this location. A blood trail should lead to the original scene. If a scene is lacking a trail and cast-off blood stains, a reconstructionist would have to consider a "staged" crime scene or that the premise that there was a beating is incorrect. The wrong statement at the crime scene can send the investigation and conclusions completely off track.

A man had reportedly committed suicide by pouring gasoline on himself inside a house and igniting it. The reconstructionist was not at the crime scene but was presented with the facts later. The man had run from the hallway where the gasoline can was located into a bedroom, onto the bed, then jumped through a window before being overcome by the flames. In looking at the sketch of the house (floorplan) the reconstructionist asked where the heater was located. It was a floor heater right where the fire started. This was no suicide; it was an accident. When the fumes from the gasoline reached the pilot light on the gas heater, they caused the gasoline can to explode and saturated the arsonist with gasoline.

As in this case, the use of physical evidence for a reconstruction may determine if the death is an accident, suicide, homicide, or natural. The determination of a natural death is left to the pathologist and the toxicologist. In the following case, the bloodstain patterns, the direction of the shot, and the way clothing was arranged were the clues that yielded information to prove a homicide.

A second-grade student came home from school to find the doors locked. Because her mother was 9 mo and 1 d pregnant, she was sure her mother went to the hospital. She went into the garage to get the house key and saw a shape that looked like a person. She ran two blocks to her grandparents and told them that her mother had gone to the hospital and someone was in the garage. Because they were supposed to take their daughter to the hospital they were very concerned. The grandfather went to the garage and found his daughter in a lawn chair with her head split down the middle and a shotgun at her feet. He called the police.

Examination of the crime scene led the reconstructionist to the conclusion that this was a staged crime scene. The following clues were the basis for this conclusion:

The bloodstains on the arms and hands were not consistent with the blood that would result from a shotgun blast to the head. The shot was directed parallel to the floor as evidenced by the blood spatter on the wall behind her. Finally, her belt was above her breasts.

These clues show that the victim was beaten elsewhere then placed in the chair and then shot with the shotgun. Later, a search warrant was obtained allowing entry to the house. Inside the house there were blood cast-off and spatter patterns on the walls and ceilings of the dining room and kitchen. There were two heavily bloodstained cast iron skillets with the bottoms broken out. A similar cast iron saucepan had the handle broken off, and a second saucepan was also spattered.

The husband had a perfect alibi; he was seen at work 1 h before his daughter left for school and was not missing at any time during the day. The investigation led to an old Army buddy of the husband's, who had been staying at the home for a couple of weeks. He had been paid $10,000 worth of cocaine by the husband to kill his wife. He stated, "She didn't want to die." Her husband and his buddy were convicted of two counts each of murder for hire. The actual killer was sentenced to two life sentences; the husband to two death penalties.

This was another staged crime scene. If the "plan" had succeed and she had been knocked unconscious with the first blow and no blood shed in the house or on her clothing, would the responding officer have been able to recognize the clues that showed this was a homicide? Probably not. This would have been a "perfect crime." Fortunately, if anything can be fortunate in a homicide, the victim did not respond as planned.

7. RECONSTRUCTION IN BEHAVIORAL ANALYSIS

Criminal profiling, or analysis of the behavior of the criminal at the scene, is a relatively new approach in criminal investigations. Crime reconstruction is an important component of these profiles. The Academy of Behavioral Profiling has stated that a reconstruction must be made before a behavior analysis is rendered *(8)*.

Cooley wrote an on-line article titled *Crime Scene Reconstruction: The Foundation of Behavioral Evidence Analysis (4)*. He stated in the introduction, "The chief goal of this report is to argue that the foundation of any competent criminal profile is that of a complete crime scene reconstruction, brought about by the physical evidence documented and collected at the crime scene(s)." In other words, the profile is based on the evidence and what it can "tell" the reconstructionist about the actions at the crime scene. Cooley also compared the processes of reconstruction and profiling: "Crime scene reconstruction like behavioral evidence analysis is both a science and an art. The process is founded on the scientific method, while the practice and degree of success is dependent upon the skill and experience of the reconstructionist. The important aspect being that its foundation is that of the scientific method. With reconstruction and behavioral evidence analysis both relying upon the scientific method the end result of one's analysis will be shielded from attacks on its reliability and validity" *(4)*. Both processes use the scientific method; however, one process is dependent on the other. If the reconstruction is flawed, it follows that the profile will also be flawed.

8. ETHICS

Reconstruction experts must be aware that the analysis rendered is, in many cases, going to be the deciding factor in how justice is dispensed. They cannot afford to allow speculation into their findings. They must pursue as much information as they can about a case. A reconstruction cannot be made without all the evidence.

It is also necessary to know the limitations of one's abilities. A disagreement between experts can usually be traced to one of them lacking knowledge about a type of evidence or the cause and effect. For example, arterial spurting is a known phenomenon, but when the torso is upright or is clothed, this is not a factor because the chest cavity fills or the clothing absorbs the energy of the blood stream. Therefore, the expert who "sees arterial spurting" from a chest wound on an upright person is misinterpreting blood that has been cast off from the hands or weapon.

The understanding of critical thinking and logic is absolutely necessary for the reconstructionist. Even with a clear understanding of these processes, not knowing how to interpret a piece of evidence will result in a faulty analysis because a wrong premise is the starting point in the process. It is also important to remember the difference between inductive and deductive logic because starting with a faulty premise will lead to wrong conclusions. As John Thornton states, "Induction is a type of inference that proceeds from a set of specific observations to a generalization, called a premise. This premise is a working assumption, but it many not always be valid. A deduction, on the other hand, proceeds from a generalization to a specific case, and that is generally what happens in forensic practice. Providing that the premise is valid, the deduction will be valid. But knowing whether the premise is valid is the name of the game here; it is not difficult to be fooled into thinking that one's premises are valid when they are not.

"Forensic scientists have, for the most part, treated induction and deduction rather casually. They have failed to recognize that induction, not deduction, is the counterpart of hypothesis testing and theory revision... too often a hypothesis is declared as a deductive conclusion, when in fact it is a statement awaiting verification through testing" *(9)*.

The reconstruction can also be faulty because evidence was not available for analysis. This can be because law enforcement did not think the evidence would be of value and, therefore, did not submit it for laboratory analysis. But more frequently, it is because the analyst did not ask for photos and reports to help interpret the evidence.

9. CONCLUSION

For reconstruction purposes, the value of physical evidence and documentation of the crime scene by competent personnel cannot be over-emphasized. The reconstruction analyst relies on correct, complete information to render a reconstruction of the events of a crime. Not all cases can or need to be reconstructed and the evidence in some of the cases does not need to be collected. In others, competent personnel are not available to respond to the crime scenes. Therefore, a reconstruction will not be possible. "The value of physical evidence varies from type to type and case to case. In some investigations, its potential may never be fully appreciated. In some jurisdictions it is a matter of the availability of trained personnel who can respond to crime scenes and collect the appropriate evidence" *(10)*.

The workload at the crime laboratories has become so great that many laboratory workers no longer respond to crime scenes. They do not develop the expertise necessary for crime reconstruction. The forensic scientist should understand the uses of the physical evidence and the importance of reconstructing the crime.

GLOSSARY

BAC:	Blood alcohol concentration. Usually reported in gram percent (g%). The legal limit for driving in most states is 0.080 g%.
DUI:	Driving under the influence, usually restricted to situations involving driving under the influence of alcohol.
DUID:	Driving under the influence of drugs. Usually used for situations involving driving under the influence of any drug other than alcohol.
FID:	Flame ionization detector. A device used to detect compounds that have been isolated by a gas chromatograph. An FID essentially detects anything that burns.
GC:	Gas chromatography. A separation technique that is used to separate mixtures of chemical compounds. A GC is usually run at relatively high temperatures (100–300°C) and uses helium to help move the unknown compounds through the system. A GC is coupled to any one of a number of different detectors, including NPD, FID, and MS detectors.
GC/MS:	A GC coupled to an MS detector.
HPLC:	High-performance liquid chromatography. A separation technique that is used to separate mixtures of chemical compounds. An HPLC is usually run at relatively low temperatures and frequently uses aqueous solutions so that the analysis of temperature sensitive and water-soluble substances may be detected. An HPLC is coupled to any one of a number of different detectors, including UV and MS detectors.
IA:	Immunoassay. A detection technique relying on the interaction of an antibody with a drug or poison.
LC/MS:	Also called HPLC/MS. An HPLC coupled to an MS detector.
ME:	Medical examiner.
MS:	Mass spectrometer. A device used to detect compounds which have been isolated by a gas chromatograph, a liquid chromatograph (HPLC), or can be used alone to identify pure substances. A mass spectrometer provides a great deal of information to help identify unknown substances, information which may include the molecular weight, a unique mass spectral fingerprint, presence of nitrogen or other halogens, and some information on how the molecule is structured.
NPD:	Nitrogen-phosphorus detector. A device used to detect compounds that have been isolated by a gas chromatograph. An NPD essentially detects anything that contains nitrogen or phosphorus and is useful for detecting drugs, poisons, and explosives.
OTC:	Over the counter. Drugs that are available without a prescription.
Toxicology:	The science of poisons.
UV:	Ultraviolet detector. A device used to detect compounds that have been isolated by a liquid chromatograph. A UV detector detects anything that absorbs ultraviolet light.

REFERENCES

1. Lee, H, ed. Crime Scene Investigation. Taoyuan, Taiwan: Central Police University Press, 1994, p. 1.
2. Chisum WJ. An introduction to crime reconstruction. In: Turvey, B, ed. Criminal Profiling: An Introduction to Behavioral Evidence Analysis. London: Academic Press, 1999.
3. Cooley C. "Crime Scene Reconstruction: The Foundation of Behavioral Evidence Analysis." http://www.law-forensic.com/behavioral_evidence_analysis.htm
4. Doyle AC. "The Adventures of Sherlock Holmes: XI. The Adventure of the Benyl Coronet." The Strand Magazine, May 1892. Republished in The Original Illustrated Sherlock Holmes. New Jersey: Castle Books, 1991, p. 164.
5. Scott DD, Connor M. Context Delicti: Archaeological Context in Forensic Work. In: Haaglund WD, Sorg MH, eds. Forensic Taphonomy. New York: CRC Press, 1997, p. 37.
6. Ogle Jr RR. Crime Scene Investigation and Reconstruction. Upper Saddle River, NJ: Prentice Hall, 2004, pp. 251–252.
7. Turvey B. Criminal Profiling: An Introduction to Behavioral Evidence Analysis, Second Edition. London: Academic Press, 2002.
8. Baeza J, Chisum WJ, Chamberlin TM, McGrath M, Turvey B. Academy of Behavioral Profiling: Criminal Profiling Guidelines. J Behavioral Profiling. 2000;1: e-pub: http://www.profiling.org/journal/subscribers/vol1_no1/jbp_abp_cpg_January2000_1-1.html. 2000;1(1).
9. Thornton JI. The general assumptions and rationale of forensic identification. In: Fraigman D, Kaye D, Saks M and Sanders J, eds. Modern Scientific Evidence: The Law and Science of Expert Testimony, Vol. 2. St. Paul, MN: West Publishing, 1997, p.13.
10. Ragle L. Crime Scene. New York, NY: Avon Books, 2002, p. 42.

Chapter 4

Digital Evidence

Robert P. Bianchi, BS and Mark Pollitt, MS

1. INTRODUCTION

Since the advent of the microprocessor, affordable storage devices, and networks, more of our daily lives are being recorded in the ones and zeros of the digital world. So it is not surprising that when crimes and torts are committed, there is often evidence of probative value stored or transmitted in digital form. This, in fact, is the definition of digital evidence (DE) according to the Scientific Working Group on Digital Evidence (SWGDE) *(1)*. This DE can be probative in virtually any criminal or civil matter. As a result of this, it appears DE will likely become the predominant form of evidence in the 21st century.

DE can be found in an ever-increasing number of places in a wide variety of formats. It may be useful to define a brief taxonomy of DE at this point in its history. Doubtless, this definition will change and evolve over time but will serve to provide a framework for the further discussion of the science.

In the definition of DE, we refer to information stored or transmitted in digital form. Thus, information is converted to ones and zeros (digital form) and placed into one of two states: static (stored) or dynamic (transmitted). One of the key advantages of the digital world is the simple transition from one state to another. Information does not have to be translated between states. This easy transmission allows us to easily move and replicate information and so it is not unusual for the same information to change states numerous times between the creation of the information and its recipient.

A document written using word processing software is initially created by digital signals emanating from the keyboard and stored temporarily in the

From: *The Forensic Laboratory Handbook: Procedures and Practice*
Edited by: A. Mozayani and C. Noziglia © Humana Press Inc., Totowa, NJ

computer's random access memory (RAM). When the document is saved, it is transferred from the computer's RAM as a file to the hard drive or other storage device. This file can then be sent via e-mail to another person who, using his or her e-mail software, opens the e-mail, saves the file to his or her hard drive and subsequently reads the document by opening it in his or her word processing program. It can be converted into printed form by sending the file to a printer.

We can see from this example that the information goes through a number of transitions in what is otherwise a simple process. From a forensic perspective, each location at which the information appears, in either state, is a potential location for evidence. Even the fact that a transition took place may provide probative information.

The forensic examination or analysis of static data is often called computer forensics, media forensics, or media analysis. The most common form of forensic examination and analysis of dynamic data is called *network forensics*.

DE is latent in the same way that fingerprints, firearms, and tool mark evidence are latent. DE is not visible to the naked eye and requires careful handling and specialized training to efficiently and effectively preserve it. It is easily altered, damaged, or destroyed. When processed by qualified examiners using hardware and software, information that is valuable to legal proceedings can be obtained. Failure to adequately preserve the original evidence can render it unusable by the prosecution or the defense. Improper examination, review, or analysis by unqualified persons can yield inaccurate or misleading results and opinions. Because it takes qualified examiners using high-technology equipment to process, DE often requires expert testimony to make both the process and the results understandable to the judge or jury.

Collectively, these characteristics suggest that the examination of this type of evidence is a forensic process that should be performed by qualified forensic personnel, ideally in a forensic laboratory setting.

2. TYPES OF EVIDENCE EXAMINED (SEE FIG. 1)

The examination of computers and their associated storage devices such as hard drives, floppy disks, and optical disks are the most obvious forms of DE. But they are, by no means, the sole sources. DE can be found embedded in or attached to a wide variety of devices, such as personal digital assistants, music players, cameras, watches, navigation units, mobile phones, fax machines, and security access devices. Many new credit cards come with an embedded computer chip and, as a result, are often called "smart cards." New devices are invented nearly every day and each generation of devices is faster and has more storage capacity. The available storage in a single device

Fig. 1. Digital storage devices.

often exceeds the capacity of large libraries. This trend, first articulated by Moore *(2)* in the 1960s, recognized that the density of semiconductors, which are the building blocks of computer chips, would double every 18 mo. This increase would similarly translate to digital storage and the size of storage devices has been following a similar curve *(3)*.

Static data is not the only source of probative information. The data that is transmitted over both wired and wireless networks can be intercepted. In the dynamic arena, there is a similar variety of physical media, such as coaxial and braided wires, infrared and radio frequency carriers that conduct signals formed into "packets." These packets are constructed in an ever-increasing number of formats designed for various purposes.

3. FORENSIC EVIDENCE PROCESSING

The nature of DE is such that it poses special challenges for admissibility in court. To effectively respond to these challenges, proper forensic processing must be followed. The process consists of four distinct but related activities: collection, examination, analysis, and reporting *(4)*.

Collection (acquisition and preservation) starts with the request for a search warrant and includes identifying evidentiary items and proper collection, documentation, packaging, storage, and delivery. Search warrants for electronic storage devices typically focus on two primary sources of information *(5):*

1. Electronic storage device search warrant.
   - Search and seizure of hardware, software, documentation, user notes, and storage media.
   - Examination/search and seizure of data.

2. Service provider search warrant.
   - Service records, billing records, subscriber records, etc.
   - Request for information from service providers such as utility companies, financial institutions, telephone or cable companies, etc.

After the scene has been secured restrict access to the area, preserve potential fingerprint evidence, and identify potential DE. *Do not turn any electronic devices on or off.* Turning a device off could activate a "lock out" feature and turning a device on could alter the evidence. Document the scene by taking photographs, making a diagram, or recording the location and condition of electronic devices. The information on the visual display should also be documented as it may prove useful during the examination or analysis activities.

Electronic devices must be handled in a certain manner to preserve their physical integrity, as well as the electronic data they contain. Whenever possible, personnel trained in the collection of digital evidence should be allowed to collect the evidence in compliance with agency policy. All actions taken should not add, change, or destroy data stored on any electronic device. Because electronic devices are sensitive to temperature, humidity, physical shock, static electricity, and magnetic sources, special care must be taken while packaging, transporting, and storing electronic devices. Do not transport or store any electronic device near a radio transmitter, speaker magnets, or heated vehicle seats.

Evidence must be secured in this manner in order to protect it from loss or contamination and to provide visible evidence if the container or seal were damaged or altered. This can be achieved by placing the items in a static free transparent bag and sealing the opening or by placing the items in a box and sealing the openings with evidence tape or stickers.

3.1. Planning the Examination

DE is unique in the forensic science arena. Owing to the variety of sources and types and volume of DE, it is necessary to apply adequate planning at each stage of the process from acquisition to testimony. This planning has both an investigative and a technical component. Neither the investigator nor the examiner usually has sufficient information or knowledge to conduct a thorough and efficient collection and examination. As a result, the forensic examination requires teamwork between the examiner and the investigator.

Examination is only one stage in the process that makes DE available to the court. This process consists of several definable stages. Like most forms of evidence, it must first be collected. Because it is found in such a wide variety of places, in such large quantities, some means of limiting the intake is required by both the law and practicality. This is both an investigative issue that seeks to identify where probative evidence is likely to be found and a technical issue of how that evidence can be effectively and efficiently collected. Like most crime scenes, the investigator is responsible for all activities conducted. Even when the investigator is well trained in the collection and preservation of evidence, he may benefit from either consultation with forensic examiners or the participation of a forensic examiner on scene where the evidentiary environment is complex.

Because of the ease in creating a digital duplicate of the original evidence, the acknowledged best practice *(6)* is to create one or more duplicates of the original either by creation of duplicate media or of a file containing a bit-for-bit copy of the original.

Once the evidence has been acquired and preserved, the next step is the forensic examination. This step is the sole responsibility of the examiner; however, it is not possible to conduct an effective and efficient examination without substantial participation by the investigator. Because there is so much evidence and it can be looked at in so many ways, there must be a clear set of goals and criteria to limit the examination. These goals and criteria must be established in concert with the investigator prior to the commencement of the actual examination.

Using these goals and criteria, the examiner designs an examination process that will effectively and efficiently meet these requirements. In most cases, this will begin by a thorough documentation of the physical and logical structure of the original DE. The next step is often to recover data that is deleted, damaged, or hidden. In an effort to minimize the amount of data to be analyzed, a data reduction process is usually applied. This can take the form of comparing file or packet signatures with known, nonpertinent data, eliminating duplicates, filtering files and packets by format or headers, and applying string searches. The goal of this step is to include all pertinent information while minimizing the nonpertinent.

Following the documentation and data reduction steps, the examiner reviews the stated goals and criteria to determine if the information produced from the examination meets these goals and criteria. If the goals of the examination include examining the data to answer questions concerning the source or methods used to store, alter, or delete the data or if there are questions concerning the order in which activities occurred, then the examiner will conduct further examination to answer these questions.

3.2. Reporting

Once all of the goals have been met, the examiner produces a report of the examination, which, accompanied by the information exported from the examination, is provided to the investigator. The final report of examination must contain enough detail to allow another competent examiner to reproduce the same extracted results. All activities, from receipt of the evidence to its return to the submitter, must be documented. Each step executed in preparing the evidence for examination, such as making and working from a duplicate of the original evidence to the software utilized and the results obtained, must be accurately and clearly presented in the report.

3.3. Analysis

The documentation, data recovery, data reduction, and extraction that comprise the examination phase are focused on the characteristics of the data in the technical context. Analysis is the evaluation and organization of the information provided from the examination in the investigative context. This phase is largely the providence of the investigator and/or the investigative analyst assigned to the case or the program. They will determine if the material is pertinent, the level of confidence in the material, and where the information "fits" in the investigative context. The forensic examiner often plays an advisory role in this phase by assisting the investigative team with determining alternative scenarios that would account for the data and advice concerning the degree of reliability of the data about the data, referred to as metadata.

3.4. Presentation

The goal of the forensic process is to provide knowledge that will assist in the investigation. The ability to communicate the distilled results of the DE process is called the presentation phase. The actual presentations may take the form of reports, oral presentations, or testimony. It is important that the forensic examiner be able to communicate to a jury with limited technical knowledge not only the process that was utilized in the particular examination, but also the underlying science and technology which allows the examiner to make factual and opinion statements. It is also important to be able to clarify the difference in roles between the examiner, the analyst, and the investigator. If each has done his or her part and communicated with each other, then the judge, jury, or

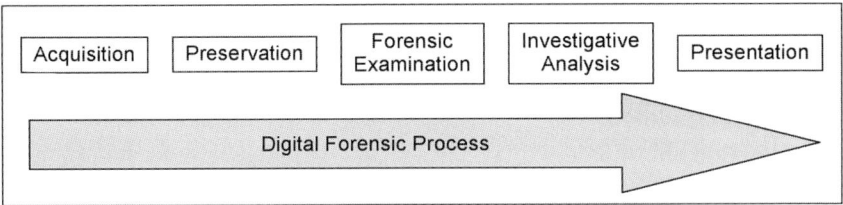

Fig. 2. Digital forensic process.

customer gains as complete and truthful a picture as is possible. *See* Fig. 2 for a diagram of this digital forensic process.

4. QUALITY ASSURANCE

A goal of a DE laboratory should be to provide high-quality results through the use of accurate, reliable, reproducible, and legally defensible procedures. This is accomplished through documented activities that assure that quality control procedures are in place and are being properly administered. The quality management system defines and documents the organizational structure, responsibilities, procedures, processes, and resources for implementing an effective program. The success of a quality system depends on the commitment of management and active participation by each member of the laboratory. The personnel responsible must be clearly designated and have access to the highest level of management responsible for approving policy. Ideally a quality assurance manager should be selected who has mastered the technical requirements of DE collection and examination and is not currently performing case work. More commonly, a member of the staff assumes quality assurance as a collateral duty.

Serious deficiencies can occur when insufficient attention is given to the quality of the work product. Applying the necessary controls to assure high-quality results is no simple matter. It requires not only a thorough knowledge of the laboratory's mission, but also the commitment to excellence by the management and operating staff. This commitment may be based in part on the need or desire for accreditation. To achieve this level of performance, the laboratory personnel will find it necessary to operate under a quality assurance system that requires extensive documentation of its procedures.

4.1. Establishing a Program

When management decides to financially and administratively establish a quality assurance program, a plan must be written to document all of the requirements of the program. Although there is no generally accepted plan to establishing a program, many of the principles are applicable to most programs. It is critical to the success of the program to have the entire staff involved in development and implementation. Top management is responsible for committing resources, establishing policy, assigning responsibilities, and developing an overall accountability for the program. Supervisors must seek consensus approval from the operating personnel as the plan is developed, obtain cooperation of the staff in assuring success of the program, and oversee the implementation of changes to the plan. Operating personnel provide technical input and advise management when changes must be made to the plan based on daily operations. The quality assurance manager monitors the program, recommends changes, evaluates maintenance records, conducts quality audits, and assists in problem resolution.

4.2. The Quality Assurance Manual

This manual identifies the policies, organizational objectives, functional activities, and quality activities designed to achieve the quality goals of the program. The manual must be flexible enough to accommodate changes in methodology, technology, and personnel. It must be reviewed periodically to maintain its relevance and to assure compliance. In addition to the general quality assurance principles (e.g., competency and proficiency testing, personnel training, safety and health maintenance, evidence control, report writing, deviations, and deficiencies), DE laboratories must address the uniqueness of DE when developing controls. Of primary importance is the use of validated software to conduct examinations. Off-the-shelf software and in-house developed software should not be used until they have been properly validated and the results of the validation documented.

The use of standards and controls for DE laboratories is substantially different than those used in other forensic disciplines. DE examiners do not compare unknown evidence with known reference materials obtained from a reliable source. Additionally, DE examiners cannot run known material in conjunction with the unknown evidence. These differences do not negate the need to run DE controls; however, the process is different form other forensic disciplines and will vary among laboratories.

5. TECHNOLOGY: EXISTING AND FUTURE

The current technology utilized in digital forensics is a combination of hardware and software tools that are designed to perform each of the functions described in the examination process. As each new technology appears in the market place, the forensic practitioner must acquire the tools required to deal with this new technology. Consequently, this discipline is driven by the market.

In the acquisition phase, the forensic practitioner must have the hardware that will allow for connection to the storage media or transmission media utilized by the original evidence. In many situations, existing software collection tools can be used. If they cannot, they will either have to be modified or new tools developed. The tools used in the documentation step of the examination phase must be updated to correctly interpret new file systems and packet structures. Likewise, data recovery and data reduction tools must be "aware" of the evolving technologies.

Currently, examiners typically utilize top-of-the-line desktop computers with a complex array of data inputs and removable storage. The average cost to set up a DE laboratory is $25,000 per work station. Network attached storage devices are becoming commonplace tools for allowing the processing, in an automated fashion, of a number of pieces of evidence in either parallel or sequence. Storage attached networks an even more complex and expensive technology, are being explored to further reduce the time required to process evidence.

Forensic software is also going through an evolutionary process. The software tools first used in conducting examinations were products that were produced by manufacturers of hardware, operating systems, and network operating systems to troubleshoot their products. Software tools followed, often written by forensic practitioners, to perform specific steps, or even substeps, in the forensic process. These tools became more numerous and complex over time and evolved into the complex graphical user interface tools that are the backbone of current practice. In the static evidence arena, tools, such as EnCase *(7)*, Ilook *(8)*, and Forensic Tool Kit *(9)*, are most commonly used. In the dynamic data area, tools, such as Ethereal *(10)*, Etherpeek *(11)*, and DCS-1000 *(12)*, are utilized.

Moore's law and the insatiable demand for more information in modern society will serve to continuously push the capabilities of forensic examiners. Whenever and wherever new technology appears, the DE forensic specialist will have to acquire, preserve, examine, analyze, and present DE. Likewise, each new technology will be examined to see if it can be applied to perform these tasks better, faster, and cheaper.

6. COMPUTER DATABASES AVAILABLE

One of the applications of new technology has significantly assisted the data reduction step in the forensic examination phase. A mathematical algorithm can be applied to files, packets, messages, or even complete storage devices, which, therefore, creates a unique value for that data. The algorithm is designed such that any alteration, however minor, will change the resulting value of the algorithm called a "hash." This hashing methodology allows for the authentication of original evidence and verification that the original evidence has not been tampered with to a mathematical precision. When applied to single files, it allows the confirmation of files to be identical if their hash value is the same. The National Institute of Science and Technology developed and published, with the assistance of the digital forensic community, a reference of known file hashes for commercial software *(13)*. By utilizing this database in the data reduction step of the forensic examination phase, a very high percentage of files can be eliminated from consideration because they have been positively identified as being part of a commercial software product and, therefore, not unique to the examination at hand.

7. USES AND LIMITATIONS OF PROCEDURES

As we have demonstrated, a series of ones and zeros exists either on a physical piece of media or in a data stream should be evaluated in several different contexts. The operating system, network protocol, file system, application, and location all contribute to the "truth" which is the technical meaning of the data. The data itself is then evaluated in investigative contexts, such as who are the creators and/or recipients of the data, what is the time sequence, and is the data pertinent to the current investigative questions. Clearly, this lends itself to opportunities for misinterpretation and error.

Examiners, analysts, and investigators must rigorously evaluate their conclusions and ensure that the "truth" as presented is clearly identified within a context and that the limitations of that context are stated. Professional ethics demand that, when there is any doubt as to the accuracy of the result or the interpretation of the results, this doubt be clearly stated. Chalk et al. stated, "Professional Ethics refers to those principles that are intended to define the rights and responsibilities of scientists in their relationship with each other and with other parties including employers, research subjects, clients, students, etc." *(14)*

The need for ethics in the DE discipline is no different than the requirements for other forensic disciplines. The results of DE examinations may be pivotal in determining a person's guilt or innocence. It is equally important that examiners maintain the highest standards of ethics when generating criminal investigative information or when involved in civil matters.

Ethical issues begin at the evidence collection site and persist until the evidence is destroyed. Because DE is latent, it can easily be altered, damaged, or destroyed by improper handling. The person collecting DE must be able to recognize items that may contain potential DE and to assure proper handling. The devices discussed earlier in this chapter may be contraband, fruits of the crime, a tool of the offense, or merely a storage device containing evidence of a crime. Agency standard operating procedures, statutory requirements, and best practices must be followed whenever possible and deviation policies must be followed when exceptional situations are encountered. In the field and in the laboratory, personnel must be aware of the conditions of the warrant and assure that all conditions are satisfied.

Every examiner should refrain from providing any material misrepresentation of education, training, experience, or area of expertise. Examiners must reveal any conflict of interest. They must resist any pressure from attorneys, investigators, or superiors in the acquisition of evidence, preparation of reports, and during the presentation of testimony. Should an examiner uncover evidence that was not requested by the investigator, is within the scope of the search warrant, and is of probative value, he is obligated to present that information in the report of the findings.

GLOSSARY

Digital Evidence: Information of probative value, stored or transmitted in binary form.

Hash: A mathematical formula that generates a numerical identifier based on input data. If any bit of the input data changes, the output number changes.

Meta Data: Data frequently embedded in a file that describes a file or directory, which can include the locations where content is stored, dates and times, application-specific information, and permissions.

RAM: Random Access Memory. Computer memory that provides the main internal storage available to the user for programs and data.

REFERENCES

1. Scientific Working Group on Digital Evidence. Digital evidence: standards and principles. Forensic Sci Commun 2000;2.
2. Moore G. Cramming more components onto integrated circuits. Electronics 1965;38.
3. http://sims.berkley.edu/research/projects/how-much-info-2003/. Last accessed on 7/15/2005.
4. Electronic Crime Scene Investigation, NIJ Publication, July 2001. http://www.ncjrs.org/pdffiles1/nij/187736.pdf
5. United States Secret Service. Best Practices for Seizing Electronic Evidence Version 2.0. http://www.secretservice.gov/electronic_evidence.shtml. Last accessed on 7/15/2005.

6. http://www.cops.org/html/forensicprocedure.htm. Last accessed on 7/15/2005.
7. http://www.guidancesoftware.com. Last accessed on 7/15/2005.
8. http://www.ilook-forensics.org. Last accessed on 7/15/2005.
9. http://www.accessdata.com. Last accessed on 7/15/2005.
10. http://www.ethereal.com. Last accessed on 7/15/2005.
11. http://www.wildpackets.com. Last accessed on 7/15/2005.
12. http://www.fbi.gov/congress/congress00/kerr090600.htm. Last accessed on 7/15/2005.
13. http://www.nsrl.nist.gov/. Last accessed on 7/15/2005.
14. Chalk R, Frankel MS, Chafer SB. AAAS Professional Ethics Project. American Association for the Advancement of Science Washington, DC 20005. AAAS Publication 80-R-4, 1980.

Chapter 5

Explosives and Arson
Boom and Flame

James B. Crippin, BS

1. INTRODUCTION

Explosive and arson cases, as they relate to forensic science, are sometimes very hard to separate. When one case happens, the other usually follows. Therefore, the two types of cases will be discussed together in this chapter.

Explosive and arson cases, either the actual investigation at the scene or the evidence being analyzed in the laboratory, are difficult cases in that they are usually tedious, time consuming, and can be very dangerous to the health of the investigators. These cases are not as glamorous or glitzy as they are portrayed on television or in the movies. There is one thing that the media did get right though: forensic analysis starts at the scene with the initial investigation. Just as the computer programming adage says: GI GO (garbage in gives garbage out), if the evidence is not located and collected properly, it will be of little use when it gets to the laboratory, let alone when it is used in court.

This chapter is broken down into two parts: investigation and laboratory analysis. Sometimes the line will blur slightly because there are a few forensic analysts in the United States who do both, but there is a difference.

2. INVESTIGATIONS

Very few, if any investigations, occur as they do on television. There is no script; it is more like a puzzle with some of the pieces missing. Many agencies are now starting to send laboratory personnel to the actual scenes to help in the

From: *The Forensic Laboratory Handbook: Procedures and Practice*
Edited by: A. Mozayani and C. Noziglia © Humana Press Inc., Totowa, NJ

Fig. 1. Buildings can and do collapse.

Fig. 2. Cars are reduced to jagged pieces of metal.

identification and collection of evidence. Not all personnel are interested in doing this, but some are. The reasons for this are many. For the most part, a bombing or fire scene will be one of the most dangerous places a person can be. Generally the area can be very hazardous to ones health. This can be for any number of reasons. The main reason is the fact that once a bomb has gone off or a fire has occurred, the scene is generally no longer structurally sound. Figures 1–3 illustrate just a few of the possible hazards of the investigation scenes.

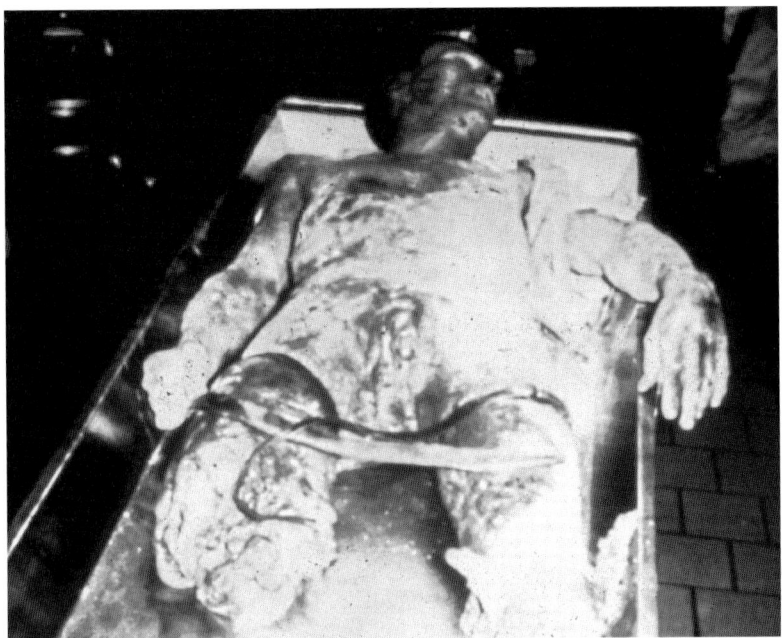

Fig. 3. People are turned into biological hazards.

In addition to the hazards depicted in Figs. 1–3, some of the "bad guys" may actively be trying to kill the responders who show up. On January 16, 1997, officers responding to the scene of a bombing incident where one person was killed and another seriously injured were targeted by the bomber. Street officers, emergency medical service personnel, and investigators of all types quickly arrived on scene. They were all in extreme danger just by doing their jobs. The bomber left behind what is called a secondary device that is set to go off approx 1 h after the first device (*see* Fig. 4).

Although the secondary device detonated, no officers were seriously injured simply because a late-arriving officer had parked his car directly in front of the device. Less than a month later the same situation occurred again. This time, however, the responding officers modified their procedures and searched the response area prior to beginning the evidence processing. Because of this alteration of their response, the secondary device was discovered and disarmed before it could detonate. Walking into an area that has a secondary device left behind which is intentionally designed to kill the responding officers can be a sobering experience. Although street officers may realize these dangers, most crime scene response personnel are unfamiliar with them.

SANDY SPRINGS PROFESSIONAL BUILDING

January 16, 1997

Metal Ammo Cans

1/8" Steel Plates

Baby Ben Alarm Clocks

Dynamite

D-Cell Batteries

Duct Tape

Electrical Tape

4d Flooring Nails

Twisted Iron Wire

Fig. 4. Secondary device.

Crime scene personnel are chosen and trained for their ability to perform evidence recognition and collection. Both bombing and arson scenes can be quite a mess with which to deal. Both can have evidence present in several physical forms, both as residues and intact material. Most people are under the false impression that when an explosion occurs, all of the components of the explosive device, as well as the explosive itself, are consumed or destroyed. The same impression is also thought of fires. Everyone, including many investigators themselves, think that ignitable liquids and other accelerants are consumed by a fire. Nothing is further from the truth. Both residues and unconsumed (intact) materials can be located at the scene and in debris recovered from the scene if the investigator knows what to collect. In addition to the residues and unconsumed explosive, there may be intentional materials left behind as well. Over recent years there have been various methods used to help in tracking explosives that could be used in bombings. One method that was tried and is still being considered is micro-taggants (*see* Fig. 5).

Micro-taggants are small, virtually indestructible layer chips that are mixed with explosives that are left behind after an explosion. Another method used is chemical taggants. Instead of actual physically inert materials, specific chemicals are mixed with the explosives as markers. After an explosion, these chemical markers can be recovered revealing what type of explosive had been used.

Code: MO292929F5

Manufacturer: A

Batch: #16234

Fig. 5. Original version of micro-taggants. (*See* color insert following p.182).

Currently this method is being used to tag several different forms of organic high explosives in the United States.

This brings us to a very important point: anyone working at a bombing or arson crime scene must be constantly aware of contamination. The techniques and equipment currently available to personnel who analyze evidence from bombings and arsons are much more sensitive than they have been in the past. This means that what could not have been detected in the past now can be found. This leads to the question: "if something is found in trace amounts, is this evidence or is it just contamination from another scene?" Boots, clothing, tools, and even vehicles can cause contamination at scenes. Agencies have to be aware of contamination problems. Most agencies have thought this through and already have procedures in place.

In addition to collecting the evidence at bombing and arson scenes, crime scene investigators are being tasked with determining what actually happened at the scene. These investigators want to determine the size of the bomb, where was it placed, how it was initiated, of what was it composed, what type of flammable liquid was used, and how it was ignited. All of these questions run through an investigator's mind when he or she arrives on scene and starts to process it for evidence (*see* Fig. 6).

Once the evidence has been identified, it must be properly collected. The evidence must be placed into secure containers for transportation to the laboratory for analysis. These containers may be plastic bags, metal cans, or glass jars. The container type is usually dependent on what type of evidence it is going to contain. Organic materials are unsuitable in plastic bags because they tend to pass through the plastic barrier and evaporate. However, there are certain types

Fig. 6. Post-blast class.

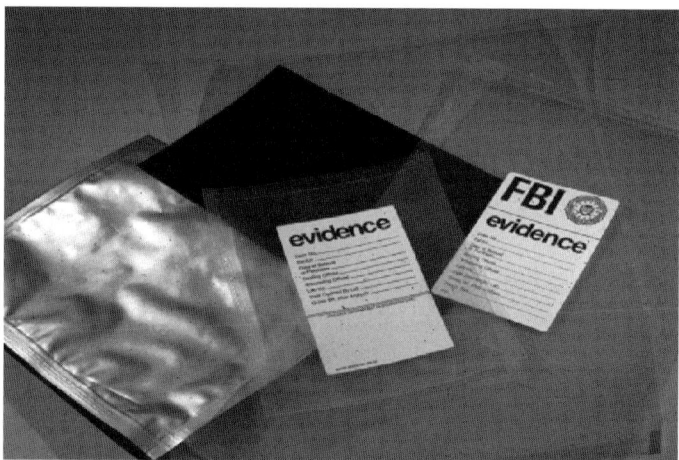

Fig. 7. Plastic evidence bags.

of plastic bags specifically made to contain organic materials. In most arson cases, evidence is generally placed into those types of bags (Fig. 7) or metal cans (Fig. 8).

Evidence from bombing scenes is collected into the same types of containers. By using the proper containers to collect and transport the evidence, any contamination or loss of the evidence can be avoided. Without good evidence, the best forensic laboratory in the world cannot produce results.

Fig. 8. Metal evidence can.

3. LABORATORY ANALYSIS

Once the laboratory receives the evidence, various types of analyses can be performed. In the case of bombing evidence, the first thing that is done is a visual examination of the debris for possible fragments of the device (Fig. 9).

Small bits and pieces are separated and, if possible, identified. The forensic examiner will be looking for, among other things, a timing mechanism, firing circuit, and device casing. By looking at the bits and pieces, their size, and what type of damage is present, an experienced forensic examiner can start to deduce many things about the device, i.e., what type/class of explosive was probably used and whether or not the device functioned properly. The examiner works on the detonated device similar to working on a jigsaw puzzle. *See* Fig. 10 for an example of a reconstruction.

While looking at the bits and pieces, the examiner is also checking for residues on the pieces, as well as signs of unreacted explosive material. At this point in time, the examiner may choose to do a simple chemical color test that will give an indication of the type of explosive. These tests are considered presumptive. That is to say they can only give an indication as to what explosive may have been used; further testing must be done in order to conclusively identify the explosive. There are no presumptive color tests for fire debris, so other methodologies must be used to determine if an ignitable is present. In some cases, a rainbow effect may be noticed in water if a hydrocarbon is present

Fig. 9. Explosive device fragments.

in fire debris. The flowchart (Fig. 11) shows a basic scheme of analysis that uses a layered approach and also utilizes almost all forms or types of explosive analyses.

No matter how the explosives are analyzed, the first step is usually a simple presumptive color test. Regardless of whether the explosive is inorganic or organically based, these color tests will lead the analyst to identification. The most widely used color test is the diphenylamine color test (*see* Fig. 12). It gives a dark blue with both organic and inorganic nitrates, as well as chlorates.

Some color tests can be used to differentiate between organic and inorganic explosives. The antazoline test reacts with inorganic nitrates, whereas methanolic potassium hydroxide (KOH) gives good color reactions with organic explosives (*see* Figs. 13 and 14).

Once the preliminary color tests have been done, the next step depends on whether or not intact particles are found. If particles are present, analysis can begin immediately. If no particles are found, a series of washes are done on the debris or fragments to recover any residues present. A water wash is done for inorganic explosives, whereas an organic solvent is used for organic explosive residues.

Fig. 10. Improvised explosive device reconstruction.

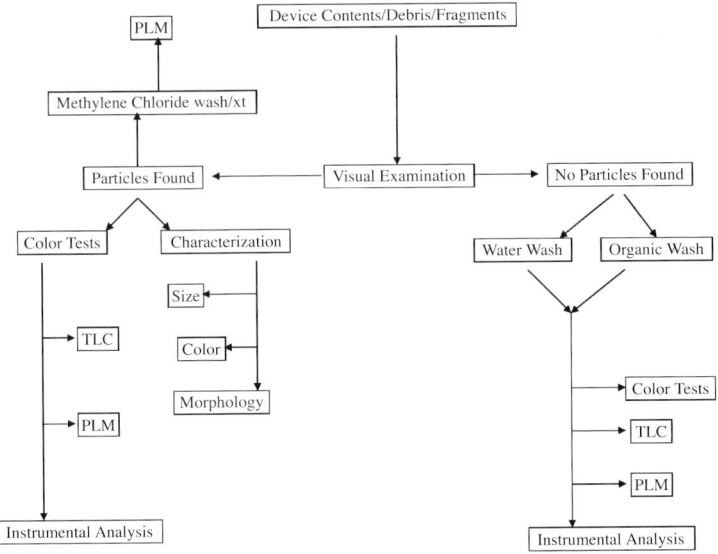

Fig. 11. Explosive analysis flowchart.

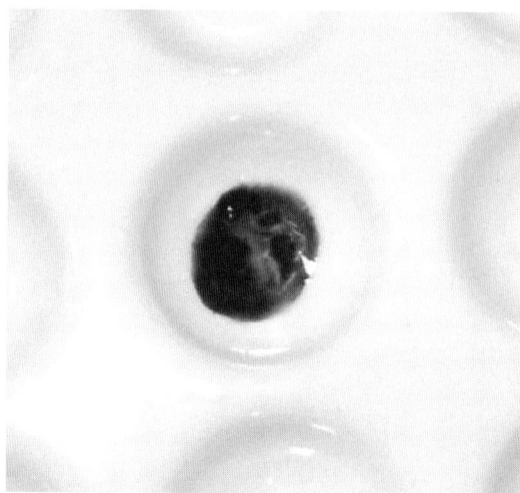

Fig. 12. Diphenylamine color test. (*See* color insert following p.182).

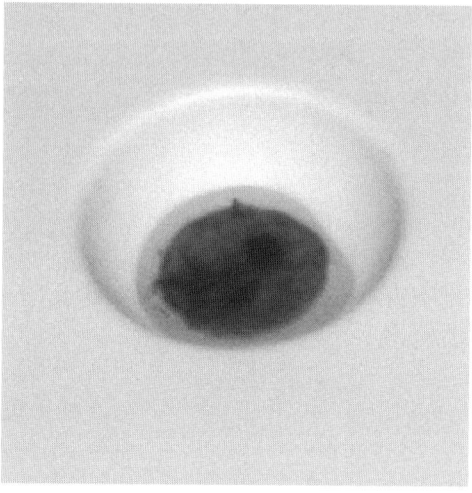

Fig. 13. Anatazoline color test. (*See* color insert following p.182).

Regardless of whether traditional instrumental analysis or microscopy is chosen as the conforming technique, the analysis is entering the final phase. For explosives, if there are no intact particles present, the fragments are rinsed to capture any residues that may be present. The fragments are rinsed with an organic solvent first and then with water. By using both an organic solvent and then water, organic and inorganic explosive residues can both be recovered. Once the residues have been recovered there are several ways to analyze them.

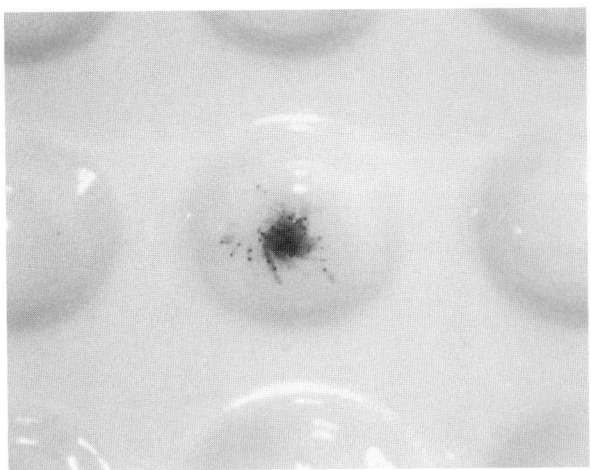

Fig. 14. KOH color tests. (*See* color insert following p.182).

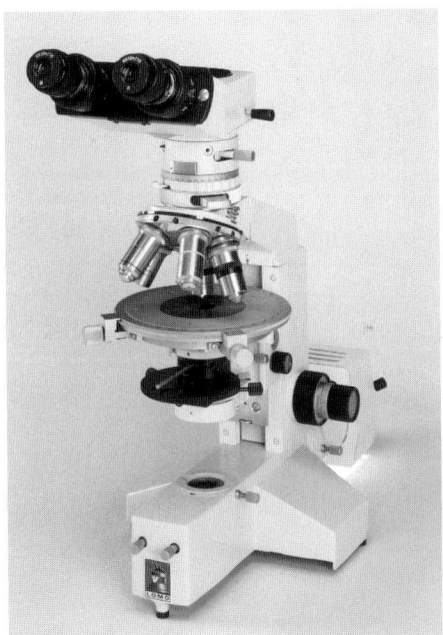

Fig. 15. Microscope.

Some laboratory personnel use polarized light microscopy (PLM) to identify explosives, whereas others prefer an all-instrumental approach.

Two examples of the different types of equipment that can be used to analyze explosives and explosive residues are represented in Figs. 15 and 16:

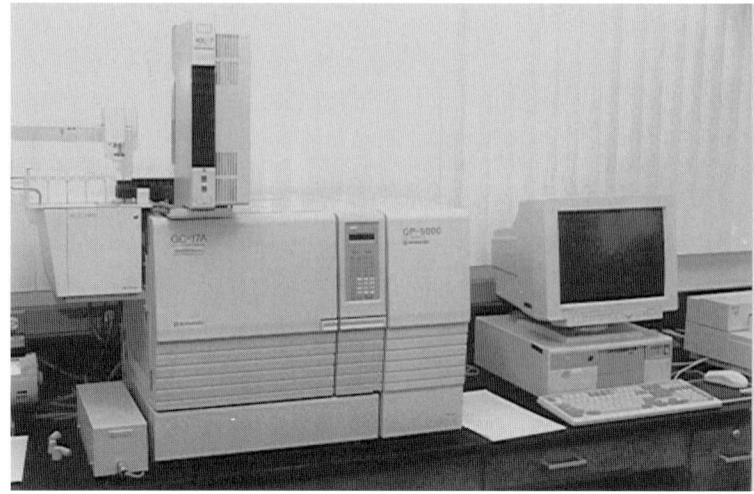

Fig. 16. Gas chromatograph/mass spectrometer.

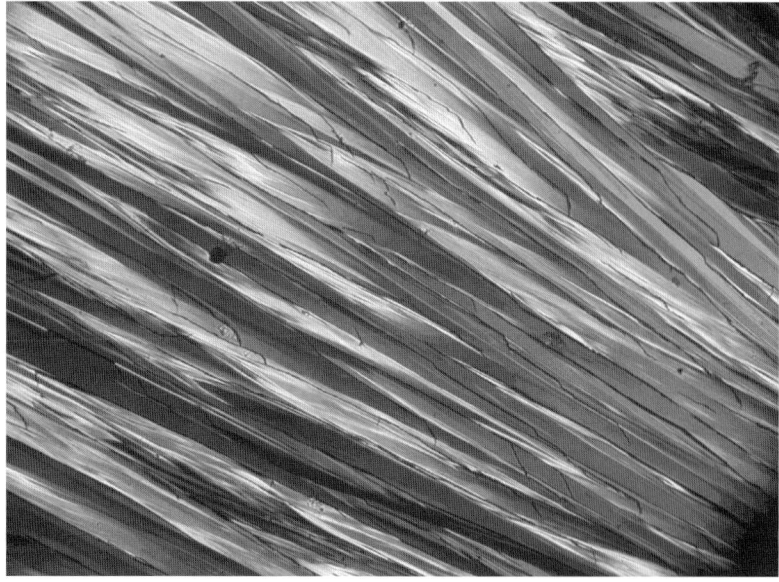

Fig. 17. TNT fusion melt. (*See* color insert following p.182).

the microscope and gas chromatography/mass spectrometry (GC/MS). Although both methodologies are considered conclusive, the data obtained varies greatly. The PLM gives data that must be examined visually and relies on a highly trained individual to make the determination of what it means. Figures 17 and 18 represent examples of the different forms of data that are interpreted.

Fig. 18. Sodium nitrate under crossed poles. (*See* color insert following p.182).

Instrumental analysis gives a different type of data. These data types are referred to as spectral data or spectrums. This data may be in the form of infrared (heat radiation absorbance/transmittance) using a Fourier transform infrared spectrometer, or data that show the actual molecular make-up of a compound, such as mass spectral information using GC/MS (*see* Figs. 19 and 20).

Fire debris or arson analysis has been done for years. Initially, ignitable liquids were extracted from fire debris by steam distillation. As time progressed, new and more efficient methodologies were developed. Currently most laboratories utilize a method referred to as passive absorption/elution. This entails placing an absorbent material sensitized to organics inside a container of fire debris and sealing the can. As the container temperature is raised, any ignitable liquids will volatilize and be absorbed by the absorbent inside of the can. The material is then rinsed with another organic solvent that extracts any absorbed ignitable liquids out of the absorbent material. This sample can then be run by either of two methods: GC GC/MS. The main difference between the two techniques is the difference in the detectors that are used to identify the compounds as they elute from the gas chromatograph. Figures 21 and 22 demonstrate the data derived from these two methods.

GC utilizes the amount of time that a compound takes to reach the end of a column and be detected. This means that, although rare, two compounds could come off of the column at the same location and, consequently, the analyst would be unable to differentiated between them. This method was the standard method of analysis back in the 1980s and is still in use in many laboratories within the United States today. Data obtained were compared with

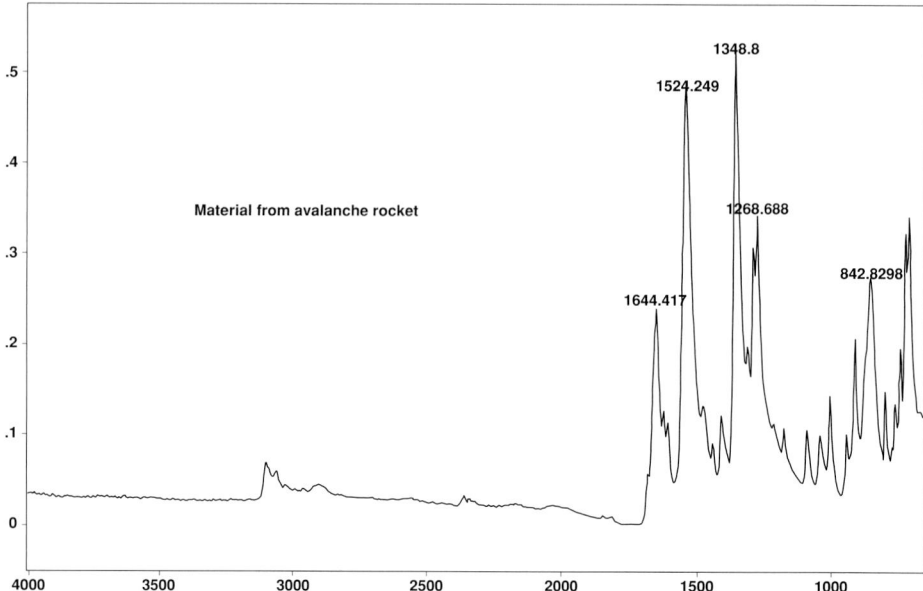

Fig. 19. FourieTransformed infared spectrophotometer data.

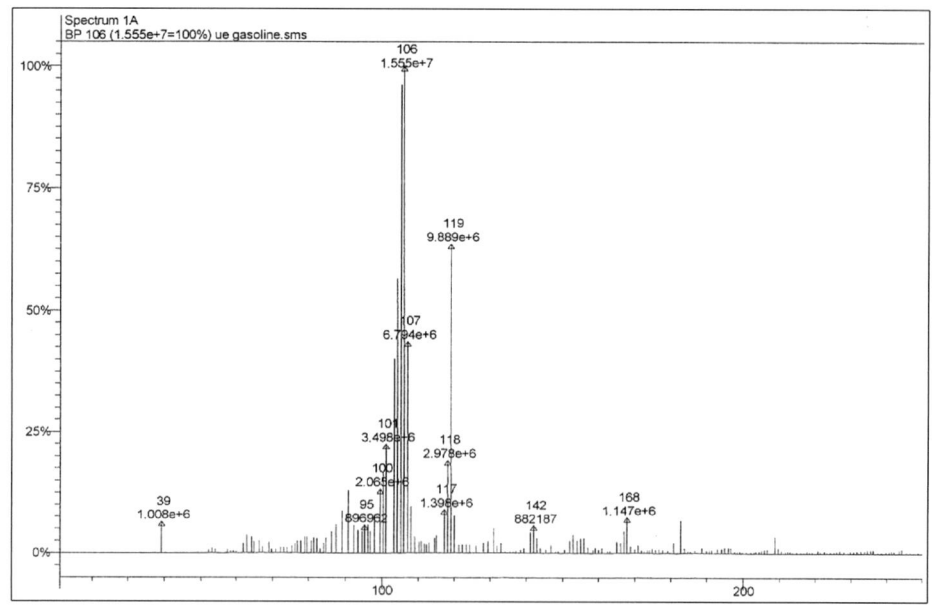

Fig. 20. Gas chromatography/mass spectrometry data.

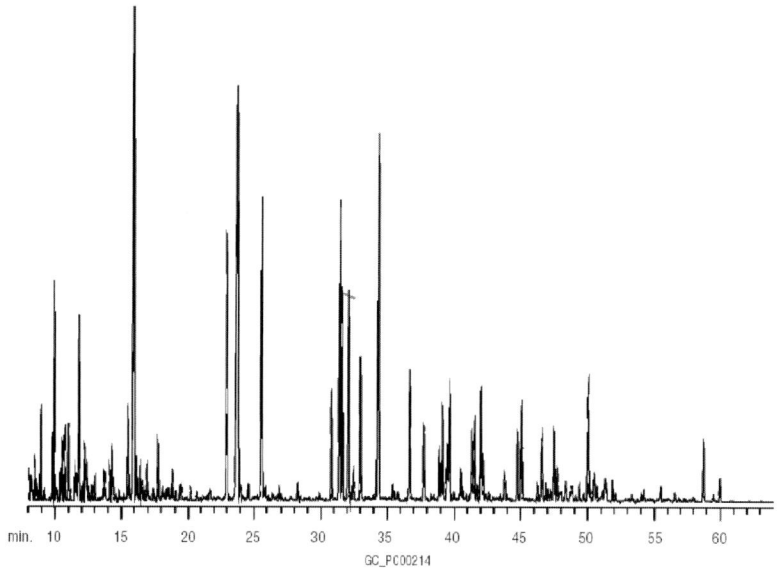

Fig. 21. Gas chromatography data.

classification systems developed in the late 1970s and early 1980s by the Bureau of Alcohol, Tobacco, and Firearms:

Class 1: Light petroleum distillates. Distillates in the range of C_4 (butane) to C_{12} (dodecane) + with a major alkane peak less than C_9(nonane). Examples include many cigarette lighter fluids.

Class 2: Gasoline. All brands and grades of automotive gasoline.

Class 3: Medium petroleum distillates. Distillates in the range C_8 (octane) to C_{12}. Examples include some mineral spirits and charcoal starters.

Class 4: Kerosine. Distillates in the range of C_9 to C_{16} (hexadecane). Examples include home heating oils.

Class 5: Heavy petroleum distillates. Distillates in the range of C_8 to C_{23} (tricosane). Examples include diesel fuel.

Using GC methodology, everything was classified as a petroleum distillate. This methodology did not work well for synthetic compounds and other types of naturally occurring materials that could be used as an accelerant.

If we look at GC/MS, GC is used to separate the compounds, but MS is the detector in this case. It does more than simply look at the amount of time it takes a compound to come off the column. It causes each compound to fragment into its ions and then graphs the ionic structure. Each compound will fragment the same way time after time. Because of this we can classify the

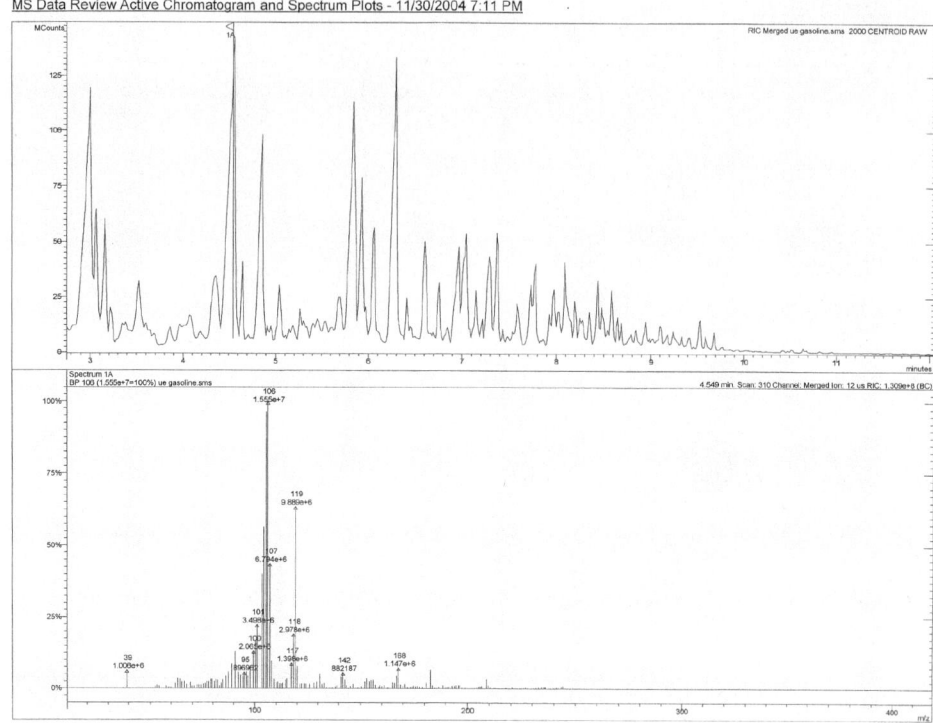

Fig. 22. Gas chromatography/mass spectrometry data.

compounds by they way they fragment making it a much more definitive type of identification.

The American Society of Testing Materials (ASTM) developed a new classification system that utilized all the information that could be obtained by GC/MS analysis. It is called ASTM 1387-95 and all ignitable liquids are separated into six classes—the first five of which are the same as the Bureau of Alcohol, Tobacco, and Firearm's classes of ignitable fluids—with the sixth class (class 0) having five subclasses as follows:

Class 0: Miscellaneous compounds. This class encompasses all non-distillate products except for automotive gasoline. The miscellaneous class is further divided into five sub-classes.

Class 0.1: Oxygenated solvents. Single component and blended products that contain an oxygenated component. Examples include many lacquer thinners.

Class 0.2: Isoparaffinic products. Products comprised solely of branched chained alkanes (isoparaffins). Examples include many odorless paint thinners and charcoal starters.

Class 0.3: *n*-Alkane products. Products comprised solely of normal alkanes. Examples include candle oils.

Class 0.4: Aromatic products. Products comprised of aromatic compounds. Examples include some specialty cleaning solvents and insecticide vehicles.

Class 0.5: Naphthenic-paraffinic products. Products comprised of cyclic and branched chained alkanes. Examples include some odorless lamp oils, charcoal starters, and specialty solvents.

This new classification system is much better and allows almost every type of ignitable liquid to be classified.

ASTM is currently proposing a newer classification that better incorporates the distillate classes 1–5 with the miscellaneous classes. This new classification system has 25 different classes that are based on a combination of distillate range and GC/MS/chemical data. This looks to be a great improvement over past classification schemes because of its flexibility.

4. REPORTS AND COURT

Once the analysis is done, a report must be written no matter what type of analysis has been done or what the results are. Reporting procedures vary among agencies. Many have a standardized form that can even be used. An arson report may read like the following:

- Analysis conducted on item(s) disclosed the presence of a flammable/combustible liquid(s) from the medium petroleum distillate (MPD) class. The following are some examples of this class: paint thinners, some types of charcoal starters, mineral spirits, and cleaning napthas.
- Analysis conducted on item(s) disclosed the presence of a flammable/combustible liquid(s) from the miscellaneous class. This class includes isoparaffins, alcohols, terpenes/turpentine, single component solvents (benzene, pentane, xylene, etc.), and specially formulated mixtures of alkanes or aromatics.
- No flammable/combustible liquid(s) were detected in item(s). This does not preclude the possibility that those types of liquids were present at an earlier time. Analysis conducted on item(s) was inconclusive at this time.

An explosives report may look like this:

- Results of analysis disclosed the presence of potassium nitrate on the pipe fragments. Potassium nitrate is a major component of gunpowder. When confined and ignited in a pipe, gunpowder will produce an explosion. This type of improvised explosive device (IED) is capable of causing serious injury and sometimes death.
- Results of analysis disclosed large square fragments of a galvanized pipe, 1 in. in diameter. Physical characteristics determined that these fragments were part a pipe

bomb filled with a low explosive/explosive compound and ignited. Some types of low explosives commonly used in IEDs are gunpowder, flashpowder, or potassium chlorate/sugar. This type of IED is capable of causing serious injury and sometimes death.

• Analysis on the debris did not detect the presence of an explosive/explosive residue or any fragments/components of an IED.

All of the above are merely examples of how reports could read. A report must clearly state the results and what they actually mean. It is also very helpful to the investigator to give examples of what kind of flammables a class may contain, such as a MPD in arson analysis.

Once the report is generated, it may or may not have to be explained in court. Many times the report itself will be entered as evidence (it will be stipulated) and the analyst who generated it will not have to testify. In my own personal experience, there have been very few times in the hundreds of bombing and arson cases I have worked over the last 26 years in which I actually testified. In that time, I probably have testified in less than 20 cases. In most situations the report is not attacked so much as the chain of custody.

However in today's contamination-conscious legal system, laboratory procedures are coming under more and more scrutiny. That is why accreditation and certification have become such hot topics among forensic personnel. Some feel it is an intrusion and others feel it is a blessing. Personally, I feel it is a good thing for the most part. Forensic science has become so specialized that no one can know it all as we thought we could in the past. However, these accrediting bodies themselves must be monitored to make sure they are working for the good of the forensic field and not empire building. One of the newest organizations solely devoted to fire debris and explosive investigation/analysis is the Technical Working Group for Fire and Explosions. It is made up of working personnel at all levels who deal on a day-to-day basis with these types of evidence. They are currently working on setting the standards against which all forensic laboratories will be measured by the accrediting organizations when it comes to fire and explosive evidence analysis.

GLOSSARY

ANFO:	A mixture of ammonium nitrate and fuel oil.
Base Charge:	The main high explosive charge in a blasting cap.
Binary Explosive:	Two substances which are not explosive until they are mixed.
Binary weapon:	Chemical weapon in which the last stage of the production process is moved from the factory to the warhead where the mixing of two generally non-toxic precursor substances takes place in flight just before deployment, creating a toxic product. Advantages are that manufacture, storage, and transport are much safer for personnel

	handling of binary chemical weapons, such as Sarin (BG-2), Soman (GD-2) and VX (VX-2).
Black Powder:	A low explosive tradsitionally consisting of potassium nitrate, sulfur and charcoal. Sodium nitrate may be found in place of potassium nitrate.
Black Powder Substitutes:	Modified black powder formulations such as but not limited to: Pyrodex, Black Canyon, Golden Powder, Triple 7, Clean Shot, and Clear Shot.
Blasting Agent:	A high explosive with low sensitivity usually based on ammonium nitrate and not containing additional high explosive(s).
Blasting Cap:	A metal tube containing a primary high explosive capable of initiating most explosives.
Bomb:	A device containing an explosive, incendiary, or chemical material designed to explode.
Booby Trap:	A concealed or camouflaged device designed to injure or kill personnel.
Booster:	A cap sensitive high explosive used to initiate other less sensitive high explosives.
Brisance:	The shattering power associated with high explosives.
C4:	A white pliable military plastic explosive containing primarily Cyclonite (RDX).
Cannon Fuse:	A coated, thread-wrapped cord filled with black powder designed to initiate flame-sensitive explosives.
ChemBio:	Chemical/Biological weapons.
Chemical agent:	Substance that can cause physiological changes in humans and animals.
Chemical weapons (CW):	There are several types of munitions and other delivery systems that contain substances intended to injure or kill or incapacitate personnel or to deny access or use of area, facilities and materials.
Combustion:	Any type of exothermic oxidation reaction, including, but not limited to burning, deflagration and/or detonation.
Deflagration:	An exothermic reaction that occurs particle to particle at subsonic speed.
Detasheet (Det Sheet):	A plastic explosive in sheet form containing PETN, HMX or RDX.
Detonation:	An exothermic reaction that propagates a shockwave through an explosive at supersonic speed (greater than 3300 ft/s).
Detonation Cord (Det-Cord):	A plastic or fiber wrapped cord containing a core of PETN or RDX.
Detonator:	A device used for detonating many types of high explosives, radiological/radioactive shrapnel.

Double Base:	A smokeless powder which contains both nitroglycerine and nitrocellulose.
Dud:	An explosive device which has undergone a complete arming and firing cycle but has failed to explode.
Dynamite:	Originally a mixture of nitroglycerine and absorbent filler that is now used to designate an entire class of high explosives.
Ethylene Glycol Dinitrate (EGDN):	Material replacing nitroglycerine in dynamites.
Electric Match:	A metal wire coated with a pyrotechnic mixture designed to produce a small burst of flame designed to initiate a low explosive.
Electric Squib:	A metal wire surrounded by a pyrotechnic mixture and encased within a metal tube which produces a small jet of flame designed to initiate a low explosive.
EMS:	Emergency Medical Services.
EOD:	Explosive Ordnance Disposal.
Explosion:	A rapid expansion of gases resulting from a chemical or physical action that produces a pressure wave.
Explosive:	An energetic material capable of producing an explosion.
Explosive Compound:	A single chemical compound capable of causing an explosion.
Explosive Mixture:	A mixture of chemical compounds capable of causing an explosion.
Explosive Train:	A series of combustible or explosive components arranged in order of decreasing sensitivity designed to initiate explosives.
Firing Train:	*See* "Explosive Train."
First Responder:	The first trained emergency response person on scene.
Flex-X:	*See* "Det Sheet."
Frag:	Any item(s) produced and cast away from an explosion.
FTIR:	FourieTransformed Infared Spectrophotometer.
Fuel:	Any substance capable of reacting with oxygen or oxygen-carriers (oxidizers).
Fuse:	A fiber wrapped cord of black powder used to initiate blasting caps or low explosives.
Fuze:	A mechanical, chemical, or electrical device designed to initiate an explosive train.
GC/MS:	Gas Chromatograph Mass Spectrophotometer.
Gunpowder:	*See* "Black Powder."
HAZMAT:	Hazardous material(s).
High Explosive:	Generally a chemical substance or mixture capable of detonation.

HMX:	Octagen, a high explosive formed as a by product during the manufacture of RDX.
Hoax:	A "dummy" device intended to appear as a bomb but not containing an explosive.
Hobby Fuse:	*See* "Cannon Fuse."
IED:	Improvised Explosive Device.
Improvised Explosive Device (IED):	A non-commercially produced device designed to explode.
Incendiary:	A compound, metal or mixture capable of producing intense heat.
Inert:	A simulated explosive or device that contains no explosive, pyrotechnic, or chemical/biological agent.
Initiator:	The part of an explosive train which starts the reaction.
Large Vehicle Bomb (LVB):	A vehicle containing large quantities of explosives and designed to act as a WMD.
Low Explosive:	Generally a chemical compound or mixture that can deflagrate without the addition of atmospheric oxygen.
Main Charge:	The main or final explosive component in an explosive train.
Munitions:	Any and all military explosives.
Munroe Effect:	The focusing of the force produced by an explosion resulting in an increased pressure wave.
NFPA:	National Fire Protection Association.
Nitrocellulose (NC):	Main component in smokeless powder, i.e., guncotton.
Nitroglycerine (NG):	Explosive material originally the basis for dynamite.
Ordnance:	*See* "Munitions."
OSHA:	Occupational Safety and Health Administration.
Oxidizer:	A chemical compound which supplies the oxygen in a chemical reaction.
PENO:	Plastic explosive comprised of PETN and a binder material.
PETN:	Pentaerythritoltetranitrate, a high explosive used in many applications.
Plastic Bonded Explosives (PBX):	A high explosive in a pliable plastic matrix, i.e. C4, Det Flex.
Plastic Explosives:	Common term for PBX.
PLM:	Polarized Light Microscopy.
Primary Fragmentation:	Frag generated by the initial explosion/blast.
Primary High Explosive:	A high explosive sensitive to heat, shock, spark, and/or friction.
Primer:	*See* "Initiator."
Primer Cap:	A small metal device containing an impact sensitive primary high explosive commonly found in ammunition or used in initiators.

Pyrotechnic Fuse:	*See* "Cannon Fuse."
Pyrotechnic Mixtures:	An oxidizer/fuel mixture that produces bright or colored lights, heat, fogs, or acoustic effects.
RDD:	Radiological Dispersive Device, i.e., dirty bomb.
RDX:	Cyclonite, high explosive used in PBX and other applications.
Report:	A loud sound produced by an explosion.
Safety Fuse:	A water-proof coated, thread-wrapped cord filled with black powder designed to be used to initiate a non-electric blasting cap.
Secondary Fragmentation:	Frag produced by primary fragments striking objects and imparting explosive inertia to them.
Secondary High Explosive:	A less sensitive high explosive initiated by another explosive.
Semtex:	Plastic explosive containing Cyclonite (RDX) and Pentaerythritoltetranitrate (PETN) made in Czech Republic.
Shaped Charge:	An explosive device which is designed to direct or focus explosive energy into a narrow jet.
Shock Tube:	Hollow plastic tube coated with a thin coating of HMX and powdered aluminum used in non-electric firing systems.
Shrapnel:	Objects which are attached to the outside or included inside a device or the container walls themselves that increase the blast damage and/or injure/kill personnel.
Single Base:	A smokeless powder which contains nitrocellulose but does not contain nitroglycerine or nitroguanidine.
Smokeless Powder:	A low explosive used in ammunition as a propellant, which can be single, double, or triple based.
Triple Base:	A smokeless powder which contains nitrocellulose, nitroglycerine, and nitroguanidine.
Weapon of Mass Destruction (WMD):	Any type weapon that is capable of cause large scale destruction and/or mass casualties.

SUGGESTED READING

Arson Suggested Reading

Askari MDF, Maskarinec MP, Smith SM, Beam PM, Travis CC. Effectiveness of purge-and-trap for measurement of volatile organic compounds in aged soils. Anal Chem 1996;68(19):3431–3433.

Bertsch W. Volatiles from carpet: a source of frequent misinterpretation in arson analysis. J Chomatogr 1994;674:329–333.

Bertsch W. Analysis of accelerants in fire debris—data interpretation. Forensic Sci Rev 1997;9(1):1–22.

Bertsch W, Sellers CS. Limits in arson debris analysis by capillary column gas chromatography/mass spectrometry. HRC CC J High Resolut Chromatogr Comm 1986;9(11):657–661.

DeHaan JD, Greenfield A. Evaporation rates of volatile hydrocarbon accelerants. 44th Annual Meeting Amer Acad Forensic Sci, New Orleans, LA, February 17–22, 1992, Abstract B20.

Dietz WR. Interpretation guidelines for "problem" accelerant chromatograms. 44th Annual Meeting Amer Acad Forensic Sci, New Orleans, LA, February 17–22, 1992, Abstract B29.

Dietz WR, Mann DC. Contamination problem within polyester bags. Newsl Midw Assoc Forensic Sci 1988;17(3):34.

Frontela L, Pozas JA, Picabea L A. Comparison of extraction and adsorption methods for the recovery of accelerants from arson debris Forensic Sci Int 1995;75(1):11–23.

Fultz ML. The effect of sample preparation on the identification of class 4 and class 5 petroleum products. 46th Annual Meeting AAFS San Antonio, TX, February 14–19, 1994, Abstract B84.

Gialamas DM. Is it Gasoline or Insecticide? CAC Fall Seminar San Diego, CA, October 1993, The CAC News 1994 16–20.

Higgins M. Turpentine accelerant or natural??? Fire Arson Invest 1987;38(2):10.

Hirz R. Gasoline brand identification and individualization of gasoline lots. J Forensic Sci Soc 1989;29(2):91–101.

Howard J, McKague AB. A fire investigation involving combustion of carpet material. J Forensic Sci 1984;29(3):919–922.

Kirkbride KP, Yap SM, Andrews S, et al. Microbial degradation of petroleum hydro-carbons: implications for arson residue analysis. J Forensic Sci 1992;37(6):1585–1599.

Lentini J. Differentiation of asphalt and smoke condensates from liquid petroleum distillates using GC/MS. 48th Annual Meeting, AAFS Nashville, TN, February 19–24, 1996, Abstract no. B42.

Lentini J, Waters LV. Isolation of accelerant-like residues from roof shingles using headspace concentration. Arson Anal Newsl 1982;6(3):48–55.

Lincoln S. Charcoal lighter fluid used as an arson accelerant. Fire Arson Invest 1991;42(1):46–47.

Mann DC. Comparison of automotive gasolines using capillary gas chromatography ii: limitations of automotive gasoline comparisons in casework. J Forensic Sci 1987; 32(3):616–628.

Mann DC, Gresham WR. Microbial degradation of gasoline in soil. J Forensic Sci 1990;35(4):913–923.

Midkiff CR Jr. Brand identification and comparison of petroleum products - a complex problem. Fire Arson Invest 1975;26(2):18–21.

Midkiff CR Jr. Is it a petroleum product? How do you know? J Forensic Sci 1986; 31(1):231–234.

Moorehead W, Dickan T. Capillary gas chromatography characterization and classification of some hydrocarbon solvents and alkyl glycol ethers. 86th Semi-annual Seminar, CAC San Pedro, CA, Autumn, 1995, Abstract: Science and Justice 1996; 36(3):203.

Newman R. New and unusual ignitable liquids. Newsl Southern Assoc Forensic Sci 1995;23(2):27–31.

Newman R, Lothridge K, Dietz WR. The effects of time, temperature, strip size and concentration in the use of activated charcoal strips in fire debris analysis. Curr Topics Forensic Sci Proc 14th Meeting Int Assoc Forensic Sci, Takatori T and Takasu A, eds. Shunderson Communications Ottawa, Ont, 1977, pp. 218–224.

Nowicki JF. Control samples in arson analysis. Arson Anal Newsl 1981;5(1):1–5.

Nowicki JF. An accelerant classification scheme based on analysis by gas chromatography/mass spectrometry (GC-MS). J Forensic Sci 1990;35(5):1064–1086.

Nowicki JF. Determining the source of gasoline samples from fire scenes by gc-ms using selected ion profiles. 46th Annual Meeting AAFS San Antonio, TX, February 14–19, 1994, Abstract B85.

Small JL, Milroy S. Possible "accelerants" found in household products. 42nd Annual Meeting AAFS Cincinnati, OH, February 19–24, 1990, Abstract B55.

Stackhouse CS. Will the real lamp oil please stand up? Arson Anal Newsl 1986; 9(2):21–31.

Stackhouse CS. Lacquer thinners-rare but not forgotten. 42nd Annual Meeting AAFS Cincinnati, OH, February 19–24, 1990, Abstract B56.

Stone IC, Lomonte JN. False positives in analysis of fire debris. Fire Arson Inv 1984;34(3):36–40.

Trimpe MA. Turpentine in arson analysis. J Forensic Sci 1991;36(4):1059–1073.

Trimpe MA. What the arson investigator should know about turpentine. Fire Arson Invest 1993;44(1):53–55.

Explosives Suggested Reading

Beveridge AD. Development in the detection and identification of explosive residues. Forensic Science Review 1992;4(1):17–49.

Christian D. Examination of smokeless gunpowder particles in pipe-bomb residues. SWAFS Journal 1996;18(1):32–42.

Garner DD, Fultz ML. The ATF approach to post-blast explosives detection and identification. Journal of Energetic Materials 1986;4:133–148.

Haag LC. Shot sizes and shot charges, forensic firearms evidence: elements of shooting incident investigation, Forensic Science Services, Inc., pp. 70–71.

Hopen TJ, Crippin JB. Methylene blue microchemical test for the detection and identification of perchlorates and chlorates. Microscope 2001;49(1):41–45.

Hopen TJ, Kilbourn JH. Characterization and identification of water soluble explosives, Microscope 1985;33(1):1–22.

Huntamer DD. Microscopical characterization of an emulsion explosive. Microscope 1999;47(1):1–4.

Kilbourn JH, McCrone WC. Fusion methods: identification of inorganic explosives. Microscope 1985;33(2):73–90.

Martz RM, Lasswell LD III. Smokeless powder identification. Proceedings of the International Symposium on the Analysis and Detection of Explosives, 1983, pp. 245–254.

McCrone LB, McCrone WC. Strained crystals. Microscope 2000;48:203–206.

McCrone WC. Particle characterization by plm part i: no polars. Microscope 1982;30: 185–196.

McCrone WC. Particle characterization by plm part ii: single polar. Microscope 1982; 30:315–331.

McCrone WC. Particle characterization by plm part iii: crossed polars. Microscope 1983;31:187–206.

McCrone WC, Andreen JH, Tsang S-M. Identification of organic high explosives. Microscope 1993;41:161–182.

McCrone WC, Andreen JH, Tsang S-M. Identification of organic high explosives II. Microscope 1994;42:61–73.

McCrone WC, Andreen JH, Tsang S-M. Identification of organic high explosives III. Microscope 1999;47:183–200.

Randle WA. A microchemical test for monomethylamine nitrate. Microscope 1997; 45:85–88.

Skidmore CB, Phillips DS, Crane NB. Microscopical examination of plastic-bonded explosives. Microscope 1997;45(4):127–136.

Teetsov A. Preparation and use of needles and micropipets for handling very small particles. Microscope 1999;47:63–70.

Twibell JD, et al. The persistence of military explosives on hands. J Forensic Sci 1984;29(1):284–290.

Twibell JD, Home JM, Smalldon KW, Higgs DG. Transfer of nitroglycerine to hands during contact with commercial explosives. J Forensic Sci 1982;27(4):783–791.

Twibell JD, Home JM, Smalldon KW, Higgs DG, Hayes TS. Assessment of solvents for the recovery of nitroglycerine from hands using cotton swabs. J Forensic Sci 1982;27(4):792–800.

Whitman VL, Wills WF Jr. Extended use of squaric acid as a reagent in chemical microscopy. Microscope 1977;25(1):1–13.

Wills WF Jr. Squaric acid revisited. Microscope 1990;38:169–185.

Chapter 6

Fingerprints

Brian E. Dalrymple, AOCA

1. HISTORY

Humans' fascination with fingerprints began thousands of years ago, as evidenced by the pictures left behind. Prehistoric cave art, including a hand with ridge patterns, was discovered in Nova Scotia. Other caves in France depict images of finger and footprints dating back further than 15,000 BCE. During the reign of Hammurabi in Babylon (1955–1913 BCE), fingerprints were used as seals on contracts, indicating an awareness of the unique and personal nature of the raised patterns on the fingers. This practice is also attributed to the Chinese as early as the second or third century BCE. Throughout the world over the next 2000 years, fascination with fingerprints evolved into study and applied knowledge that has laid the ground work for one of the most powerful forensic tools available to the modern criminal investigator. Listed here is a more detailed timeline of this fingerprint history:

- Circa 1200, China: Fingerprints featured as a criminal identification tool in a novel.
- 1600s, England: Function of the pores in the hands and feet are described.
- 1600s, Italy: Friction ridges studied under the microscope, a new invention.
- 1700s, Germany: Awareness of the uniqueness of fingerprints.
- 1800s, Germany: Fingerprint patterns classified.
- 1800s, India: Fingerprints recorded to defeat fraud in pension payments.
- 1800s, Great Britain: Further studies upholding the individual nature of friction ridge detail.
- 1800s, Great Britain: Endorsement of the unchanging and, hence, reliable nature of fingerprints for identification.

From: *The Forensic Laboratory Handbook: Procedures and Practice*
Edited by: A. Mozayani and C. Noziglia © Humana Press Inc., Totowa, NJ

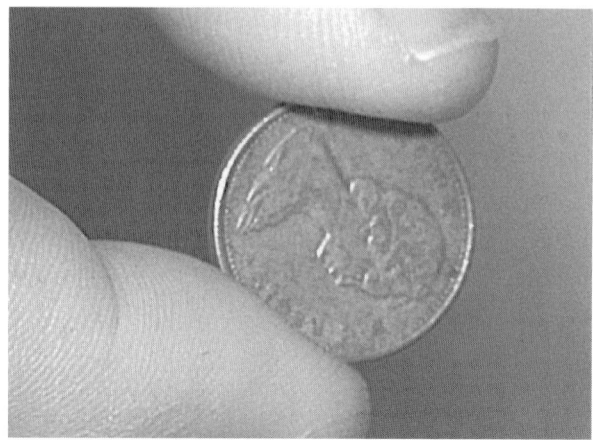

Fig. 1. Friction skin aids in grasping objects.

- 1890s, Argentina: Development of an operational fingerprint identification system for police investigations.
- 1892, Argentina: First criminal case in history to be solved by fingerprints.
- 1896, Great Britain: Development of Henry System, the method used to classify sets of fingerprints until replacement by computer databases.

2. FRICTION SKIN

The surfaces of the hands and feet on all primates are covered with a special purpose skin, adapted to the needs of primates in climbing and grasping. It is ridged like corduroy and significantly thicker than skin on any other part of the body (*see* Fig. 1). Many more sweat pores are located on friction skin than elsewhere; the secretions of which give added purchase to the fingers. In an imitation of this natural effect, we lick our finger to assist in turning the page of a book.

The tough outer layer of the skin is called the epidermis. Like a tight-fitting glove, it protects the inner layer, the dermis, which contains the nerves, sweat glands and the unique pattern of the ridge detail (*see* Fig. 2). If the epidermis is injured (and the injury does not extend to the dermis), no scarring will take place. If, however, the dermis is damaged, a permanent scar will result. This scar irreversibly disrupts the flow of the ridge detail (*see* Fig. 3). Resulting scar formations can add great weight to a conclusion of identity.

When we stay in the bathtub too long, the skin on our hands and feet absorbs water, expands, and becomes temporarily wrinkled, unlike the rest of our skin surface. The remainder of the body surface is protected from swelling by sebaceous oil glands. Oil is not an asset in applying a firm grasp

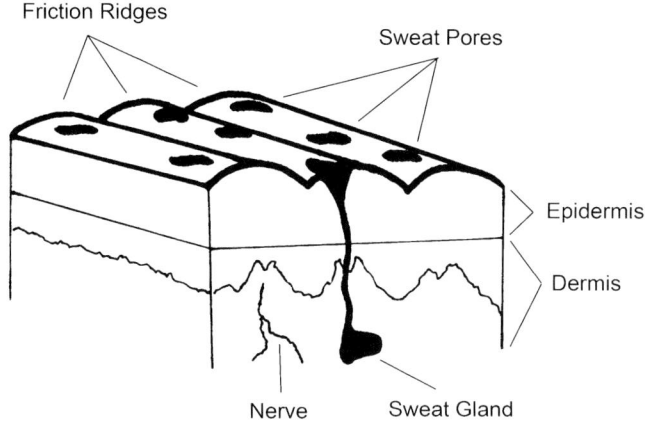

Fig. 2. Cross-section of friction skin.

Fig. 3. (A) Scarred fingerprint **(B)** Same fingerprint recorded 11 yr later.

and, consequently, there are no oil glands on the friction surfaces of the hands or feet.

Ridges generally run parallel to each other and form patterns, which are the basis of fingerprint classification. Fingerprint patterns consist of combinations of the following component parts (*see* Fig. 4):

Recurve: A recurve is any ridge that turns 180° and retraces its course, including the bend in a loop and the circular path of a whorl.

Delta: A triradius, or delta, is the point at which ridges converge from three directions. Arches do not contain deltas.

Core: The core is the central portion of the pattern and contains the point of core, all recurving ridges and the ridges that conform to them. The exact point of core is determined differently for each pattern type.

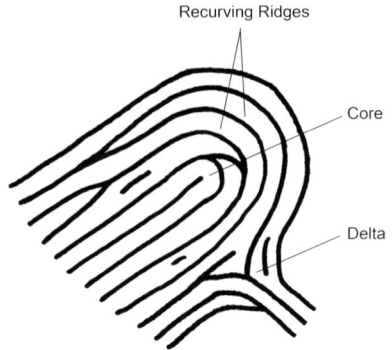

Fig. 4. Components of fingerprint.

Fingerprint patterns (*see* Fig. 5):

- *Arch*: Ridges flow one above the other in a gently arching configuration. There are no deltas or recurves.
- *Tented arch*: Arch pattern with at least one up-thrusting ridge at right angles to the ridges above it.
- *Ulnar/radial loop*: Consists of at least one free recurving ridge and one delta. These patterns are named after the ulna and radius, the bones of the forearm. In ulnar loop, recurves originate from and return to the little finger side of the hand, whereas recurves in radial loops originate from and return to the thumb side of the hand.
- *Whorl*: Consists of at least one recurving ridge and two deltas. A straight line drawn between the points of delta will cross at least one of the ridges revolving around the core.
- *Central pocket loop*: Similar to the whorl, except that none of the recurving ridges will be crossed by a straight line between the points of delta.
- *Double loop*: Consists of two looping formations and two deltas.
- *Composite*: Contains at least two of the previous described basic patterns, excluding the arch.
- *Accidental*: Contains two deltas, one in front of an up-thrusting formation and the other in front of a recurving formation.

The human body perspires for several reasons:

- Expulsion of waste products.
- Temperature regulation (cooling through evaporation).
- As a response to fear, anxiety, or anger.

The surfaces of the friction ridges (Fig. 6) on the hands and feet are covered with a perpetual film consisting of perspiration, oil (transferred to the hands by touching other parts of the body), and foreign substances acquired

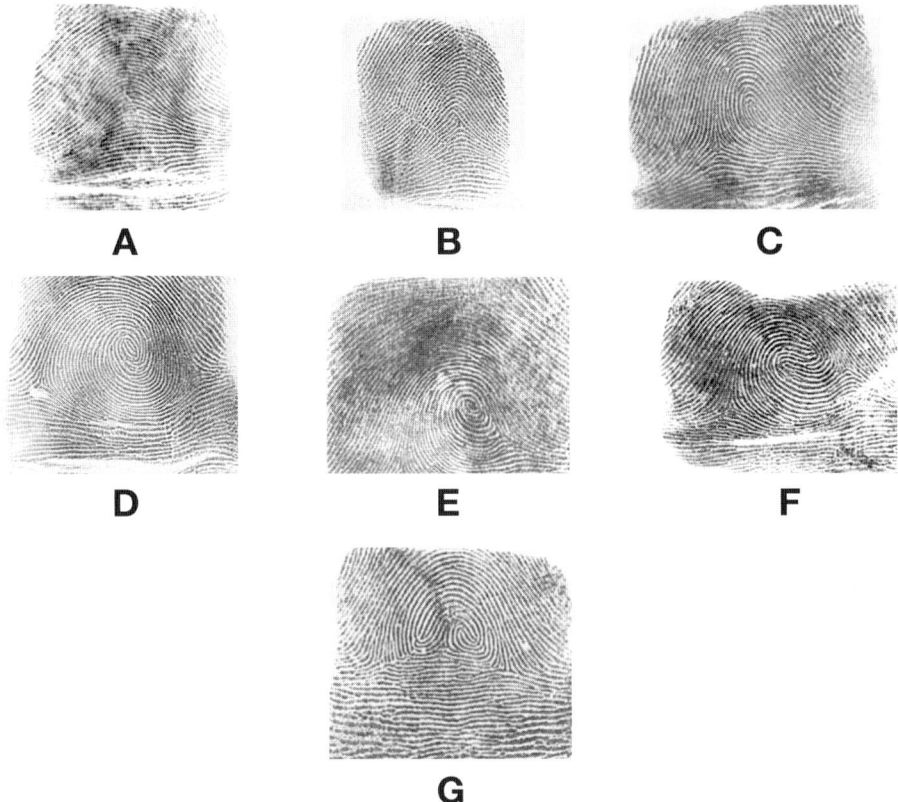

Fig. 5. **(A)** Arch, **(B)** tented arch, **(C)** loop, **(D)** whorl, **(E)** central pocked loop, **(F)** double loop, and **(G)** composite.

through contact with objects. In turn, these substances are transferred to the objects we touch, in the unique patterns on the fingers.

The main reason that fingerprints are so important in a forensic context is that our hands are sensory organs; the part of the body in almost constant physical contact with our surroundings and the part of the body that most frequently leaves our personal signature behind.

3. LOCARD'S EXCHANGE PRINCIPLE

In the late 1800s, Dr. Edmond Locard developed a theory that became the basis of modern forensic analysis. Whenever a person comes in contact with another person, an object, or a location, a cross-transfer of physical evidence occurs. In other words, the person takes away something from the contact

Fig. 6. Close look at friction skin.

and leaves something behind. What is exchanged is virtually an unlimited list of possibilities from fingerprints, hairs, saliva, and other material from the body, to shoeprints, tool marks, and chemicals. Skill, thoroughness, and tenacity play a large role in the detection of the evidence, but it is often a question of chance as to whether the transfer will be sufficient in clarity or extent to be forensically significant. It is uncommon, but not unheard of, to process amenable exhibits for fingerprints without revealing the slightest evidence of handling. Finding fragments of ridge detail with no evidential value is far more frequent.

4. IDENTIFICATION PROCESS

As previously mentioned, friction skin is arranged in patterns of generally parallel ridges that form patterns. Technicians assess fingerprint detail in three categories:

1. *Level 1 detail*: Loops, arches, and whorls, as previously described, are familiar words to anyone who has watched a crime drama or read a murder mystery. These are classed as level 1 detail and are used to group fingerprints in general categories. In and of themselves, they have no identification value. Knowing that a latent fingerprint is a loop is comparable to looking for someone in a blue suit. There are many people who have loops on their fingers; the information is useful only to eliminate those who do *not* have loops.

2. *Level 2 detail*: Friction ridges are not unbroken parallel lines. They frequently split to form two ridges or simply come to an end. These ridge characteristics or minutiae, are referred to as bifurcations and ridge endings, respectively. Their location, direction, and sequence form the basis of fingerprint identification.

3. *Level 3 detail*: The third level detail includes the shape of the characteristics and the location of sweat pores.

    Fingerprints developed in connection with crimes may exhibit one, two, or all three levels of detail. Two fingerprints under scrutiny are initially compared on the basis of first-level detail. It is obvious that if the crime scene impression is a whorl and the suspect's fingerprints are all loops, the comparison need go no further.

    Next, the level 2 details (the ridge characteristics) are compared for presence and agreement in location and direction. Finally, third-level detail is compared if present, including the shape of the characteristics and the location of pores.

4.1. Statement of Identification

    If the examination reveals the continuous agreement of ridge characteristics in sequence with no unexplainable dissimilarities, identity is established to the exclusion of any other area of friction skin.

5. FINGERPRINTS ARE UNIQUE

    The identification of fingerprints is based on two scientific axioms:

*   The friction skin on the hands and feet is formed in the fourth fetal month and does not change significantly in a person's lifetime except through injury or disease.
*   Nature does not duplicate.

    It is important to emphasize the degree and significance of this natural diversity and variation. Not only are fingerprints unique, but any given segment of ridge detail from all areas of friction skin is completely different from any other, including areas from the same host. Fingerprints are not the only part of the body that expresses our individuality. Every aspect of our being is a personal expression of uniqueness that distinguishes us from all other members of our species, living or dead. The configuration of nonfriction skin is also unique, as are the flexion creases of the lips, the arrangement and shape of teeth and ears, and the internal structure of cancellous (soft) bone.

    Identical twins, originating from one fertilized egg, are arguably the most alike of any beings on earth. They share the same DNA profile because they began existence as one entity, yet their fingerprints are as distinctive as any two unrelated persons, differing in two or, potentially, three levels of detail. The thumbprints of identical twins are depicted in Fig. 7. Although a striking resemblance in general pattern trend can be seen in the left thumbs (A and C), the right thumbs are not even the same pattern type (level one detail). When the level-2 detail is compared, no agreement can be found between the left thumbs,

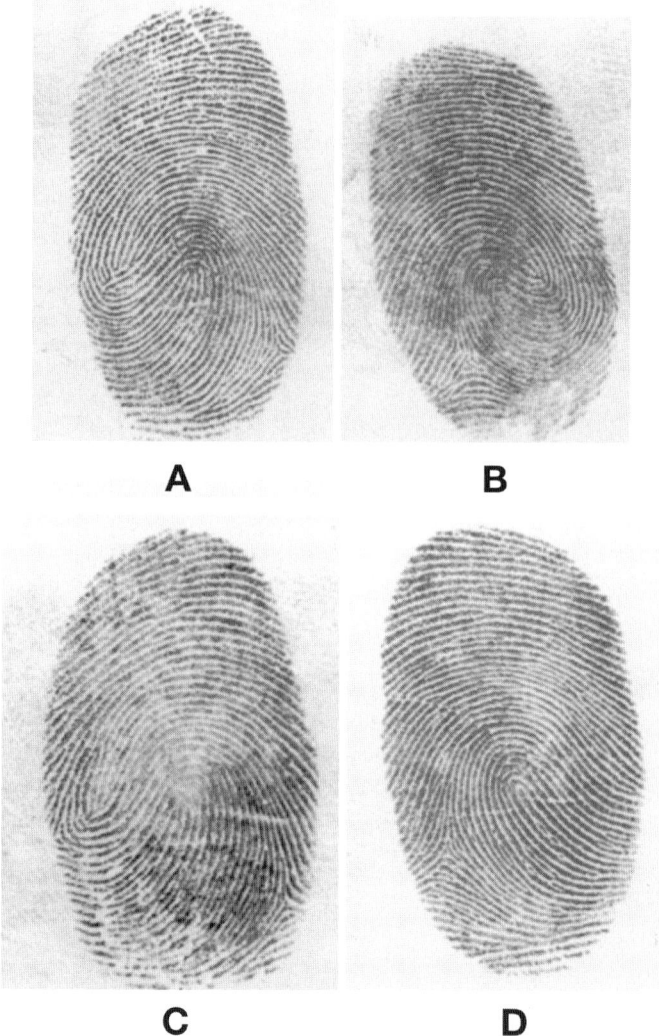

Fig. 7. Thumbprints of identical twins. (**A** and **C**) Left thumb (**B** and **D**) Right thumb

although they are both twinned loops. The location and sequence of the ridge characteristics is completely different.

The more closely we can examine an item and its detail, the more conclusive and exclusionary we can be in our findings. Consider the following scenario:

While walking to meet someone, we spot an object on the horizon, perhaps at a distance of a mile or more. We can barely discern movement and, hence, come to the conclusion that it is a living thing. As we draw closer, we are able to make the judgment that it is a person, as opposed to a dog or a horse. When we are closer still, details of the size and clothing reveal relative height, weight, gender, and, perhaps, age. We are still not close enough to scan facial features for recognition, but we may have decided that the figure is human, of average height, stocky, and definitely not a child. As we reduce the distance further, we see that the person is male. At a certain distance, which varies with the acuity of our individual eyesight, we recognize the person we seek. To take the analogy one forensic step further, if we were able to examine the subject's ridge detail, in all three levels, their teeth, ears, bone structure, and innumerable other physiological features, we would find them all narrowing down to only one possible identification. It is significant to note that far less information is required to exclude someone than is needed for positive identification. We can tell at a relatively great distance if the person is a child or the wrong body shape for the person we are meeting.

There is another aspect to the identification process that should not be overlooked. Fingerprint technicians have been visually trained through years of intense scrutiny to recognize certain spatial relationships. X-ray technicians and physicians possess a similar ability applied to radiographs. This ability illustrates the difference between seeing and evaluating what is seen. Consider a page of typed garble, random characters without spacing or order. Imagine somewhere in the central part, that an English word, such as "fingerprint," appears. Our eyes have been trained to recognize the meaning of these of letters when they appear in this order and will be drawn to them. Next, imagine that instead of the word fingerprint, the series of letters spells out your name. Even within a body of coherent information in our own language, our eyes will be riveted to this most familiar sequence of letters.

If an Indian from the Amazon rainforest were standing beside a city dweller at a busy intersection, they would "see" the same things in that the image on their respective retinas would be composed of the same information. However, it is likely that the sense they would make of this visual data would be very different. Similarly, if the same two people were side by side in the Matto Grosso, they would have radically different evaluations of the view.

5.1. ACE-V

The identification process is composed of three separate stages, referred to as ACE-V, which stands for Analysis Comparison, Evaluation, completed by Verification.

Analysis: Trained fingerprint technicians scan exhibits and must first decide if what they are looking at is friction ridge detail. Once that determination has been made, the ridge detail located within the impression is located and assessed.

Comparison: The details present in the crime scene impression are compared to details in the known (suspect) fingerprint.

Evaluation: Based on the quantity, quality, and clarity of detail in the two impressions, a conclusion of either identity or nonidentity is reached.

Verification: A colleague of equal or greater qualifications and experience must verify conclusions of identity.

There are three possible conclusions a fingerprint technician may reach:

- *Positive certainty*: Based on the detail present, no other reasonable conclusion can be reached other than that the two impressions originated from a common source.
- *Negative certainty*: Based on the detail present, no other reasonable conclusion can be reached other than that the two impressions did not originate from a common source.
- *Inconclusive*: There existed insufficient clear detail on which to basis an opinion of either identity or elimination.

6. FINGERPRINT DETECTION

The vast majority of fingerprints are latent, or hidden, but the word "latent" has come to be applied to all fingerprints related to police investigations. All methods for revealing latent fingerprints target one or more ingredients of the residue commonly found on the fingers, including water, salt, lipids, B vitamins, urea, uric acid, sebaceous oil, and amino acids. In addition to the natural compounds produced and expelled through our pores, we acquire soil, dyes, pigments, and other material from the objects we touch. This list is virtually unlimited and may help or hinder the detection of fingerprints. Some detection methods target the presence of oil in fingerprints. Consider the possible results if a culprit had just eaten fried chicken and not washed his hands. Drug traffickers occasionally leave clear recordings behind in hashish oil, whereas the fingerprints of counterfeiters have been discovered in printer's ink.

The classic and most familiar method from books and television for revealing fingerprints is dusting powder (*see* Fig. 8), which adheres readily to anything sticky, such as oils and water. This method is still used extensively on nonporous exhibits like glass, metal, and painted surfaces, but it does not always detect older fingerprints because the ingredients on which it relies do not stay sticky indefinitely.

There has been an explosion of technological advancement in fingerprint detection in the last 30 yr based on other residue properties resulting in a list of techniques too numerous to describe here in detail. Today, more fingerprints are being found on more varied surfaces. Fingerprints are routinely found on many surfaces including plastics, metal, glass, paper, and the sticky side of tape.

Fig. 8. "Powder and Brush." Courtesy of Lynn Peavey Company.

One exciting development over the past half century has been the detection of fingerprints on murder victims. Human skin is not an ideal surface for fingerprint as it is an active site of chemical activity both in life and after death. Fingerprints do not last long on such a surface, but for a short window of opportunity in specific cases, they can be recovered. Despite the adverse conditions, there are at least eight documented cases worldwide in which the fingerprint of a murderer has been detected on the skin of his victim (*see* Fig. 9). It is obvious that a court will assign enormous weight to such a fingerprint. It is rare indeed that there be innocent explanations as to how such an impression came to be discovered on a body.

A forensic identification specialist must first decide what method or methods to apply based on the nature and condition of the exhibit. Some techniques can be used on any exhibit, whereas others are designed for use on either porous or nonporous surfaces. Several techniques can be used on the same exhibit, provided they are applied in the right order. This approach increases the chance of detecting any fingerprints that are present.

Some of the ingredients routinely found in finger residue are fluorescent, which means that they emit a specific color of light when they are examined with another specific color of light, produced by laser or forensic light source. A forensic light source consists of a lamp producing white light, combined with a series of filters, each emitting a very specific range of wavelengths. Each filter selection can excite fluorescence in diffrent types of evidence. Special filters are used to view and record these fluorescent fingerprints, which are not visible

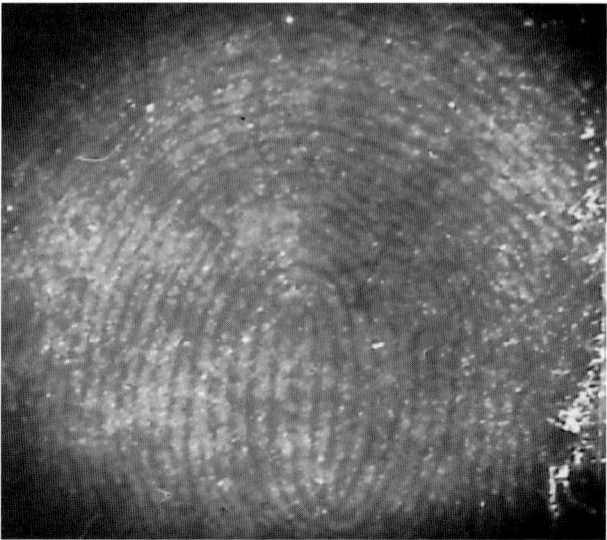

Fig. 9. Fingerprint revealed on skin by argon laser.

without the correct light sources and filters. Several types of lasers and custom forensic light sources are used to detect fingerprints in this way. Figure 10 depicts the first such laser.

There are several advantages to this initial fluorescence examination (*see* Fig. 11).

- The exhibit is not harmed.
- Both porous and nonporous items can be examined.
- Fingerprints not revealed by this method are not altered or degraded.
- All other methods can still be used successfully.
- Items can be examined without leaving any sign that they have been examined (crucial in some sensitive investigations).
- It can be used successfully on exhibits for which chemical techniques are not practical.

Police discovered by accident in the 1970s that the fumes of cyanoacrylate (the active ingredient in superglue) react with ingredients commonly found in latent fingerprints and make them visible. Since that time, the reaction has been researched and optimized, resulting in the application of superglue as a major detection technique used worldwide for nonporous exhibits.

There are certain conditions under which superglue fuming alone may not be fully effective at revealing fingerprints that are present.

- The fingerprints are old.
- They contain very little of the target ingredient(s).
- The background color or tone of the exhibit obstructs the fingerprint.

Fig. 10. First forensic laser (1977), Ontario Provincial Police GHQ.

For all of these reasons, superglue fuming is routinely followed by the application of a fluorescent dye, which is absorbed by the glue-developed fingerprint. When the surplus dye is removed by rinsing, a laser or forensic light source is used to reveal the fluorescing dye in the fingerprint. This follow-up process reveals many more fingerprints than were evident after glue alone.

Other chemical methods target the amino acids commonly found in fingerprints. The reaction either stains the fingerprint a visible color or makes it fluorescent. Ninhydrin has been the major detection method for paper exhibits for over a quarter century. A pale yellow solution, ninhydrin reacts with the amino acids routinely present in fingerprints. After the treated exhibits are exposed to heat and humidity, magenta-colored fingerprints will appear (*see* Fig. 12).

More recent research has resulted in the development of new reagents based on fluorescence, which is much more sensitive as a detection approach than simple staining. Fingerprints usually contain less than 1 ng (one billionth of a gram) of matter. These include 1,8-diazafluoren-9-one (DFO) and 1,2-indanedione. This means a staining technique may react with a faint fingerprint, but the resulting coloration is not strong enough to be visible.

If a fingerprint is developed with gray powder on a white surface, it will have a fixed dynamic range, that is, the difference between the lightest and the darkest tone in the subject. Adding more light will not change this dynamic

Fig. 11. Fingerprint revealed by argon laser.

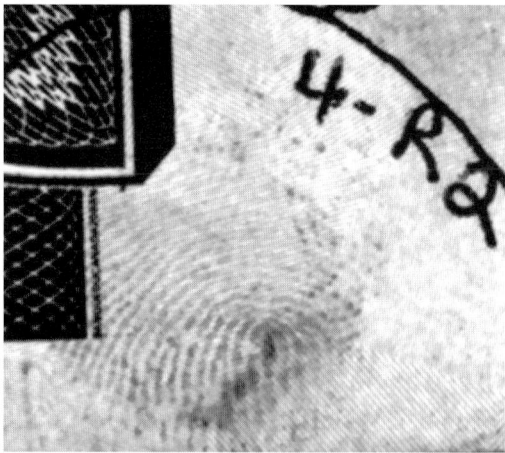

Fig. 12. Fingerprint revealed by ninhydrin.

range. If it is not wide enough, the fingerprint may not be seen. Fluorescence techniques are entirely different. When a fingerprint ingredient fluoresces, it absorbs light and re-emits light of a different wavelength; it becomes a light source. Imagine trying to see an object on the shore of an island, by flashlight, across water, in the dark of night. Compare that situation to searching for the beam of the flashlight itself directed at you. With no competition from the surrounding darkness, the light can be seen from great distances.

Another detection technique of great sensitivity is vacuum metal deposition. Thin layers of gold and zinc are evaporated onto crime exhibits in a vacuum chamber. This process reveals fingerprints on a wide variety of surfaces and has been particularly effective on older impressions.

6.1. AFIS

There are three possible stages of latent fingerprint comparison. First, they are compared to (and potentially eliminated as) the fingerprints of those who may have legitimately touched the items in question. Next, they are compared with known suspects in the occurrence, if there are any. The last stage is for those instances where no suspects are known.

Police services across North America, at all levels, maintain computer databases of fingerprints taken of all persons who have committed certain specified offenses. This technology is referred to as AFIS, the Automated Fingerprint Identification System. The fingerprints are digitized and computer coded for entry into the database. A highly trained AFIS technician plots the location and direction of each ridge characteristic appearing in the impression. The result is an array of circles with tails—the circles indicating the position of the ridge characteristic and the tail showing its direction. This is a language that the computer can understand. Crime scene impressions are coded for search in the same way. Figure 13 provides an example of AFIS coding.

Using the power of sophisticated software, the computer has the ability to compare a crime scene impression against many thousands of fingerprints in the database in a matter of seconds. On the basis of the information entered, the computer will eliminate all of the prints in the database that *cannot* be the same. The technician is left with a short list of possibilities that the computer could not eliminate. The technician makes the final comparisons and determination of identity or nonidentity. Unidentified crime scene impressions form another part of the database, waiting for comparison and possible identification to fingerprints from future crimes. AFIS is a pivotal forensic tool, responsible each year for the resolution of thousands of crimes for which there existed no known suspects.

6.2. Digital Enhancement

When everything has been done with chemical techniques and conventional photography to reveal and optimize evidence like fingerprints, the final result may still fall short of being useful. Digital image enhancement is another example of computer power that can extend the forensic reach of a

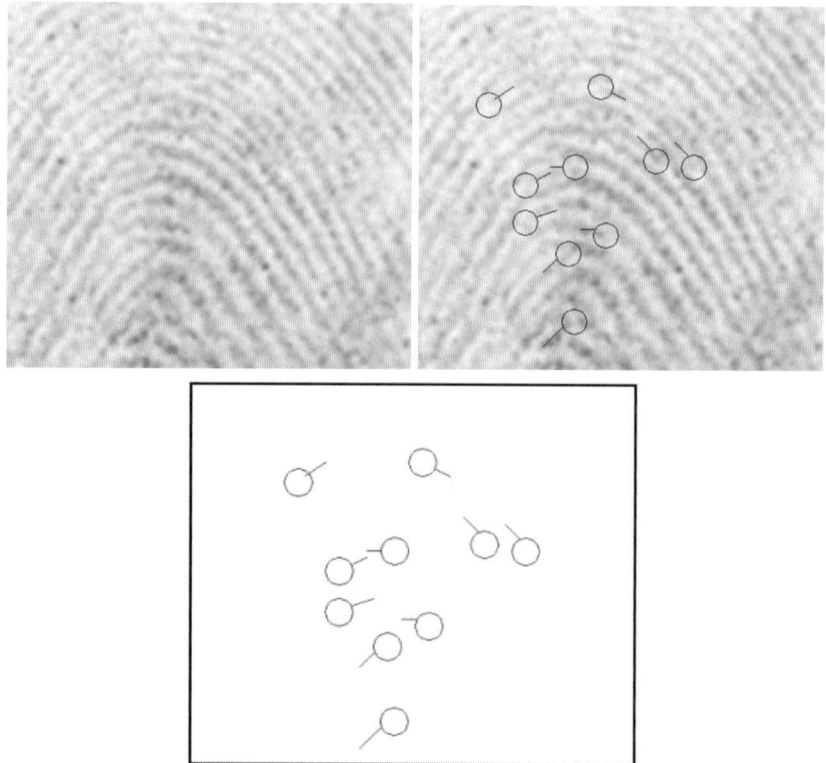

Fig. 13. AFIS coding applied to fingerprint minutiae.

technician beyond what is possible with analog techniques. In other words, digital techniques have the potential to reveal more evidence than was possible with the conventional methods. In order to understand this extended reach, one must have a grasp of the fundamental differences between analog and digital.

Analog imaging, which includes conventional photography, consists of a *continuous modulation of tones,* from black to white, and a representation of color hues based on separate layers of the film emulsion. Digital imaging is based on a *series of discrete steps, each separate and independent from the others.*

The two attributes of digital imaging responsible for this extended reach are control and sensitivity. A digital image is composed of independent blocks of information called picture elements, or *pixels*. The pixels contain the tonal and color values for that small piece of the image (*see* Fig. 14). They also contain their "address." The pixels are arranged in rows and columns, similar to the children's game Battleship. This is why a file on the hard drive (which is

Picture Element (Pixel)

Fig. 14. Pixel (picture element).

composed entirely of combinations of numbers) can be displayed on the screen and will be seen as the same image that was originally captured.

We are accustomed to seeing our e-mail inbox displayed on our computer screen, usually in chronological order. Imagine that you wish to view a specific message from a friend that was sent at some time in the past. Also imagine that your inbox contains several hundred messages. Going through the messages one by one can be a time-consuming task. With a single touch, the messages can be arranged alphabetically, allowing you to find your friend's message quickly and easily. This is the power of control over each building block of the image that is inherent to operations in the digital domain.

The second great digital asset is sensitivity. The human eye is capable of discriminating between 30 and 32 shades of gray between black and white when, in reality, there are an infinite number of light intensity gradations. We do not possess great tonal sensitivity, although our ability to discern subtle color change is far better. Photography is even less sensitive at approx 16 values. An 8-bit digital gray scale image has the potential to contain 256 separate gray values, each of which is recognized by the computer as distinct from the others. The significance of this fact is enormous. Important evidence, hidden from the eye in an area of apparent uniform gray, can be easily made visible with computer techniques.

As previously mentioned, digital images are numbers in great quantity and complex arrangements. The following is a simple arithmetical operation:

$$\begin{array}{r} 7+2 \\ -2 \\ \hline 7 \end{array}$$

A forensic image is typically composed of two elements: signal and noise. The signal is the desirable part (the fingerprint), whereas the noise is whatever interferes with or obscures it. Because a digital image is composed exclusively of numbers, one image can be subtracted from another, frequently with an increase in clear detail. Substitute the simple subtraction shown above with the following:

$$SIGNAL + NOISE$$
$$-NOISE$$
$$\overline{SIGNAL}$$

If one can obtain an image of just the interference in the image, in exact register to the first image, it can be subtracted and, hence, eliminated from the first (Fig. 15).

There are many other computer techniques that can be used to exploit the power of digital imaging.

7. ABSENCE OF FINGERPRINTS

"Since my client's fingerprints do not appear on the gun, doesn't that mean he didn't touch it and, consequently, that he didn't commit the murder?" This question, with variations, is among the most commonly asked of finger-print specialists. To answer it accurately and truthfully requires a deep knowledge of fingerprints and how and when we leave them behind. If this premise were true, the following would have to be true:

- Everyone always leaves fingerprints on everything they touch.
- The fingerprints always contain enough detail to be identifiable.
- The fingerprint detail always consists of enough of the ingredients targeted by the methods used to find them.
- When we touch things, the fingers are never obstructed or obscured by anything, including dirt, grease, water, and gloves.
- The surfaces on which we leave fingerprints are always capable of receiving fingerprints and contain or include no chemicals that would react with and destroy them.
- The surfaces on which we leave fingerprints are never subjected to wiping, abrasion, cleaning, intense light, intense humidity, or anything harmful to the fingerprints *after* we have left them.

Perhaps if all of these statements were true, it might be possible to form an opinion that a subject had not touched an item, but it is not possible to know the full history of a fingerprint before it came to our attention.

8. WHY DOES IT STILL WORK?

Fingerprint identification has been a powerful forensic tool for over a century. Countless investigations during that time have been resolved through

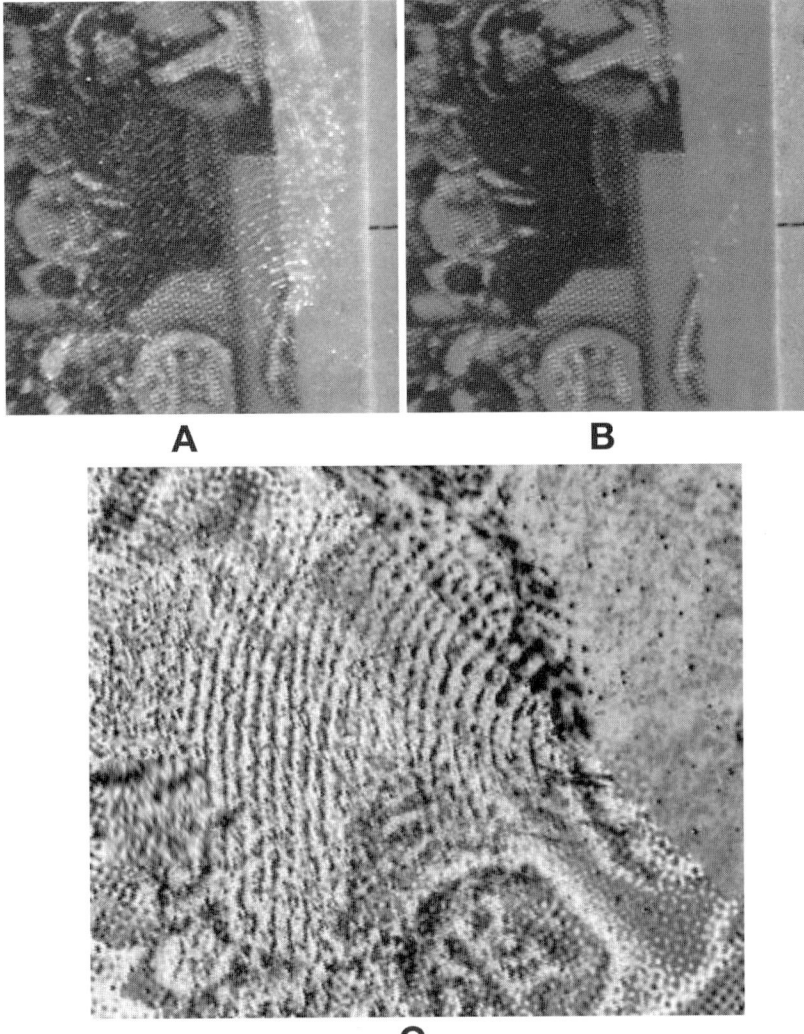

Fig. 15. Subtraction Example. **(A)** Original fingerprint image, **(B)** image with fingerprint erased, and **(C)** digitally subtracted image, background suppressed.

linking criminals to their crimes by their fingers and what they touch. Solving crime with the telltale fingerprint has been dramatized in books, on television, and in movies. How then can it still be effective when everybody knows about it?

Sir Walter Scott once wrote, "Oh what a tangled web we weave, when first we practice to deceive." When a person commits a crime, they must establish a fictitious alibi. It is an enormous task to suppress or eliminate all of the inter-related evidence of what *really* happened in a slice of time, while creating false evidence of what did *not* happen. There are so many types of evidence that may contribute to an investigation, it is difficult for a criminal, even a mastermind, to eliminate or alter all of them successfully. Consider just some of the evidence covered in this book that a criminal must be aware of (and may well overlook) in attempting to conceal a crime:

- Shoeprints.
- DNA.
- Eyewitness.
- Ballistics.
- Toolmarks.
- Surveillance cameras.
- Hair/fiber transfer.
- Chemical transfer.
- Tiremarks.

We touch things out of necessity in our daily lives, as the hands are instruments of sensory perception. They are essential in maintaining our connection with the physical world. It would be almost impossible to list everything we have touched in any hour of a routine day. Most crimes are not carefully planned, but are committed on impulse by those who equally do not remember where their hands have been.

9. CONTINUITY AND ETHICS

An everyday object like a soft drink can takes on a special importance the instant it is designated as an exhibit during a criminal investigation. From that moment until presentation in court, its life history, including who possesses it and what is done to it, must be recorded in an unbroken chain. This chain of custody assures the court that nothing could have altered the exhibit or any evidence it might bear, except the documented procedures of those who seek that evidence. It guarantees the integrity of this evidence.

It may well be necessary for one exhibit, such as a firearm, to be examined for fingerprints, fibers and blood, as well as ballistics. Time and date are recorded and signed every time the exhibit changes hands. A fingerprint technician protects the integrity and the usefulness of the fingerprint evidence he finds by including his initials, the date, and a scale in his photographs. This practice allows him to make comparisons with known fingerprints at the correct size, as well as identify his work and the fingerprint at a later date in court.

Just as Locard's Exchange Principle has provided law enforcement with so much critical evidence over the last century, it can also work against the investigation unless analysts take special care in the handling and storage of evidence. Wearing gloves at all times prevents the transfer of unwanted fingerprints which may cloud the waters and lead investigators away from the true course of events. It is ironic that the same human reflex of handling and touching things that has impelled criminals to leave evidence also affects those who seek it. Complacency is a threat to sound laboratory procedure and to evidence which may be contaminated or destroyed through a momentary lapse.

Every person who follows a career in forensic science is well aware of the phrase "fruit of the poisoned vine," meaning that if the vine is poisonous, one would do well to avoid eating the fruit. In law, the phrase suggests that if one aspect of evidence is found to be suspect, it will bring all of the related evidence into disrepute. The poisoned vine argument is one of the most effective rebuttal strategies in the hands of the defense and explains why cross-examination tactics often avoid the direct implication of physical evidence and focus instead on one or more of the following questions:

- Is the procedure both reliable and recognized by the forensic community?
- Does the witness have the training and experience to support his/her conclusions?
- Is the witness of good character without previous blemish in his/her forensic career?
- Has he/she ever made a mistake?
- What was not done?
- What was done incompletely?
- What was done carelessly?
- Was there a lapse in the continuity of the evidence at some point in its history as an exhibit when its condition or anything that may have happened to it cannot be accounted for?

All of these questions must be addressed, with regard to each piece of evidence and opinion tendered, to avoid presenting "bad" evidence to the court and tainting the prosecution case. The poison vine argument is also a safeguard built into the system that provides a measure of protection for an accused person against implication by faulty or improper evidence. The conclusions tendered in court can be pivotal in ending a defendant's liberty or even ending his life.

10. EVIDENCE

Direct evidence is the result of what a witness said, observed, or heard. An example of direct evidence presented in a witness's testimony would be, "I saw the defendant point the gun and shoot the victim." Circumstantial evidence is fact or expert opinion that can be used to infer another fact. All physical evidence, including fingerprints, falls into this category. Movie versions of defense attorneys will cavalierly dismiss evidence as being "purely circumstantial," as though the words were synonymous with weak or meaningless. On the contrary, circumstantial evidence can be the most convincing persuader to a court that an alleged event actually happened. It is a vital link in a chain of evidence that can lead to an inescapable conclusion of guilt or innocence. Physical evidence, properly prepared and presented, offers another advantage: the objectivity of a scientific finding. There is no emotion or bias in the statement of conclusion. The physical evidence found at crime scenes routinely vindicates persons under investigation as suspects.

It is absolutely crucial, however, that the inference drawn from a piece of physical evidence goes no further than what the evidence supports, for the court as well as the proponent of the said evidence. Imagine a scenario in which a young woman appears at a police station, distraught and disheveled, stating that she had been given a ride while hitchhiking and that the driver had assaulted her. Acting on her statement, the police seize and examine the suspect's car. A fingerprint, identified as the victim's, is located on the dashboard. It is perhaps most useful in this scenario to review what has *not* been proven:

- That a crime was committed.
- That the suspect committed the alleged crime.

It can be stated purely on the strength of the fingerprint evidence that at some point in history, under undetermined circumstances, the alleged victim touched the dashboard of the suspect's car. Depending on the location and direction of the fingerprint, it may not even be possible to place the victim *inside* the car. Like all circumstantial evidence, this fingerprint identification must be one fact in a chain of facts which all point in a specific direction. Many investigations ending with insufficient evidence have included fingerprint evidence that could be explained by innocent or legitimate access.

There are occasions, however, in which an innocent explanation of a fingerprint is not easy. In the 1980s, a man in the United States was accused of connection with war crimes during the Second World War. He denied the charges and the State Department initiated an investigation which led them to archival documents in Germany. Permission was granted for the forensic examination of these documents on the condition that they not be defaced or destroyed. All chemical techniques were therefore ruled out, but laser scrutiny is nondestructive because nothing touches the object but light. A single fingerprint was revealed by laser on one of these documents; an impression ultimately identified as belonging to the man under investigation. The recipient of the document was a high level Nazi official. Perhaps the most significant fact about this case is that the document was dated 1942 and had been in storage since that time, placing the age of the fingerprint at more than 40 yr.

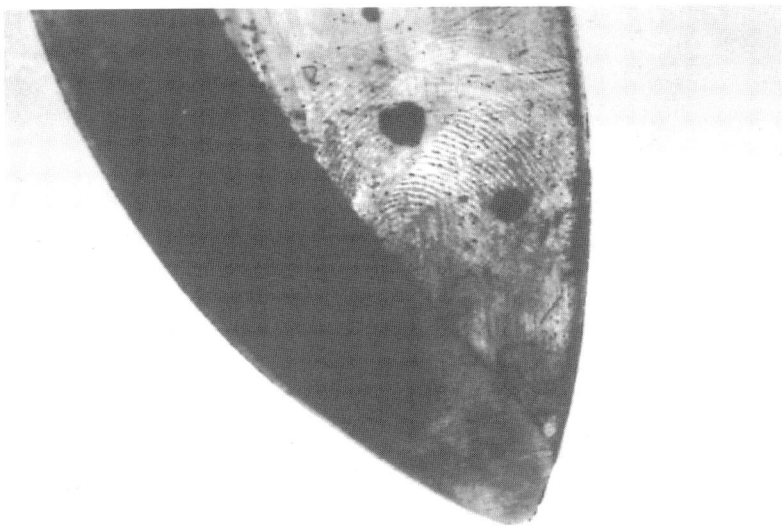

Fig. 16. Fingerprint on knife blade.

10.1. Court Challenges to Fingerprint Evidence

In 1993, a civil case initiated a turning point for fingerprint identification—*Daubert v. Merrell Dow Pharmaceuticals*. The name "Daubert Hearing" has come to be synonymous with challenges to fingerprint evidence, although it really applies to the admissibility of any scientific evidence.

The Daubert opinion states that the trial judge must screen scientific evidence to ensure its relevance and reliability. Factors the courts consider include:

- Testing and validation.
- Peer review.
- Rate of error.
- General acceptance.

At the midway point of 2004, there were 40 legal challenges to finger-print evidence, with none succeeding. The ruling has placed a greater (and proper) obligation on the proponent of fingerprint evidence to satisfy the courts that scientific process has been followed. An error in fingerprint identification was made in the investigation of the March 11, 2004 terrorist bombing in Madrid. Several experts misidentified a fingerprint developed on evidence from the bombing.

It is important to distinguish error in the science from human error committed by practitioners. Any science, regardless of its reliability, can be adversely affected by those who lack sufficient training or who deviate from accepted practice. The history of fingerprint identification over the past century has included many millions of identifications with only a handful of errors. Intensified scrutiny from the courts will require that greater attention be paid to training, the adherence to ACE-V, and the confirmation of findings.

A Canadian man, who was under investigation for the murder of his girlfriend in 1988, sensed that the investigation was drawing close to him. He was observed throwing items into Lake Ontario after dark. Police divers later recovered a number of knives, one of which yielded a single fingerprint (*see* Fig. 16). It proved to be made by the suspect who was ultimately convicted of the murder.

11. CONCLUSION

Fingerprints display a complex combination of fragility and persistence. There is no other more profound reminder of man's individuality and uniqueness than the intricate patterns found on his fingers that are left behind as signatures on things he touches. There is also no more powerful tool in the forensic arsenal to link a criminal with his crimes.

GLOSSARY

ACE-V:	Acronym for analysis, Comparison, Evaluation, and Verification; the accepted procedure for fingerprint identification.
AFIS:	Acronym for Automated Fingerprint Identification System, the use of powerful computer technology to search latent impressions against a database of offender fingerprints, and produce a shortlist of possible matches.
Chain of custody:	The continuous, unbroken possession of an object, from the time it becomes an exhibit until presentation in court, which ensures the integrity of the evidence found thereon.
Circumstantial Evidence:	Testimony given that infers another fact; includes all physical evidence, including fingerprint identification.
Cyanoacrylate:	The active ingredient in superglue, found to react with and make visible, some of the compounds routinely found in fingerprint residue.
Dermis:	The layer of skin just beneath the epidermis, which contains the sweat ducts, nerve endings and, in friction skin, the unique pattern of ridge characteristics.
Direct Evidence:	Testimony given of what was seen or heard, alleging a fact; requires no special skill or training, only the requirement to tell the truth.

Epidermis:	The tough outer layer of skin.
Expert Evidence:	The permission given to a witness by the court to give opinions in evidence, in recognition of specialized, pertinent training, experience and expertise in a specific discipline, such as fingerprint identification.
Fingerprint residue:	The material found on friction skin and left behind as fingerprints; composed of sebaceous oil, water, organic and inorganic salts, amino acids, lipids, urea and foreign substances touched by the fingers.
Fluorescence:	The property of a compound to absorb light of one wavelength and emit light of a different, longer wavelength: the basis of many fingerprint detection techniques.
Friction skin:	The ridged skin found on the inner surfaces of the hands and feet of all primates, so named for its assistance in grasping and holding.
Latent:	Hidden, unseen; used to refer generally to evidence fingerprints.
Ridge Characteristics:	Also called minutia, the locations in friction skin where ridges either come to an end or split to form two ridges.

SUGGESTED READING

Ashbaugh DR. Quantitative–Qualitative Friction Ridge Analysis, An Introduction to Basic and Advanced Ridgeology. Boca Raton, FL: CRC Press.

Lee HC, Harris HA. Physical Evidence in Forensic Science. Tuscon, AZ: Lawyers & Judges Publishing Co, pp. 131–145.

Siegel JA, Saukko PJ, Knupfer GC, eds. Encyclopedia of Forensic Sciences. San Diego, CA: Academic Press, pp. 854–899.

Chapter 7

Firearms and Tool Marks

Edward E. Hueske, MA

1. INTRODUCTION

The field of firearms identification is typically associated with tool mark identification in the context of two related but different entities. Much of firearms identification entails a specific area of tool mark identification. By definition, a tool mark results from the contact of one surface with another, the harder of which is the "tool." Thus, in the case of a firearm and a bullet, the firearm (e.g., the interior of the barrel) is the tool that produces tool marks on the surface of the bullet as it moves through the barrel upon discharge of the firearm. Likewise, the examination of firing pin impressions, magazine marks, extractor marks, ejector marks, breech face marks, and chamber marks on fired cartridge cases all constitute tool mark examinations.

The fact that firearms identification also involves examinations other than tool marks accounts for the distinction between the two disciplines. The analysis of gunpowder patterns on clothing, the determination of cartridge case ejection patterns, and the measurement of trigger pull or establishing bullet trajectory are examples of other examinations. Likewise, weapons function testing, shot pellet pattern testing, and serial number restoration are additional nontool mark comparison aspects of firearms identification.

Firearms identification is often referred to as "forensic ballistics" or just "ballistics." This is actually a misnomer because ballistics is limited to the study of projectile behavior. Ballistics, in the true sense, includes three different aspects: interior ballistics (bullet behavior within the confines of the barrel), exterior ballistics (bullet behavior upon exiting the barrel), and terminal ballistics

From: *The Forensic Laboratory Handbook: Procedures and Practice*
Edited by: A. Mozayani and C. Noziglia © Humana Press Inc., Totowa, NJ

(bullet behavior on impacting a target). Wound ballistics is a specialized area of terminal ballistics relating to the behavior of bullets striking human or animal targets.

Tool mark examination, on the other hand, is limited to the determination of whether or not a tool mark was made by a particular tool. Tools commonly examined and compared to questioned (evidence) tool marks include pliers, saws, screw drivers, pry bars, hammers, chisels, in addition to firearms and ammunition components.

Tool marks are of two different types: impressed and striated. Impressed tool marks result when a tool leaves an impression on another surface. An example would be the result of a blow from a hammer on soft wood. Striated tool marks are the result of a combination of force and motion. The example of a gun barrel producing a tool mark on a bullet illustrates the production of striated tool marks. A cut in metal with a pair of shears is another example. The striations that are produced are often visible only under magnification (i.e., with a microscope).

Tool identification is based on the fact that a particular tool will leave behind random/unique marks that only it could have made. In order to be able to properly evaluate firearm/tool mark evidence, an examiner must have extensive training and knowledge about manufacturing techniques of firearms and tools. This is required so that the examiner can distinguish between what are random/unique marks or "individual characteristics" and what are merely "class characteristics" or "subclass characteristics."

Class characteristics are those characteristics exhibited by an entire group or class of tools. An example would be the width of the blade of a particular brand of screwdriver or the cross-sectional diameter of a gun barrel (caliber) of a certain brand and model firearm. Subclass characteristics are produced incidental to manufacture and can change over time. Thus, only certain members (a subset) of a class or group will exhibit them, such as tools made using a mold, or dye having some defect that would carry over to the tool. If the dye/mold were to wear away and disappear or be replaced, the subclass characteristic would not appear on subsequently manufactured tools.

Individual characteristics are unique to a particular tool (to the exclusion of all similar tools). They are accidental or random characteristics that provide a basis for individualization. Individual characteristics may be produced in manufacture or through use (wear).

The actual comparison and ultimate identification of individual characteristics is a combination of quantitative and qualitative evaluations of the present surface contours. Identification is the result of the examiner determining that "sufficient agreement" exists in the surface contours of a test tool mark

Fig. 1. Revolver.

and an evidence tool mark. After decades of court acceptance, challenges to the scientific validity of tool mark examination have been made. The basis for the challenges is the lack of clearly articulated criteria for identification (i.e., a specific number/quality of marks). Various studies have been undertaken in an effort to resolve this apparent shortcoming. Further discussion of criteria for identification appears in a following section.

2. *Types of Firearms*

The broadest category of firearms includes two types: handguns and long guns. Handguns are designed to be fired while held in the hand, whereas long guns are designed to be fired from the shoulder. Handguns include revolvers and pistols, examples of which appear in Figs. 1 and 2.

2.1. Handguns

Pistols are either semiautomatic (autoloading) or fully automatic (machine pistol); the difference is that a semiautomatic requires that the trigger be pulled for each shot, whereas a fully automatic pistol continues to fire until all its ammunition is expended following an initial pull of the trigger. Pistols use magazines, sometimes erroneously referred to as "clips," to feed cartridges into their actions. Revolvers rely on a rotating cylinder to hold cartridges and place them into a firing position. Revolvers are classed as either single action or double action. Single action means that the hammer must be manually cocked in order to fire the weapon. Double action means the hammer will be

Fig. 2. Pistol.

cocked as the trigger is pulled and the cylinder is simultaneously rotating. Pistol actions function by stripping a cartridge from the magazine, seating it in the chamber, firing the cartridge, extracting the fired cartridge case, and ejecting it from the weapon. Each of these events potentially leaves identifiable tool marks on the cartridge case.

2.2. Long Guns

Long guns include rifles, shotguns, machine guns, and submachine guns. Rifles and shotguns can have a variety of actions including bolt action, lever action, and semiautomatic. Submachine guns and machine guns are capable of fully automatic fire. The difference between machine guns and submachine guns is that machine guns fire rifle cartridges and submachine guns fire pistol cartridges. A typical rifle and shotgun are shown in Figs. 3 and 4.

Handguns and long guns, with the exception of most shotguns, have spiral grooves cut or formed into the interior surface of the barrel. These grooves are designed to impart a spin on the bullet as it moves down the barrel on discharge of the weapon. This spin stabilizes the bullet in flight to improve accuracy and increase the effective range. The areas between the barrel grooves are known as "lands." There are an equal number of lands and grooves in a gun barrel. The number of lands and grooves typically ranges from 2 to 16. The lands and grooves in a gun barrel are illustrated in Fig. 5. The interior of a gun barrel is best described as a helix. Various methods of creating the barrel grooves (rifling) are used. Traditional methods involve cutting using hooks, carbide buttons, or broaches, whereas more recent methods rely on hammer forging or electrochemical etching.

Fig. 3. Rifle.

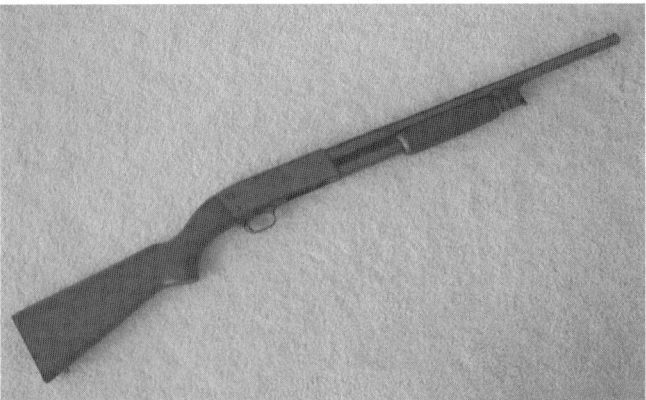

Fig. 4. Shotgun.

The direction of twist of the lands and grooves may be either clockwise or counter-clockwise. The degree of twist is the rate at which the rifling creates bullet spin per unit length. Common rates of twist for small arms would be 1 in 12 or 1 in 14. This means the bullet makes one revolution in 12 in. or one revolution in 14 in. (even though the barrel may not actually be that long). The number and widths of lands and grooves, the direction of twist, and the degree of twist are among the class characteristics of a given make and model of weapon.

The cross-sectional dimension from land to land is the caliber of a weapon and represents another class characteristic. People sometimes confuse caliber with cartridge designation. For example, 9-mm Luger, .38 special, and .357 Magnum are designations for specific cartridge configurations. The calibers of

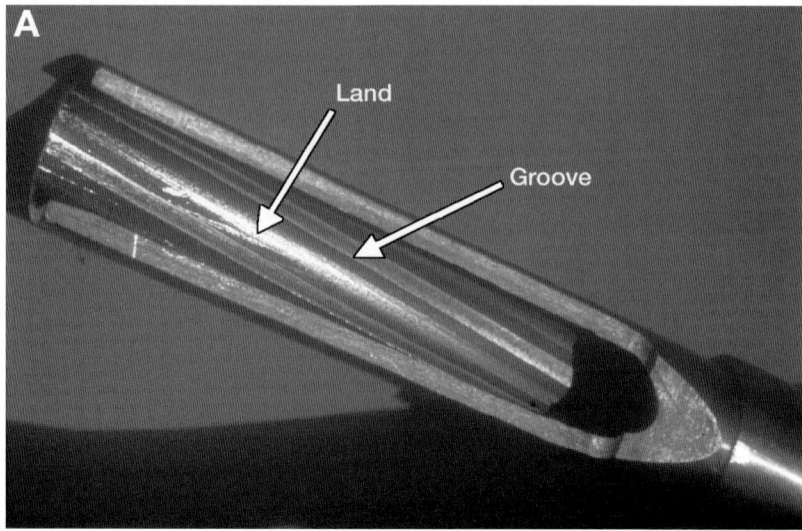

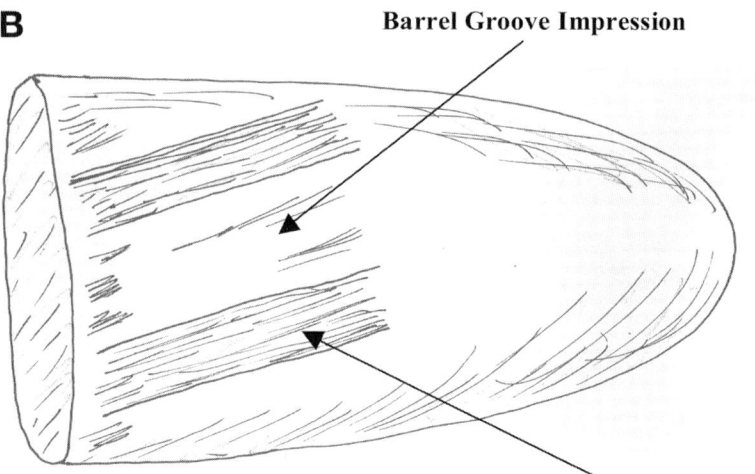

Fig. 5. (A) Cut-away of barrel showing lands and grooves. **(B)** Example of rifling marks engraved on bullet by barrel (left twist).

the weapons that fire these cartridges are all essentially the same, however. Caliber determination is illustrated in Fig. 6.

Shotguns, on the other hand, are usually smooth bore (without lands or grooves). Because spherical pellets are most often fired, spin stabilization and rifling are unnecessary. Shotguns may also be used to fire "slugs" (single, large

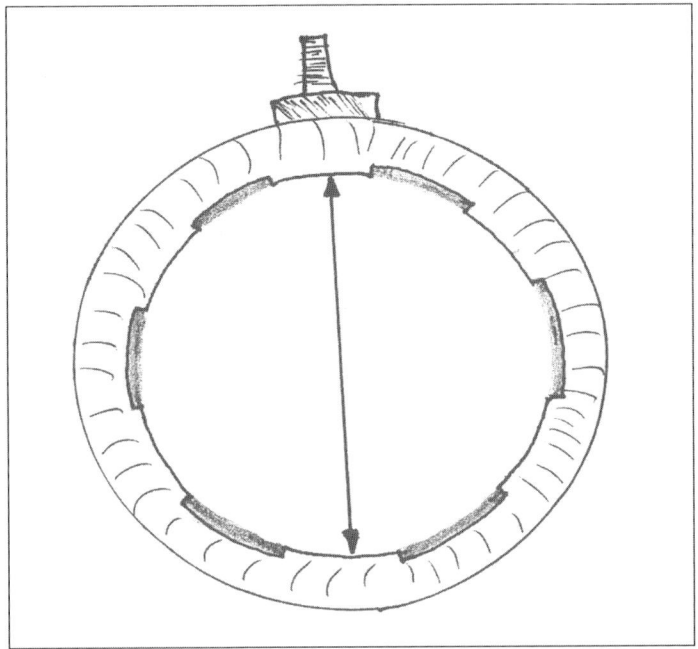

Fig. 6. Illustration of the caliber of a gun barrel (land-to-land dimension).

projectiles), in which case spin stabilization is desirable. This may be accomplished by having spiral grooves cast into the body of the slug itself. There are also shotguns with true rifling in the barrels. Rather than by caliber, most shotgun barrels are distinguished according to "gauge." Commonly encountered gauges include 12, 16, 20, and 28. The gauge designation is a holdover from Old English terminologies. Gauge represents the number of lead shot of a particular diameter to the pound. Thus, a 12-gauge shotgun barrel has a diameter such that 12 lead shot of that same diameter would weigh 1 lb. Because a 16-gauge shotgun represents a barrel diameter equivalent to 16 shot to the pound, a 12-gauge shotgun has a greater diameter than a 16-gauge which is greater than 20 and so on. The 410 shotguns are the exception in that they are actually designated as to caliber (0.410-in. diameter) rather than gauge.

Shotgun pellets leave the barrel in a cylindrical column that gradually begins to spread into a conical pattern. Various constrictions can be built into the muzzle end of the barrel of shotguns. The purpose of these constrictions, or "chokes," is to increase the distance from the muzzle that the pellet spread begins. Chokes range from "full choke" to "cylinder bore" (no constriction at all). In between are modified, improved, and improved—modified. In general, the

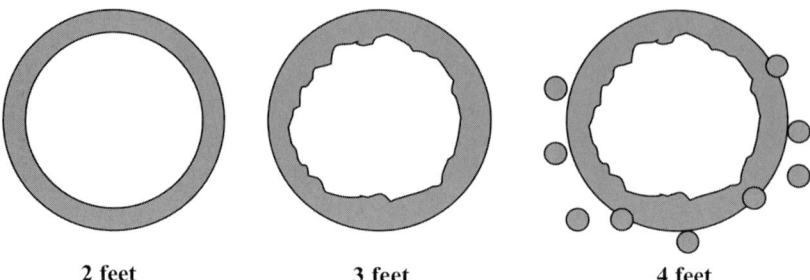

| 2 feet | 3 feet | 4 feet |

Fig. 7. Appearance of shotgun impacts at various distances.

greater the choke, the greater the distance of pellet travel before spreading occurs. At muzzle-to-target distances of approx 2 ft, all shotguns typically produce a singe hole. At about 3 ft, the margins of the hole show a ragged or scalloped effect as the pellets start to move apart. At approx 4 ft, signs of pellet spread first appear as individual pellet holes around the main central hole. This is illustrated in Fig. 7. A rough approximation of shotgun muzzle-to-target distance can be made by measuring the overall pellet spread and allowing 1 yd of muzzle-to-target distance for each inch of pellet spread. This is useful for providing a starting point at a crime scene to begin looking for other evidence of shooter presence such as ejected shot shells, footwear impressions, or perhaps even cigarette butts. Different chokes, barrel length, and shot size can and do affect the pellet pattern diameter. This requires that actual test firing be conducted using the same weapon and shot shells like those used in the shooting incident.

3. AMMUNITION COMPONENTS

Small arms ammunition is divided into two categories: cartridges and shot shells. Cartridges consist of a metallic case containing a priming mixture in the base, a powder charge (gunpowder) in the body, and a bullet seated in the mouth.

3.1. Priming Mixture

The priming mixture is either found in the annular rim of the cartridge case (rim fire) or encased in a metal cup seated in the center of the base (center fire). Figures 8 and 9 illustrate rim fire and center fire cartridges. Modern rim fire ammunition is mostly 22 caliber, although 17 caliber is rapidly gaining popularity. All modern larger caliber metallic cartridges are center fire.

Modern priming mixtures have typically consisted of compounds of lead, barium, and antimony. The presence of lead, barium, and antimony on the

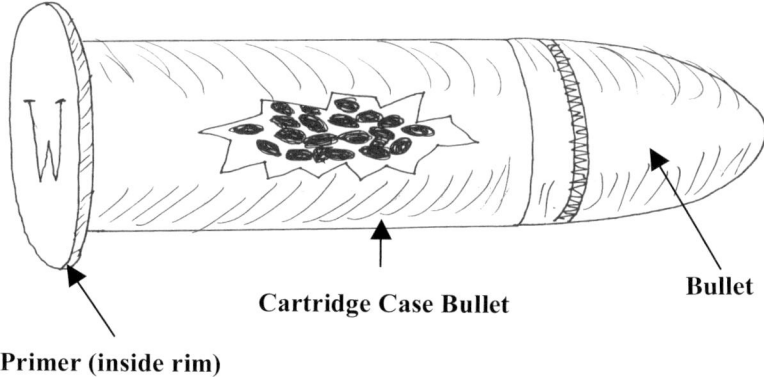

Primer (inside rim)

Fig. 8. Typical rim fire cartridge (cut away shows propellant).

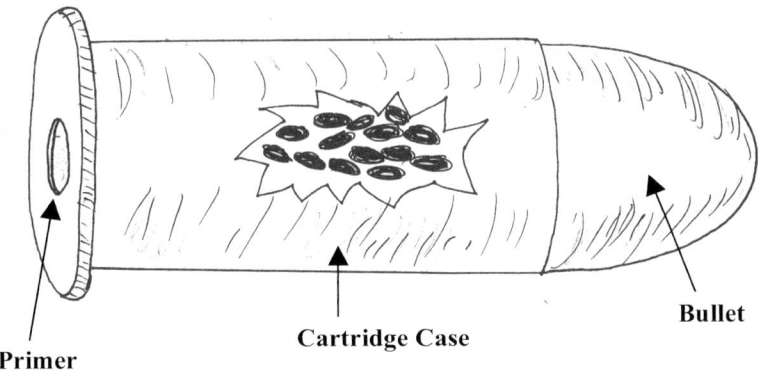

Fig. 9. Typical center fire cartridge (cut way shows propellant).

hands is then used to state that a suspect either fired a weapon, handled a weapon, or was in close proximity to a weapon that was fired. The environmental concerns about lead have resulted in the introduction of "lead-free" primers. Lead-free ammunition also includes copper bullets or lead bullets fully encased in nylon or copper. Other elements, such as zinc and titanium, are used in the priming mixture and are tested for in the event lead-free ammunition was used in a shooting.

3.2. Bullet Designs

Bullet designs vary greatly depending on their designated use. Round nose or flat nose lead bullets are most often used for target practice. Hunting bullets and bullets for law enforcement/personal protection typically consist of an inner lead core and either a partial or total covering (jacket) of copper or brass. This

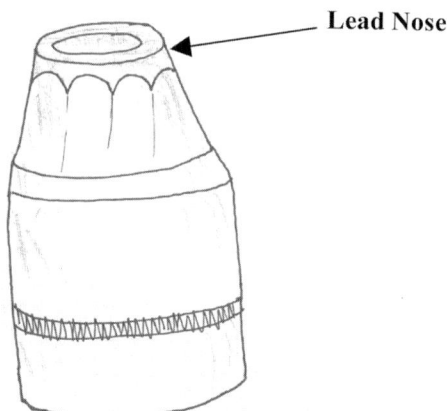

Lead Nose

Fig. 10. Semi-jacketed hollow-point design bullet (copper jacket with lead nose).

jacketed design allows for controlled expansion upon impacting a target. This results in maximum tissue destruction and maximum likelihood for incapacitation. Maximum expansion is achieved through the so-called hollow point design in which the bullets have a cavity in the nose (Fig. 10). A myriad of various shapes and designs of bullets are available. The fact that there are so many different designs can assist the examiner in identifying a particular source.

From a forensic standpoint, the hollow-point bullet is most desirable. This is because intermediary target material tends to accumulate in the hollow-point cavity. This material can be recovered by the examiner and used to establish a "history" of the bullet path.

Gunpowder consists of several different shapes and formulations depending on its intended use. It takes more gunpowder to push a bullet out of a long barrel than a short barrel. Ammunition manufacturers must take into consideration all possible weapons that their ammunition might be used in. For that reason, they incorporate more than enough gunpowder to do the job. This is good news for the firearms examiner because it means that, at close range, there will likely be unburned or partially burned gunpowder spewed from the end of the barrel. The presence of this gunpowder can be determined through examination/testing and used to estimate the distance of the shot.

3.3. Gunpowder

The shape or morphology of gunpowder particles designed for small arms ammunition includes spherical (ball powder), flattened ball, disk or flake, and cylindrical. Two different chemical formulations are used. Single base powders use nitrocellulose. Double base powders use nitrocellulose in combination with

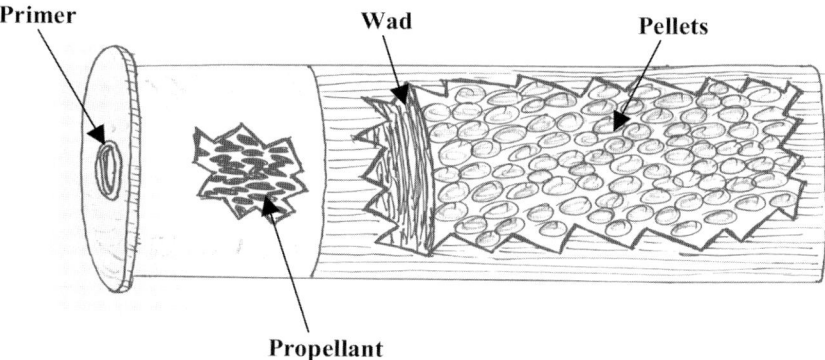

Fig. 11. Typical shot shell (brass base and plastic body).

nitroglycerine. Various stabilizers, plasticizers, and anti-static agents are also usually present.

The chemical composition and morphology of the gunpowder particles can be determined and compared to gunpowder found in ammunition confiscated from shooting suspects. The examiner can then make a determination as to whether the suspect's ammunition is consistent or inconsistent with the evidence.

3.4. Shot Shells

Shot shells consist of a paper or plastic tube with a brass base and center primer. Shot shells constructed entirely of plastic are also manufactured. The shot or pellets are separated from the powder charge by a paper or plastic wad. Some shot shell designs incorporate the wad with a plastic cup that contains the shot and is known as a shot cup. A typical shot shell is shown in Fig. 11. At close range (less than about 10 ft), the shot cup/wad is often found inside the wound. The characteristics of the shot cup/wad can provide the examiner with information as to the gage and manufacturer.

3.4.1. Shotgun Pellets

Shotgun pellets are designated as either birdshot or buckshot. The shot is made of either lead, steel, bismuth, or tungsten (nonlead shot is required to accommodate environmental concerns in some areas of the country). Lead shot is of three general types: soft shot (pure lead), hard shot (hardened with antimony), and plated shot (plated with copper). Shotgun pellets range in size from 0.05 in. (No. 12 birdshot) to 0.36 in. diameter (000 buckshot); the specific size is designated by number. Shot shells can contain two different shot sizes (duplex loads) or three different shot sizes (triples loads), although most contain

Fig. 12. Buffered shot shell loads (l. slug, r. buckshot)

only one size. Shot shells, particularly buckshot loads, often contain polypropylene or polyethylene particles known as buffer. Buffers may also be present in slug rounds. This is illustrated in Fig. 12. The presence of buffer material on the clothing or body assists the examiner in determining the shot distance because the buffer material will only travel a limited determinable distance. Because buffer material varies in composition and morphology (shape), the examiner is able to make some determination as to the source (manufacturer and specific load).

4. MANUFACTURING PROCESSES

The firearm/tool mark examiner must have knowledge of manufacturing processes for firearms and tools in order to properly assess the significance of marks that are present on ammunition components and other surfaces. Without knowing how a firearm or tool was made, the examiner could erroneously conclude that a class or subclass characteristic was an individual characteristic. Early manufacturing techniques relied heavily on hand production and hand finishing. Interchangeable parts were a concept that had not yet been developed. The individuality that was inherent in the firearms and tools that resulted was an examiner's dream. Modern manufacturing techniques have resulted in closer tolerances as well as parts interchangeability. Computer controlled machine tools have taken much of the hand work out of the manufacturing processes. On the surface, the demise of individuality would seem to be the inevitable, if not desired, outcome. Despite all the mechanization, however, individuality is still alive and well. Hand finishing, in the form of grinding and polishing, is still used in the manufacture of most firearms and tools. Even automated machining processes involve the use of bits, blades, grinders, and other tools with surfaces that are subject to wear and change. As these surfaces come into contact with the firearms parts or tool parts, they leave random/unique manufacturing marks. The result is that modern firearms and tools can and do produce unique and random marks that can be used for positive identification. It is just more incumbent on the examiner to become familiar with the admittedly less common sources of individuality.

5. THE EXAMINATION

5.1. Types of Examinations Conducted

The firearm/tool mark examiner is capable of answering a wide range of questions through the examination of evidence recovered at a crime scene in addition to "Did this tool make this mark?" These questions include the following:

- Did this weapon fire the bullet/cartridge case/shot shell recovered?
- Did this weapon chamber the cartridge/shot shell?
- If no gun was recovered, what type of weapon could have fired the recovered bullet/cartridge case/shot shell?
- Was the recovered bullet/cartridge case/shot shell fired from the same weapon as that used in other crimes?
- What was the approximate muzzle-to-target distance of the shot?
- What was the directionality of the ricochet mark/crease?
- Is the firearm functional?
- Is the firearm capable of accidental firing (mechanical malfunction)?
- How does the firearm eject fired cartridge cases/shot shells?
- What was the serial number on a defaced weapon?

Additionally, many firearm/tool mark examiners are trained and experienced in the reconstruction of shooting incidents. Reconstruction involves determining positions of shooters and victims, sequences of shots, and other aspects relating to how the shootings took place. This frequently involves other disciplines, as well as firearms/tool marks (i.e., footwear/tire tread evidence, bloodstain pattern analysis, latent prints, trace evidence, and DNA).

5.2. Planning and Carrying Out the Examination

Unlike the examiners portrayed on popular television dramas, firearm/tool mark examiners usually have evidence come to them by way of the investigators who collected it rather than being at the scene themselves. Some examiners, however, are actively involved in crime scene analysis/reconstruction and collect evidence at the scene themselves. This activity is usually restricted to major crimes because of manpower considerations and the heavy workload most crime laboratories have. Typically, there will be a lead detective (case officer) in charge of the crime scene who has the responsibility of seeing that all appropriate evidence is collected and transported to the crime laboratory for examination and testing. An Evidence Submittal sheet and a Request for Analysis form accompany the evidence and help maintain a record of where the evidence has been from the point of collection until it is presented in court. These forms also give direction to the examiner. The record of evidence transmission/ receipt is known as the chain of custody. Because the examiner is the expert who is most familiar with laboratory capabilities and limitations, it is important that the Request for Analysis be critically evaluated. If, in the examiner's opinion, additional and/or different tests are more appropriate, this must be communicated to the case officer. Blindly following the Request for Analysis without considering the possibility of other testing does a disservice to the case officer and is unprofessional. Examiners are sometimes tempted not to stray from the indications of the Request for Analysis form owing to the pressures of heavy caseloads and the subsequent motivation of not wanting to "create any extra work." Given the fact that lives are often hanging in the balance and depend on the outcome of the laboratory examinations, this attitude can simply not be tolerated.

5.3. Equipment

5.3.1. Microscopes

The firearm/tool mark examiner primarily uses two different types of microscopes on a regular basis. The first is the stereomicroscope. This microscope sits on the work table and is usually mounted on a boom or arm extending from a stand. It usually has zoom capabilities for magnification from about ×3 to about ×10. Initial examinations of weapons, ammunition components, tools, and objects with tool marks on them are done with the stereomicroscope. The relatively low power provides lots of working room so that the examiner can manipulate various cumbersome objects into the field of view. The workhorse of the firearm/tool mark section is the forensic comparison microscope. This is actually two microscopes that are connected by an optical bridge. As a result, both stages are visible via a split screen as one looks through the eye pieces. In this way, evidence tool marks on a surface can be compared directly to test tool marks on a similar surface.

Forensic comparison microscopes have special holders that fit on the stages so that a wide variety of evidence items can be examined (i.e., bullets, cartridge cases, shot shells, tools, firearms/parts). Creative fixtures must some times be fabricated by the examiner in order to get a desired part under the microscope. Comparison microscopes are fitted with multiple objectives so that a range of magnification is available to the examiner. A maximum of about ×40 magnification is typically adequate for firearm/tool mark examination. The comparison microscope is usually fitted with a video imaging system for use in training and for case documentation purposes. Digital images showing the specific areas of identification provide visual support for the examiner's written notes and conclusions. An argument against photographing identifications has been made on the basis that photographs do not fully represent what the examiner sees because they are only two-dimensional when the actual tool marks are three-dimensional. Although this may be true to some degree, such images are useful for refreshing the examiner's memory of the comparison at a later date and for allowing a defense expert to see the basis for the identification. Of course, some tool marks have no perceptible depth and, thus, the argument is completely lost in those cases.

5.3.2. Measuring Tools

Firearm/tool mark examiners use a number of different measuring tools in the process of examining evidence. Dial calipers allow accurate measurements of the thickness and depth to one-thousandth of an inch. Micrometers are also used to measure thickness and are accurate to one-thousandth of an inch as well. Such measurements are used with firearms and ammunition components in particular where various comparisons of size are being made. Trigger pull weights, scales, and/or electronic measuring devices are used in the testing and evaluation of functionality of firearms. Extremely light or extremely heavy trigger pulls can be a factor in whether a shooting was intentional or not.

5.3.3. Water Trap

In order to have test bullets for comparison to evidence bullets, the examiner must have a bullet trap that is capable of catching/preserving fired bullets. Water traps typically consist of large (approx 30 in. × 48 in. × 96 in.), stainless steel boxes filled with water, and have a pipe attached to one end to fire into. Filter systems for both the air above and the water help keep the working environment safe.

5.3.4. Reference Collections

In examining weapons, ammunition, and tools, there are frequent needs for exemplars. With regard to weapons, it is sometimes necessary to have parts available so that an evidence weapon received with a broken part might be test fired anyway by replacing the part. Ammunition of known origin assists the examiner in identifying various ammunition components submitted for examination. Having reference bolt cutters, saws, pliers, screwdrivers, and other tools can provide information as to the presence of class, subclass, and individual characteristics.

5.4. Case Example

The following example illustrates the basic process of evidence examination for a firearms case. In this example, we will assume there has been a shooting incident in which a person has one superficial wound to the arm with the bullet entering, exiting, and getting lodged into a wall. The fatal shot strikes the victim in the chest, first passing through the shirt. A weapon is found at the scene.

5.4.1. Evidence Receipt

The firearm/tool mark examiner first receives the Evidence Submission/ Request for Analysis form that alerts him/her to the evidence submission. A typical excerpt from this type form appears below.

Evidence Submission/Request for Analysis

Items Submitted:

1. *38-Caliber Smith & Wesson model 36 snub-nose revolver, serial number K37653.*
2. *3 live rounds (2 R-P, 1 W-W) and 2 fired cartridge cases from item 1 (1 R-P, 1 W-W).*
3. *Bullet recovered from the NW bedroom wall at the crime scene.*
4. *Bullet recovered at autopsy (removed from victim's chest).*
5. *Black T-shirt from victim with apparent bullet hole in chest.*

Request for Analysis:

Examine the weapon for latent fingerprints. Compare the weapon to the bullet from the scene and the bullet from the victim. Examine the victim's shirt for gunshot residue and determine the shot distance.

5.4.2. General Evidence Examination

The examiner begins by checking out the evidence from the property and evidence unit where the case officer or crime scene investigator had submitted it. The evidence is then taken into the examiner's work area where examination of the evidence commences and a work sheet is begun. The stereomicroscope and measuring tools are used. Some typical work sheet entries appear below:

Evidence Examination Worksheet

Item 1:	*Tape sealed paper sack bearing the initials "AMP" and the ID # 3296 and containing a black steel Smith & Wesson .38 special model 36 revolver, s/n K37653, 5 shot.*
Visual exam:	*No blood or other trace evidence observed in/on weapon; 2 prominent cylinder flares (chamber under*

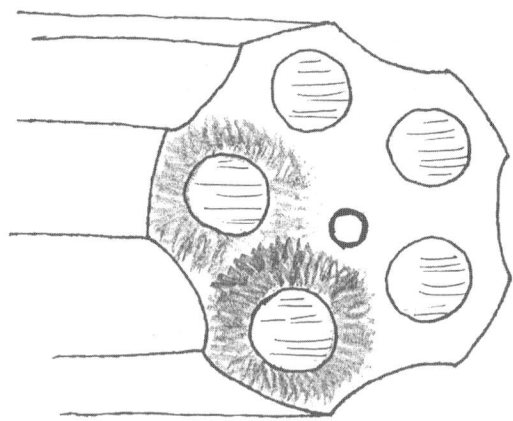

Fig. 13. Face of revolver cylinder showing powder flares.

	hammer, 1 to immediate left); cylinder rotates clockwise, 5 lands/grooves (right twist).
Superglued weapon:	*No identifiable prints obtained.*
Trigger pull:	*11–12 pounds (double action) 6–7 pounds (single action).*
	Test fired 6X using lab ammunition (R-P semi-jacketed hollow point, 120 grain—3X and W-W round nose lead—3X).
	Weapon functions normally.
	Marked "EEH" under left grip.

The evidence examination worksheet shows that no trace evidence was present on the weapon as received. It is important to make this determination prior to conducting any sort of testing to avoid loss or contamination. It was noted that there were "2 prominent cylinder flares." Cylinder flares are deposits of soot that appear on the cylinder face around the margins of chambers in which cartridges have been discharged. Each successively produced flare overlaps the previous such that sequence of shots can be determined. This is illustrated in Fig. 13. In this example, the clockwise rotation direction of the cylinder and the location of cylinder flares under and to the left of the hammer indicate that the cylinder has been rotated from its original position. Were this not the case, the cylinder flares would be under and to the right of the hammer or the cylinder flare under the hammer would overlap the one to the left. The first step the examiner takes is to determine whether or not one of the investigators is responsible for the cylinder rotation. Often times, investigators cannot resist the urge to open the cylinder of a revolver found at the scene. Without realizing it, they rotate the cylinder as they open it and then close it back. In the event that an officer is not responsible, it

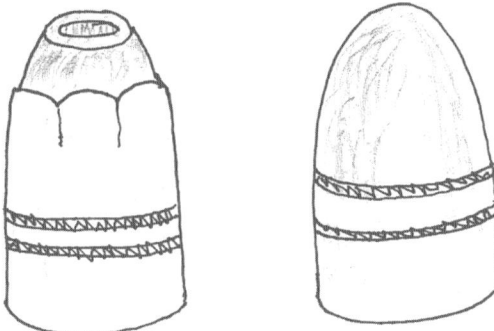

Fig. 14. R-P (left) and W-W (right) bullets.

must be assumed that the cylinder was rotated between the firing of the first and second shots. Because two bullets were recovered, one from the scene and one from the victim, the question is which was first? The answer is found by using the crime scene investigator's notation as to which chamber had the "R-P" cartridge case (Remington-Peters) and which had the "W-W" (Winchester-Western). Because the bullet designs will be different (*see* Fig. 14), it will be possible to determine which was fired first (i.e., if the W-W cartridge case is to the left of the R-P, it was fired first).

Once those observations are made, the weapon is tested for the presence of latent fingerprints using the technique of superglue (cyanoacrylate ester) fuming. No "identifiable prints" means there may have been a few friction ridges and/or smudges, but no potentially identifiable fingerprints. In my experience, identifiable fingerprints are found on firearms in less than about 10% of the cases. It is also possible to detect DNA on the surfaces of weapons and, thus, identify the person or persons who handled the weapon.

The worksheet indicates that the trigger pull was determined both in single action and double action mode. This is done to test for the possibility of an extremely light pull ("hair trigger"). Trigger pulls below 1–1.5 lb are considered dangerous and can contribute to unintentional firing. In this example the trigger pulls are within the range expected for a weapon of this type. Trigger pull may be determined either by hanging special weights from the trigger or by using a spring scale or electronic tester.

The worksheet entry regarding test firing indicates that three each of two different brands of ammunition were fired in the weapon. This was done because these same two different brands of ammunition were fired in the weapon during the incident under investigation. It is imperative that the examiner duplicate the actual conditions of the crime as closely as possible when carrying out tests such as these. This is because different brands of ammunition can have different bullet and cartridge case compositions. Different compositions can mean different degrees of hardness and that can affect how the various markings (rifling, breech face, etc.) will be imparted. The firing of three test rounds is done to allow the examiner to intercompare the tests so that reproducibility of markings can be established. This will help the examiner in examining the evidence bullets and cartridge cases by knowing what markings to expect and to look for. In this example the weapon was recovered at the crime scene and, being a revolver, did not eject the fired cartridge cases but retained them in the cylinder. Despite of what would seem obvious, the examiner cannot assume anything and must compare the fired cartridge cases to known test fires to verify their source.

5.4.3. Cartridge Case Comparison

Test-fired cartridge cases are obtained by firing the weapon into a water trap. The examiner begins the cartridge case comparison by intercomparing the test cartridge cases. This is followed by a comparison of the evidence cartridge cases to the tests. This is all done using the comparison microscope. A sample cartridge case worksheet for this example case is shown below:

Cartridge Case Examination Worksheet

Item	Headstamp	Type	Case	Primer
2a	W-W	.38 spl	Nickel	Nickel
2b	R-P	.38 spl	Brass	Nickel

Comparison Result:
1. *Test fires T1, T2, T3; T1 identified to T2/T3 by firing pin impressions and breech face marks.*
2. *Test to 2a; 2a identified to T2 by breech face marks.*
3. *Test to 2b; 2b identified to T1 by firing pin impression.*

Note: Both cartridge cases received with "AMP" engraved in mouth.

The cartridge case examination worksheet indicates that all three test-fired cartridge cases were identified to one another on the basis of firing pin impressions and breech face marks. Either of these is sufficient for positive identification. Both the firing pins and the breech faces of weapons receive random/unique marks during manufacture and through use (wear). These, in turn, may be impressed upon the cartridge cases as in this example.

Breech face marks result from the expansion of the cartridge case back against the breech face on discharge. This expansion can also produce chamber marks along the sides of the case. Firing pin impressions in the outer area

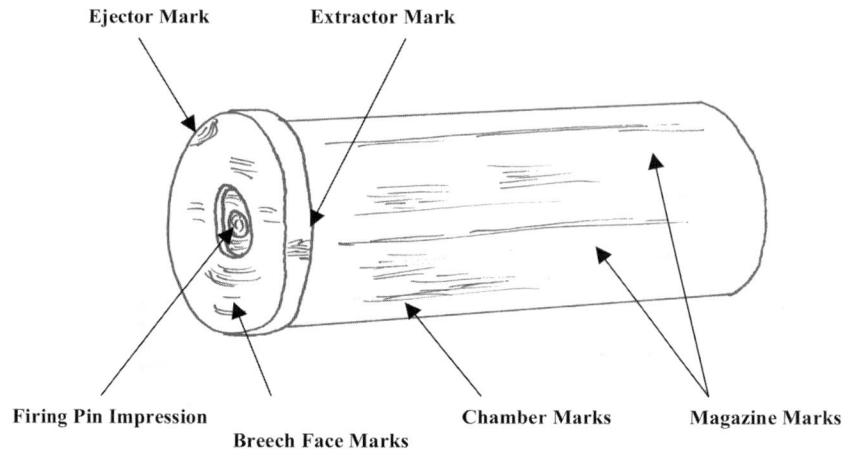

Fig. 15. Cartridge case markings that may be present.

of the base of rim fire cartridges and in the primer of center fire cartridges result when the firing pin impacts these areas during discharge. The shape and size of firing pins constitute class characteristics only. It is the tiny gouges, scrapes, and other random markings produced by manufacture/wear that must be present for identification. It is possible for a cartridge to be inserted and/or cycled through a weapon but not fired. Thus, the presence of magazine marks, extractor marks, and ejector marks do not necessarily indicate firing. On the other hand, breech face marks, firing pin impressions, and chamber marks can only result from firing and, therefore, positively confirm firing. These various markings are illustrated in Fig. 15. The worksheet reflects that evidence cartridge case 2a was identified to test T2, whereas evidence cartridge case 2b was identified to Test T1. Because all three test-cartridge cases were intercompared and identified, this is fine. The net result is that it has been confirmed that 2a and 2b were fired from the same weapon, albeit having been done indirectly. This process is summarized below:

T1 and T2 were matched. Then T2 was matched to 2a and 2b was matched to T1.

Therefore, 2a matches 2b.

The two evidence bullets will, of course, have to be compared to test fires as well. The fact that the weapon was fired twice and two bullets were recovered might also appear to make it obvious that this is the responsible weapon. Once again, however, the examiner must verify this. There is always the possibility that the weapon/ammunition was altered in some way or that another weapon and or other ammunition components were used.

5.4.4. Bullet Comparison

Test-fired bullets are recovered from the water trap they were fired into. The bullet comparison follows in the same manner as the cartridge case comparison in that the test fires are intercompared first and then the comparison of the evidence items to the test is conducted using a comparison microscope. A sample bullet examination worksheet for this example appears below.

Bullet Examination Worksheet

Item	Caliber	L/G no.	WT (grains)	Twist	Type	Trace evidence
3	0.357	5	158	Right	RN lead	No
4	0.357	5	125	Right	SJHP	Blood

Comparison Result:

1. *Test fires T1, T2, T3; T1 identified to T2/T3 by 2 areas of 6+ consecutive striae near base.*
2. *Test to 3; 3 identified to T1.*
3. *Test to 4; 4 identified to T1.*

Comments: Dried blood in nose of item 4 removed and placed in paper packet for exam by DNA unit:

Both bullets received with "AMP" engraved on nose.

In the comparison of the bullets, both evidence bullets were identified to the same test bullet (T1). It was noted that there were two areas of correspondence and that these areas were near the base of the bullet. Both of the two areas were noted to consist of more than six consecutive striations (striae) each. The significance of two areas of more than six consecutive striae is discussed in Subheading 5.5.1.

5.4.5. Gunshot Residue Testing

In this case example, there was a black T-shirt with a bullet hole in the chest. The examiner begins with visual and microscopic (stereomicroscope) examination of the shirt, noting the presence of gunpowder, blood, and any other trace evidence of potential value. The sample worksheet for this part of the examination appears below.

Gunshot Residue Examination Worksheet

Item: *Black T-Shirt.*

Markings: *"AMP" on tag as received; Marked "EEH" on back of tag.*

Visual Exam: *Round hole in chest 16 inches from right side, 12 inches below neck band; apparent soot/powder residue; small amount of apparent blood on inside around hole (soaked through).*

Microscopic Exam:	*no tearing/burning/melting/soot around hole margins observed; powder particles (disk) visible out to approximately 4 inches from hole.*
Griess test:	*Pattern of nitrites detected with a diameter of approximately 4 inches.*
Rhodizonate test:	*No vaporous/particulate lead detected.*

The gunshot residue examination results for this example revealed that an intermediate range shot was involved. This is based on there being a 4-in. pattern of gunpowder particles around the hole in the chest of the T-shirt but no tearing, burning, melting, or soot. At contact or near contact distance, little or no powder particles would be found (because it goes into the wound) and the muzzle blast would cause burning and/or melting of fibers and deposit soot. Distance shots, on the other hand, would not deposit gunpowder particles.

The next step for the examiner is to use the weapon and ammunition like that in evidence to establish test patterns that duplicate the 4-in. powder pattern found on the front of the T-shirt. Because there are two possible brands of cartridges (W-W and R-P), the examiner has to refer to the evidence submission form and utilize his ammunition reference collection to verify which brand produced the bullet hole in the T-shirt (and, of course, the wound). Once a determination of which type ammunition was used has been made, the examiner acquires several rounds of that ammunition and proceeds to the shooting range to conduct test firings. Test shots are fired at measured distances into white cotton twill squares. In this example, the examiner would probably begin by firing at 24 in. and then moving in or out depending on the result obtained. Six-inch increments are usually used. Once a pattern similar to the evidence is obtained, an additional shot is made at that same distance for confirmation. Finally, a swatch of the actual evidence garment is used for final confirmation firing. The reason for using the actual material is that gunpowder particles can behave differently on striking various different surfaces. For example, a powder particle might bounce off a tightly woven nylon fabric whereas, at the same distance, it might adhere to a woolen sweater. An example of the gunshot residue testing report is shown below.

Gunshot Residue Examination Report

The area around a hole in the chest of the item 5 T-shirt was examined microscopically and processed chemically for the presence of gunshot residue (gunpowder and primer residues). A pattern of gunpowder particles was obtained.

Using the item 1 revolver and ammunition like that in item 4, a similar pattern was obtained at a distance of 12–18 inches.

These results mean that the fatal shot was probably fired at a distance of 12–18 in. (muzzle to garment). The chemical tests used consist of the Griess test (a chemical color reaction for nitrites) and the sodium rhodizonate test (a chemical color reaction for lead). Nitrites result from partial burning of gunpowder (nitrates). Lead originates from the priming mixture (lead styphnate/lead azide) and/or lead bullets.

Ultimately the examiner writes a final report in which all the findings are articulated. This report is provided to both the case officer and the prosecutor (district attorney, county attorney, etc.). An abbreviated version of the final report for this example appears below.

Report of Scientific Examination

- *The item 1 revolver was examined for the presence of latent fingerprints but no identifiable prints were found.*
- *The item 1 revolver was test fired and found to be in working order.*
- *The item 3 bullet (from the crime scene) and the item 4 bullet (recovered at autopsy) were both identified as having been fired from the item 1 revolver.*
- *The item 5 T-shirt was found to have a bullet hole in the chest that testing indicates was fired from a distance of approximately 12–18 inches.*
- *The bullets and cartridge cases were entered into NIBIN and no hits were obtained.*

In this example case, the firearms examiner was able to provide useful evidence that would assist the lead investigator in reconstructing the shooting. The examination results provided information as to sequence of shots and the distance the fatal shot was fired from.

5.5. Databases

A number of useful databases have been established and are available to the firearm/tool mark examiner. Probably the most significant is the National Integrated Ballistics Identification Network (NIBIN). This system contains a database of bullet rifling marks and cartridge case base markings (firing pin impressions and breech face marks). The system is networked with law enforcement agencies throughout the United States and is administered by the Bureau of Alcohol, Tobacco and Firearms (ATF). The ATF provides the equipment to the agencies that agree to support the program with staffing and resources. According to the ATF, more than 6200 "hits" have been logged as of 2005. This means bullets/cartridge cases entered into the system that have been found to match other bullets/cartridge cases already in the system (i.e. fired from the same gun). Many agencies, such as the New York Police Department, assign individuals whose job it is to enter bullet/cartridge case data from weapons seized on the street into the database. It is here that so-called cold hits are generated. This system, though time consuming itself, still saves thousands of hours of manual searching that would have to take place when a bullet or cartridge case needs to be searched against previous submissions.

Other useful databases include trigger pull data and general rifling characteristics. The general rifling characteristics, along with the incorporated cartridge case markings file, allow the examiner to predict possible weapons that could have fired bullets/cartridge cases.

Future possibilities include the entering of bullet/cartridge case markings data from new weapons through cooperative agreements with firearm manufacturers. This would be similar to having a fingerprint file for all individuals from birth.

5.5.1. Criteria for Identification

Examiners are sometimes reluctant to present images of comparisons at trial for fear of opening the door for defense attacks where less than obvious agreement between striae exist or where there is even apparent disagreement. These arguments can be overcome by simply pointing out that there will never be 100% agreement in these marks. On this topic, Miller and McLean stated, "Nothing duplicated in nature has been reportedly found to be exactly the same, and man has not been able to produce things exactly alike"(1). The Association of Firearm and Tool Mark Examiners (AFTE) allows for "opinions of common origin to be made when the unique surface contours of two tool marks are in sufficient agreement" (2). The definition of "sufficient agreement" varies somewhat depending on who is asked to define it. This means that often the examiner, having looked at a large number of tool marks, particularly known nonmatches (tool marks known to have been made by different tools), is left to use his best judgment of sufficient agreement and identification. Studies of the number of consecutive matching striae have been conducted. Biasotti and Murdock (3) have proposed a "conservative criteria for identification" as:

1. In three-dimensional tool marks when at least three each, or one group of six consecutive matching striae appear in the same relative position in an evidence tool mark compared to a test tool mark.
2. In two-dimensional tool marks when at least two groups of at least five each, or one group of eight consecutive matching striae are in agreement."

There is on-going study and debate on this subject. It is the lack of universally accepted criteria for identification that has fostered the legal challenges to tool mark identification that have arisen (4). The problem of articulating criteria for identification results from the fact that comparisons must take into account not only the quantitative aspect (number of consecutive matching striae), but also the quality of the match. Exactly how to define "quality of match" is somewhat more difficult than establishing the minimum number of consecutive striae for an identification. Although there may continue to be legal challenges to the scientific validity of tool mark evidence, I feel the proof of the validity derives from the results of studies, such as one I participated in a number of years ago involving consecutively manufactured pistol barrels. The greatest chance for carry over of tool marks is clearly going to be found in the manufacturing process where the same machine/operator/tool/stock are used to produce items one after another. Thus, a group of consecutively manufactured pistol barrels was obtained. The purpose of the test was to see if bullets fired through the barrels could be distinguished from one another and, more importantly, if the bullets could be identified to the specific barrel that fired them. The bottom line was that the bullets were both distinguishable from one another and identifiable to the barrel that fired them.

6. COMPARING SCREWDRIVERS, PLIERS, AND OTHER HAND TOOLS

The underlying principle in comparing two objects is that "like must be compared to like" or "you can't compare apples to oranges." In other words, if a tool mark was left on a piece of copper sheet, the test tool mark should also be made on copper sheet and not lead or zinc. Although similar principles are used to compare all different types of tool marks, there are inherent differences that must be considered. For example, a common pair of shears has four different surfaces, two sides on each blade that could produce tool marks. Thus, directionality/orientation becomes an issue. If a test cut is made holding the shears opposite to the direction the evidence cut was made, the tool marks produced will not be in the same relative orientation. Comparison of hand tools begins with a stereomicroscope examination of the tool surfaces for the presence of tiny bits of material (metal, plastic, wood, etc.) from the item that was cut/drilled/sawed/scratched/gouged/indented. If this material is found, the tool can be related to it, even if the tool marks cannot provide positive identification. Test tool marks are produced and evaluated for class, subclass, and individual characteristics. This may require obtaining exemplar tools for examination/comparison. The exemplar tools should be new and unused. As already mentioned, test tool marks should be made in/on the same material as the evidence. It is possible, however, to make useful test tool marks in other media, such as lead rod or sheet, and use these to establish reproducibility. Usually three test impressions are made and intercompared for reproducibility. Once the examiner has established that the tool makes reproducible marks, comparison of the test marks to the evidence marks begins. This is an over-simplification, however, because different angles, positions, degrees of force, and other factors can affect the tool marks produced. The examiner must consider all these factors and may have to make numerous test marks in an effort to duplicate the conditions under which the evidence marks were produced.

In some instances, the examiner may make silicone casts of a test tool mark in one medium and the evidence tool mark in another medium and compare the casts to one another. In this way, apples get compared to apples, albeit with a backdoor approach.

7. SERIAL NUMBER RESTORATION

The restoration of obliterated serial numbers is typically part of the responsibilities of the firearm/tool mark examiner. Stolen items that bear serial numbers, such as firearms, motorcycles, and tractors often have their serial numbers defaced or removed in an effort to avoid identification. When the serial number is stamped into metal, disruption of the crystalline structure occurs. This disruption extends below the actual impression of the number. When the number is ground off, but not excessively, there is a reasonable chance that the number can be restored through chemical etching. This is because the compressed area of the metal reacts at a different rate than the surrounding area when subjected to chemical etching. This is illustrated in Fig. 16.

The first step in any serial number restoration process is to polish the surface where the serial number obliteration has taken place. This is done using fine sandpaper and/or polishing wheels. The purpose is to allow as much contrast as possible between the compressed and uncompressed areas. Different chemical etching solutions are used depending on the metal (i.e., steel, aluminum, or zinc alloy). The process can be sped up through the use of electrical current since the etching process is actually an electrochemical process in which electrons are being transferred as the metal is etched. The examiner must be careful, however, because too much etching can destroy the serial number remnants completely. Some success has been achieved by heating defaced metal surfaces with a torch until it is red hot and then observing the cooling process. The principle is the same in that the compressed area cools at a different rate than the uncompressed area, allowing visualization of the serial number. Another method relies on differences in magnetic properties of compressed vs uncompressed steel. This is the same technique used by metallurgists to locate defects in steel objects and is known as magnafluxing. Iron filings (magnaflux) in an oil suspension are placed on the surface under examination after an electromagnetic field has first been applied. The filings collect in the compressed area

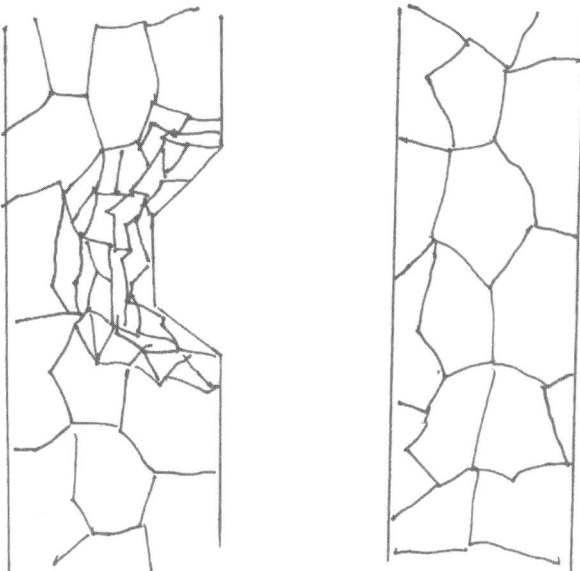

Fig. 16. Illustration of the compression of the crystalline structure of steel owing to serial number stamping (left); normal crystalline arrangement is shown on right for comparison.

of the serial number. Another technique that has been used involves an ultrasonic bath. The ultrasound technique produces etching much like the chemical process. Serial numbers in plastics can be restored by using organic solvents, such as chloroform, to cause swelling. Again, the difference in rate of reaction between compressed and uncompressed areas allows visualization.

If the serial number has been too deeply ground away or drilled out, nothing can be done to restore the number. Likewise, serial numbers that are lightly stamped or merely engraved offer little hope for restoration when defaced.

8. THE FUTURE

The future of firearm and tool mark examination is directly tied to the technology of the firearms and tools that are being and will be devised. As the technology of these items changes, the methodologies used in their identification and comparison must also change. Firearms are already being developed that use electronic ignition rather than conventional firing pin/primer mechanisms. This eliminates the firing pin impression aspect of firearms identification. Caseless cartridges have been around since before the Civil War, but there now is renewed interest in them. Obviously the markings typically utilized (extractor, ejector, breech face, firing pin, and chamber) are not available if there is no cartridge case. Alternative means of identification will have to be developed. The most probable changes on the horizon for firearm and tool mark examination will likely involve increased automation. A possible consideration would be the use of topographical analysis of tool marks and automated comparison. In this way the quality and the quantity of the marks could be related. The quality would be based on the degree of contour match of the marks (test vs evidence), whereas the quantity would be evaluated as is already being done (number of consecutive striae). A combined "degree of match" might then be derived. A push has been underway for a number of years for certification of firearm and tool mark examiners through the AFTE. In the future, universal endorsement of AFTE certification may become a reality.

9. CASE STUDY

9.1. Case Details

A man was found in the bedroom of his home shot to death. The man had an entry wound in the right chest and an exit in the lower right back such that the exit wound was lower than the entry wound. A bullet hole was discovered in the ceiling and there was blood spatter around the hole. A revolver with one fired cartridge case was found on the bedroom floor in front of a chest of drawers. The question to be answered was: is this homicide, suicide, or accidental? In order for the medical examiner to make this determination, assistance from the firearms examiner was required in evaluating the firearms evidence and reconstructing the shooting.

9.2. The Evidence

The weapon was determined to belong to the victim. Ammunition like that found in the cylinder was located in a box in the closet. No identifiable prints, blood, or other trace evidence was found on the weapon. The weapon was found to be fully functional. The weapon was a single action style that would only fire with the hammer fully cocked and the trigger fully depressed (i.e., it would not fire if dropped on the hammer). The trigger pull was found to be approx 5.5 lb (within the expected range). The man's shirt had a 6-in. pattern of gunpowder particles around the bullet hole. Using the weapon and ammunition like that found in the weapon, the approximate muzzle-to-target distance was determined to be 18–24 in. There was a linear soot deposit in the palm of both hands and powder stippling on the inside of the man's right arm. The bullet recovered from the ceiling was found to have been fired from the weapon. The fired cartridge found beneath the hammer of the weapon was identified as having been fired in the weapon also.

9.3. Additional Information

There was no sign of a struggle at the scene and no sign of forced entry. The decedent had no medical, financial, or other reasons for taking his own life. Thus, there was no apparent motive for homicide or suicide.

9.4. The Reconstruction

The reconstruction was approached from the standpoint of trying to determine if there was any way that the shooting could have been accidental because there was no reason to suggest either homicide or suicide. The most important considerations were the bullet trajectory through the victim's body and into the ceiling and the soot and powder stippling on the victim's palms and right arm. The bullet trajectory clearly indicated that the man was bent over at the waist with the muzzle of the gun pointing upward when shot. The soot deposits on the palms of both hands were from the gap between the front of the revolver cylinder and the frame (*see* Fig. 17). The weapon was test fired with a piece of white foam board bent over the top of the gun to record the soot deposition from the cylinder gap. The results confirmed that linear deposits like those in the palms would be produced. Figures 18 and 19 illustrate the position of each hand relative to the weapon. Figure 20 shows how the man's hands had to be positioned at the time the weapon discharged. It should also be noted that the location of the powder stippling found on the inside of the right forearm of the victim was simulated with a black marker pen on the arm of the examiner. The position of the weapon, as shown, lined up with the simulated powder stippling.

In order to achieve the 18- to 24-in. muzzle-to-target distance determined through gunshot residue testing, it was necessary for the arms to be extended. The question that remained was how could the weapon be fired unintentionally.

First, the hammer of the weapon had to have been cocked. Then the trigger had to be depressed in order for it to fire. But how could this take place unintentionally? With no ammunition in the weapon, the weapon was cocked and grasped by the examiner with both hands in the manner that the soot deposits indicated. By leaning forward while simultaneously bending at the knees, the butt of the weapon would strike the floor. As this happened, the forefinger of either or both hands could come in contact with and depress the trigger. This would cause the hammer to fall. This reenactment was repeated several times for confirmation.

As a result of the analysis and reconstruction, the following probable sequence of events was proposed: the man undoubtedly had the weapon loaded and cocked as he handled it. He may have been trying to place it on the chest of drawers or he could have been picking it up. He must have partially lost his grip and the weapon started to fall toward the floor. As he stooped over and

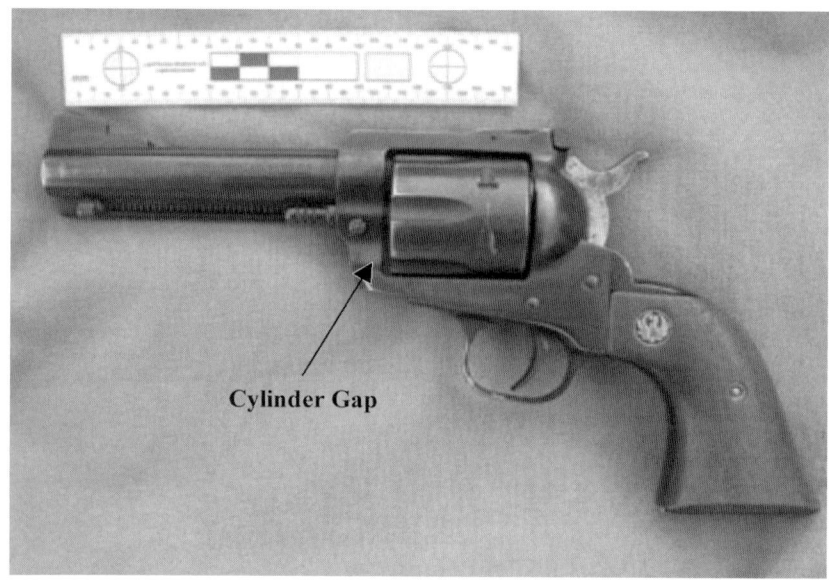

Fig. 17. The weapon.

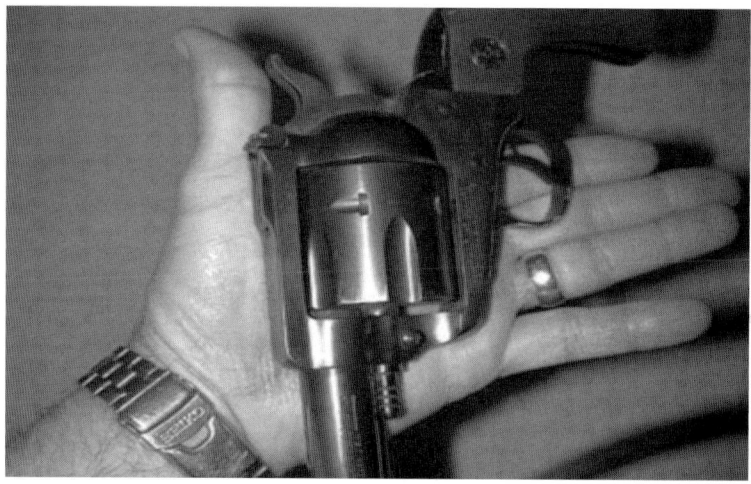

Fig. 18. Left-hand orientation based on cylinder gap deposit on palm.

tried to grab it with both hands, the butt of the gun struck the floor causing one or both of his forefingers to move forward against the trigger and discharge the weapon. The bullet struck him in the lower right chest, passed through his body, exited through his lower right back, and passed through the ceiling. Blood spatter from the exiting bullet was deposited on the ceiling.

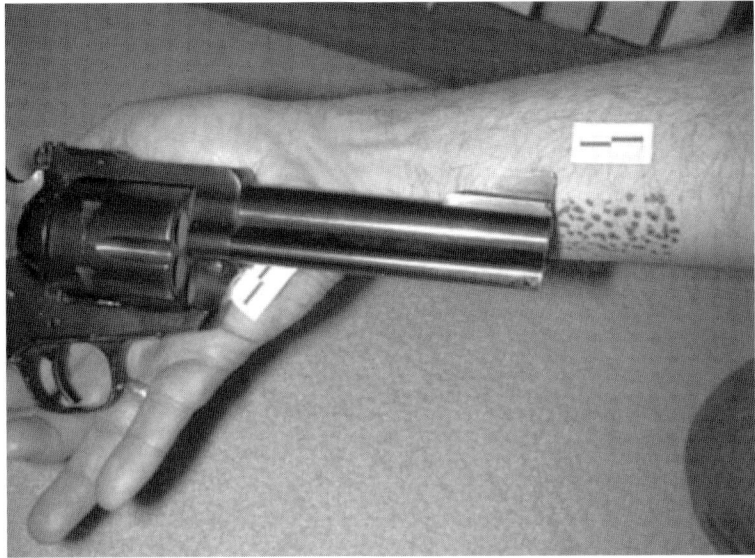

Fig. 19. Right-hand orientation based on cylinder gap deposit on palm and powder. Stippling on inside of right forearm.

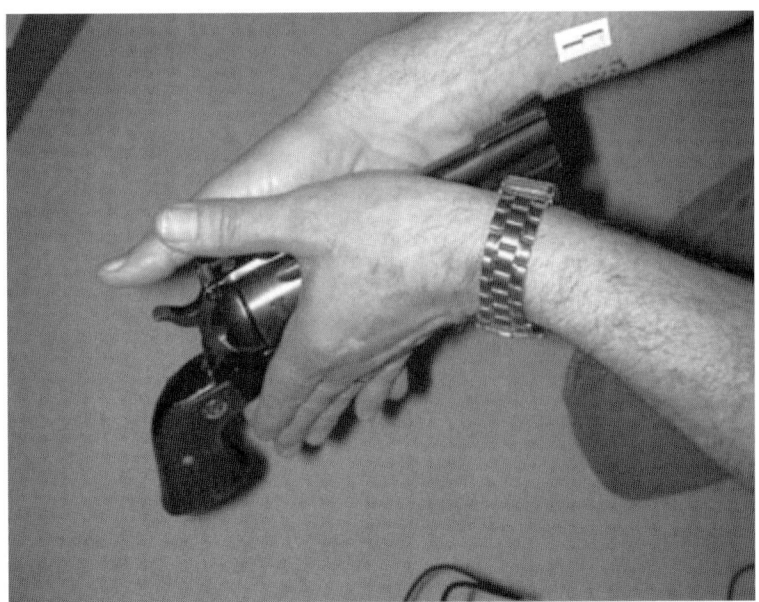

Fig. 20. Position of victim's hands when weapon discharged.

This case shows how the firearm and tool mark examiner can play a vital role in determining what happened in a shooting death with suspicious circumstances. The goal of forensic science, regardless of the particular discipline, is to assist in finding out the truth. It is equally important, if not more so, to show that a crime has not been committed or to exonerate someone as it is to bring a criminal offender to justice.

GLOSSARY

Annular rim:	The outer circumference of the cartridge case base (location of priming mixture in rim fire cartridges).
Antimony sulfide:	A component of most priming mixtures that acts as a fuel.
Ballistics:	The study of projectile motion, often confused with firearms identification.
Barium nitrate:	A component of most priming mixtures that acts as an oxidizer.
Bird shot:	A general term for any shot smaller than buckshot.
Bolt action:	A firearm in which the breech is always in line with the bore and manually reciprocates to load, unload and cock (2 principle types: rotating and straight pull).
Bore:	The interior of a barrel forward of the chamber.
Breech face:	That part of the breech block or bolt which is against the base of the cartridge case or shot shell during firing.
Broach:	Rifling cutter that cuts all the grooves simultaneously.
Buckshot:	Lead pellets ranging in diameter from 0.20 in. to 0.36 in. and normally fired in shotguns.
Bullet:	The projectile portion of a cartridge.
Bullet jacket:	Metallic covering over bullet core.
Caliber:	The cross-sectional diameter of the barrel from land to land.
Calipers:	A device consisting of two moveable jaws or legs used to measure distance, thickness or width.
Cartridge:	Ammunition component consisting of a cartridge case, bullet, powder charge (propellant) and primer.
Cartridge case:	The container for all the other components of a cartridge.
Center fire:	Cartridge with the primer in the center of the base (head).
Chamber:	The rear part of the barrel bore that has been machined for a specific cartridge (revolver cylinders are multi-chambered).
Chamber marks:	Individual characteristics imparted to the chamber walls during machining.
Choke:	Constriction in the muzzle end of a shotgun barrel.
Class characteristics:	Those characteristics exhibited by an entire class or group.
Clip:	A separate device for magazine reloading.

Cock:	To place a firing mechanism under spring tension.
Disk powder:	An extruded form of gunpowder that is cut into small disks.
Double action:	A single pull of the trigger cocks and releases the hammer.
Ejection:	The expulsion of a fired cartridge case or shot shell.
Ejector marks:	Marks left on the base (head) of a cartridge case or shot shell by the ejector during the process of ejection.
Etch:	To produce corrosive action on metal.
Falling block:	A single shot lever action mechanism in which the breech block slides vertically or nearly vertically down as the lever is worked.
Firing pin:	That part of a firearm mechanism that strikes the primer and initiates ignition.
Firing pin impression:	The impression left by the firing pin upon impact with the primer.
Function testing:	The examination of a firearm for operability and firing capability.
General rifling	The number, width and direction of twist of rifling grooves. characteristics:
Griess test:	Chemical test for nitrites used to detect gunpowder residue around bullet holes.
Grooves:	Helical grooves in the interior of the barrel to impart spin on the bullet.
Gunshot residue:	Gunpowder and primer residue resulting from discharge.
Hammer:	That part of the firing pin that imparts energy to the firing pin.
Hammer forging:	Process of forming the interior/exterior of a barrel by hammering.
Individual characteristics:	Accidental, random marks used to identify tool marks.
Lead azide:	Chemical compound used in most priming mixtures.
Lever action:	Type of firearms action that utilizes a lever to move the breech mechanism.
Micrometer:	Precision measuring device used to measure small distances/thicknesses.
Nitrocellulose powder:	A smokeless propellant whose principle ingredient is nitrocellulose.
Nitroglycerin:	A high explosive and component of double-based gunpowder.
Pellet:	Common term for small, spherical shot used in shot shells.
Polygonal rifling:	Rifling with rounded edges instead of the usual square edges.
Powder Stippling:	The result of powder particles striking the skin and imbedding and/or leaving a burn or bruise.

Primer:	Shock sensitive explosive mixture that initiates burning of the propellant.
Propellant:	The powder charge inside a shot shell or cartridge case.
Slug:	Single projectile for a shotgun.
Sodium rhodizonate:	Chemical test for lead.
Tool mark, impressed:	The result of a tool pressed against another surface with enough force to leave an impression.
Tool mark, striated:	A mark produced with a combination of force and motion.

REFERENCES

1. Miller J, McLean M. Criteria for identification of tool marks. AFTE J 1998;30:16.
2. Association of Firearm and Tool Mark Examiners, Theory of Identification, AFTE Glossary, Revision 4, 2002.
3. Biasotti A, Murdock J. Firearms and tool mark evidence. In: Modern Scientific Evidence: The Law and Science of Expert Testimony, Vol. 2. St. Paul, MN: West Publishing, 1997, p. 124–155.
4. Garcia C. Are "knife-prints" reliable evidence: an analysis of tool mark evidence and Ramirez v. State. AFTE J 1993;25:266–279.

SUGGESTED READING

Di Maio V. Gunshot Wounds: Practical Aspects of Firearms, Ballistics and Forensic Techniques, 2nd Ed. Boca Raton, FL: CRC Press, 1999.

James S, Nordby J., eds. Firearm and tool mark examinations. In: Forensic Science: An Introduction to Scientific and Investigative Techniques. Boca Raton, FL: CRC Press, 2003, p. 327–356.

Saferstein R., ed. Firearm and tool mark evidence. In: Forensic Science Handbook, Vol. 2, Upper Saddle River, NJ: Prentice-Hall, 1988, p. 393–450.

Chapter 8

Forensic Odontology
Teeth and Their Secrets

Helena Soomer, DDS, PhD

1. INTRODUCTION

When I was a little girl, I enjoyed playing puzzle games. Although fitting many small pieces carefully together may take some time and effort, the result is always fascinating—a big and truly unique picture! Forensic science is like that. By working with these "puzzle pieces"—the pieces of evidence from a crime scene—the "big picture" almost always results. The resulting picture is a provable reconstruction of what happened, how it happened, and most importantly, who did it. This reconstruction work is done by a team of forensic specialists. They work together at the crime scene to recover, document, collect, and transport the resulting evidence to the crime laboratory for further analysis. Each expert has special skills in his or her area of expertise. The forensic odontologists on these teams are dentists who have such special skills in the areas of forensic dental science, including criminal investigation and identification. They analyze any dental evidence, make forensic conclusions, and testify in court to support their conclusions. Forensic odontologists often play an essential role in identifying either victims of disasters or victims and suspects of individual crimes. They thereby assist the legal authorities in solving crimes and bringing criminals to justice. Forensic odontologists have other roles as well. For example, their activities may range from assisting in archaeological expeditions to assessing bite marks and injuries to the teeth and facial structures for plaintiffs in civil and criminal cases.

From: *The Forensic Laboratory Handbook: Procedures and Practice*
Edited by: A. Mozayani and C. Noziglia © Humana Press Inc., Totowa, NJ

2. WHO IS THE FORENSIC ODONTOLOGIST?

The forensic odontologist is first and foremost a highly trained clinical dentist, familiar with tooth development, oral anatomy, disease pathology, and dental surgery and restoration. The forensic odontologist combines this specialized clinical knowledge with additional investigative skills. For example, the odontologist is trained in collecting evidence and working closely with police investigators and the medical examiner. The forensic odontologist is familiar with the standards for evidence recovery, documentation, and analysis, such as the International Criminal Police Organization (Interpol) standards for victim identification. Thus, forensic odontology crosses the disciplines of clinical dentistry, forensic medicine, and police investigation.

3. WHAT IS DENTAL EVIDENCE?

Dental evidence may include such diverse items as a bite mark impression, the entire dentition of a victim, or just a single fragment of a tooth found at a crime scene. Dental evidence also includes the premortem, or historical evidence of dental treatment, such as textual records, diagrams, and X-rays. Because teeth are the hardest materials of the human body and strongly resist postmortem changes and adverse environmental conditions such as fire, water immersion, or explosion, dental evidence is often available in crime cases. Consequently, forensic odontologists play a vital role in investigations.

For example, our team was once called to the scene of a murder where we found a fractured tooth in a pool of blood next to a murdered man. The forensic odontologist immediately recognized the unique morphological features of this tooth fragment and identified it as the upper left second molar. However, the victim had his second molar, and indeed all 32 of his teeth, in place. The odontologist surmised that the tooth probably belonged to the assailant, who must have been injured severely to lose such a large and firmly rooted tooth so deep in the mouth. Therefore, all emergency medical facilities in the region were alerted to be on the look out for a recent traumatic facial injury. In fact, one hospital had just received a patient who had sustained a gunshot wound to his face. He claimed to have been wounded while cleaning his gun. Our forensic team rushed to the hospital and asked for his panoramic mouth X-ray. The X-ray revealed that, in addition to his other facial injuries from the gunshot, the patient was freshly missing a second molar—consistent with the tooth we found at the crime scene. The patient tried to escape from the hospital after receiving first aid, but was arrested at the door for suspicion of murder. In this case, the forensic odontologist quickly identified the criminal, who would have otherwise escaped early capture. The type of identification procedure described here is called "comparative identification," which consists of the forensic comparison of a person's known dental data (the panoramic mouth X-ray in this case) and the dental evidence found at the crime scene. The result is a determination of whether the dental evidence came from the known person (the suspect in this case). This example shows how the forensic odontologist can play a crucial role in a breaking crime scene investigation.

4. SCOPE OF FORENSIC ODONTOLOGY

Forensic odontology is broadly applicable to criminal investigation, disaster recovery, and civil law cases. Identification of unknown persons is a main focus of forensic odontology. However, forensic odontologists also participate in a wide variety of activities, including scientific research and even in the investigation of ancient civilizations and peoples.

4.1. Identification Work

Identification is one cornerstone of forensic odontology. Whether it involves estimating the age of an illegal immigrant detained in a terrorism investigation without documents, matching victim remains to premortem records in a mass disaster, or identifying a single crime victim, forensic odontologists spend most of their time trying to answer identity questions: Who is the victim with the dental bridge and a missing molar? Who is the criminal who left that bite mark? How old is that detained terrorist?

4.2. Age Estimation

Age estimation helped solve a recent European case where a man was tortured and then murdered in a brutal fashion: his hands were tied and he had received multiple flesh wounds before finally dying. After the murder, the criminal tried to hide the crime by burning the victim. As a result the victim was unrecognizable: the outer layer—hair, skin, and clothing—was completely burned away. However, the teeth were preserved because they are the hardest parts of the body. This victim had shining white teeth, which led the policemen and forensic pathologist in attendance to agree that he must have been young. Fortunately, the forensic odontologist was also in attendance and recognized that the "nice white teeth" were in fact artificial—covered by expensive porcelain veneer. The rear teeth were worn and had moderate periodontal disease. Dental age estimation by the forensic odontologist provided a completely different victim profile: this man was approx 50 yr old and was likely someone wealthy enough to have this expensive veneer work done.

In this investigation the forensic odontologist correctly recognized and correlated a variety of interrelated factors: the normal dental anatomy, the presence of subtle blended restorations, and the age-related pathology and wear patterns. This technique is called "reconstructive postmortem dental profiling." With reconstructive profiling, dental evidence collected from the body is used to determine the victim's profile, including factors such as approximate chronological age, social status (e.g., expensive restorations imply wealth), smoking and dietary habits, and even sex and race.

Dental age estimation is a common dental forensic procedure. It can be done upon intact teeth, as demonstrated in the preceding case, or even more precisely by sectioning the teeth and examining them microscopically. The microscopic exam typically assesses features such as the amount of secondary dentine (a reparative tissue), increased root transparency, root resorption, and the amount of cementum around the root—all of which increase directly with age. The gross appearance of the wear patterns and other microscopic findings are all directly related to a person's age. Several formulae have been derived to calculate age based on these observations and measurements (1–6). The application of reliable dental age estimation techniques (7), as well as assessment of other associated dental features, permit the police to narrow their search among missing persons and, therefore, identify murder or disaster victims more quickly and effectively (8).

4.3. Disaster Identification

Forensic odontologists are crucial team members when investigating small- and large-scale disasters. Dental identification is quick, highly accurate, cost-effective, and can be done on site in most cases. In contrast to other techniques, such as DNA identification, it requires only minimal equipment and logistical support. Typical requirements include electrical power, X-ray equipment, and a computer assisted identification program, such as WinID or Interpol's Disaster Victim Identification (DVI) System, when large amounts of victim data are involved. DNA analysis is a powerful adjunct technique as well, but it is not possible in all cases. For example, just as premortem dental records may be missing, premortem DNA samples may not be available. In some other cases the postmortem DNA may be degraded or contaminated, such as in the case of the fractured tooth mentioned earlier, where the DNA-rich pulp has been exposed to and contaminated with an unknown blood source. However, as that case also showed, the anatomy of the same tooth fragment may be all that is needed to provide an immediately available and crucial clue that can result in an arrest. DNA analysis also requires considerable time, often weeks or even months, because multiple postmortem samples and premortem reference samples must be processed *(9)*. In many cases DNA and dental identification compliment and confirm each other.

4.3.1. Mass Disasters

4.3.1.1. September 11th Attacks

The notorious terrorist attacks on September 11, 2001 included the World Trade Center in New York City. At this location, 2752 deaths were recorded *(10)*. The victims virtually all received severe trauma and therefore more than 19,900 body parts were recovered. Approximately 1435 victims have been positively identified. The main methods of identification were DNA (more than 700 cases), dental (more than 500) and fingerprints (approx 200). In addition, dental identification contributed in 78% of the cases where some other means of identification was conclusive *(10)*. A dental contribution to identification typically meant that there were no discrepancies between ante- and postmortem dental data, but that the dental data alone was not sufficient by itself for positive identification. For example, the dental identification was deemed to contribute if premortem dental information was not unique (e.g., could match several victims, as might be the case if only textual dental records were available and no dental X-rays). Another example of dental identification being contributory was when the premortem dental data was relatively complete but there was only limited amount of postmortem information (e.g., only a small piece of jaw or just one tooth). Dental identification was able to play such an important role in the September 11th disaster in part because premortem dental records in the United States were, generally, highly complete and readily available.

In order to handle the huge amount of data, forensic odontologists working on the September 11th disaster used a computerized dental identification system called WinID. WinID is a database that stores ante- and postmortem dental information about physical descriptors, pathological injuries, and anthropologic findings. These findings are used to match missing persons to the unidentified victims. *(11)*. WinID is one of several available forensic dental computer systems. For example, Interpol offers another computerized identification system that is used in Europe called the DVI system. Unlike WinID, DVI not only has dental identification capabilities, but also is a general purpose forensic tool to store and match other data, such as information about the victim's overall physical description, autopsy findings, personal belongings, DNA profile, etc. Computerized systems have become increasingly important in mass disasters, wherein dozens, hundreds, or even thousands of potential premortem data sets must be matched to postmortem data sets.

Although September 11th is particularly memorable because of the human and economic scale, other mass disasters occur with dismaying frequency. Although airline crashes come to mind most readily, wartime crimes, such as those in Kosovo *(12)* in the mid 1990s, ship or ferry disasters and natural disasters are also significant. Airline and other transportation disasters are particularly notorious and difficult to deal with, perhaps because of their unexpected occurrence and frequently multinational implications. The severe trauma these victims often undergo also presents particular challenges to forensic teams.

4.3.1.2. SAS 686 Crash, Milan, Italy

On October 8, 2001, at Linate Airport in Milan, Italy, an SAS MD87 airplane with 110 crewmembers and passengers on board was ready to take off. It was cleared to reposition itself onto the active runway, but simultaneously a Cessna Citation II jet with two pilots and two passengers on board was taking off on the same runway. Seconds later these two airplanes collided and crashed into an airport baggage hangar, causing the death of four additional victims among the ground staff. The planes caught fire and large pieces of airplane wreckage and multiple body parts flew into the air. Firefighters and rescue crews rushed to the scene, but nobody had survived. The accident claimed a total of 118 victims of nine nationalities *(13)*.

Following this accident, DVI teams from the respective countries involved began work. Some "home" teams stayed in the passengers' countries of origin and collected premortem data, whereas other teams arrived on site to collect postmortem data. Using passenger lists from the airline, the odontologists back in the home countries worked in pairs (checking each others' work) in order to collect and enter all available premortem dental data from dental records into the Interpol DVI system. The on-site teams simultaneously entered the postmortem data into the same system. The DVI software allowed the team members to match the pre- and postmortem data and produce possible matches. I was in Copenhagen at the time and joined the Danish DVI home team in collecting premortem data.

This multinational disaster in Milan involving nine different countries demonstrated several important points. First, forensic odontologists must be familiar with different countries' dental record keeping systems (including legal standards). Dental record-keeping standards in different countries vary widely, far beyond the obvious language differences. Some countries, such as Sweden, have elaborate clinical documentation requirements, whereas other countries have no particular requirements beyond legal minimum standards for billing *(14)*. Second, dental conventions and standards used in the dental record also vary widely. For example, European dental records refer to the right lower third

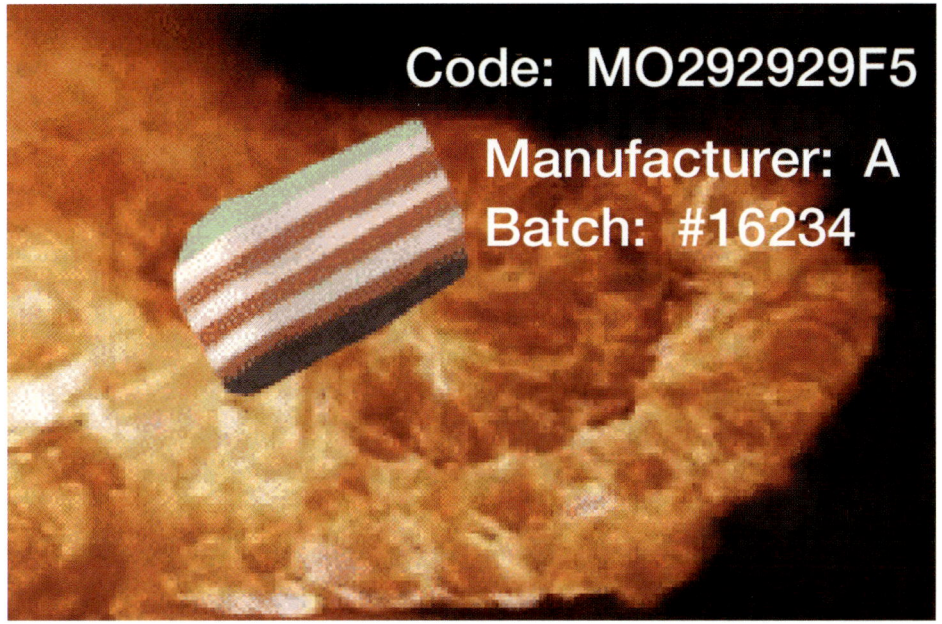

Color Plate 1, Fig. 5. Original version of micro-taggants. (*See* discussion in Ch. 5 on p. 94).

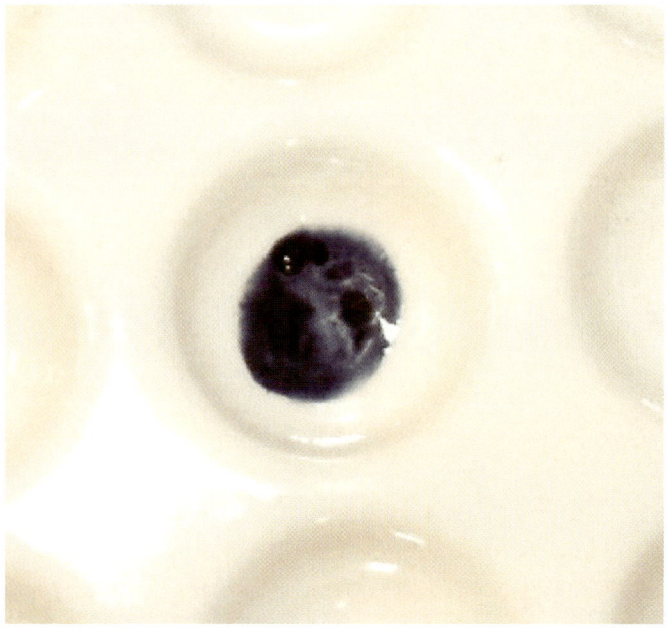

Color Plate 1, Fig. 12. Diphenylamine color test. (*See* discussion in Ch. 5 on p. 98).

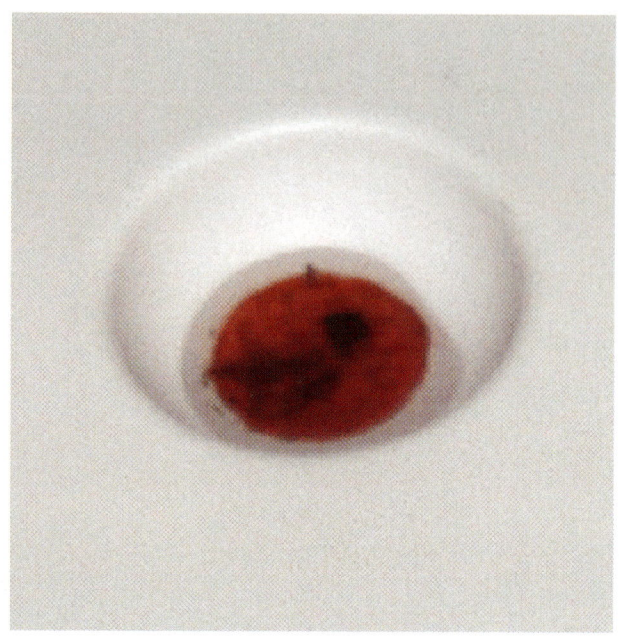

Color Plate 2, Fig. 13. Anatazoline color test. (*See* discussion in Ch. 5 on p. 98).

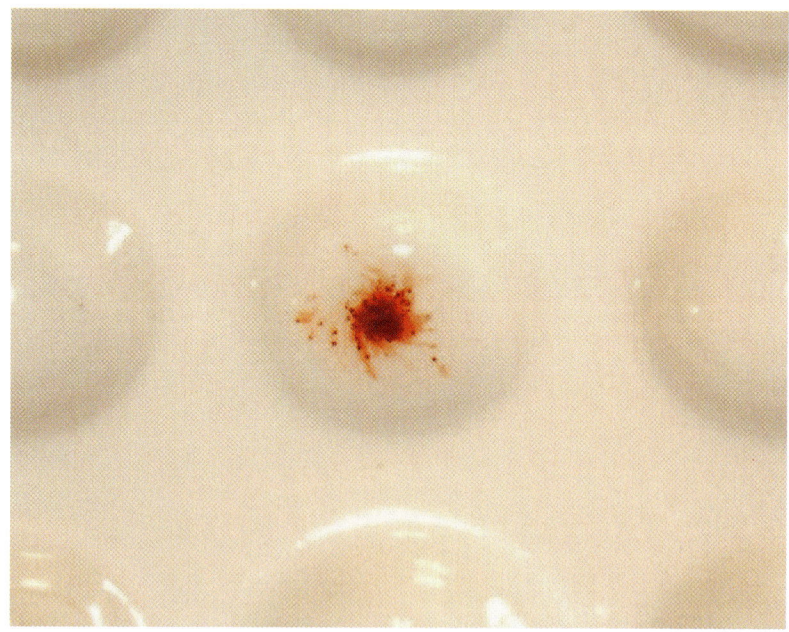

Color Plate 2, Fig. 14. KOH color tests. (*See* discussion in Ch. 5 on p. 98).

Color Plate 3, Fig. 17. TNT fusion melt. (*See* discussion in Ch. 5 on p. 102).

Sodium Nitrate
water recrystallization 100X
crossed poles

Color Plate 3, Fig. 18. Sodium nitrate under crossed poles. (*See* discussion in Ch. 5 on p. 102).

molar as tooth number 48, but in the United States it is called tooth number 32. Forensic odontologists must be aware of these different standards and the various terminology systems used. Third, the Milan disaster also indicates the need for forensic odontologists to reach agreement on international standards to collect premortem and postmortem information, such as the Interpol DVI system and WinID that were previously described. The Interpol DVI system is particularly useful because it serves to integrate the victims' dental, pathological, anthropological attributes (e.g., clothing, documents, jewelry), and personal information. Systems, such as Interpol DVI and WinID, allow the evidence to be combined and viewed in a single system. Both systems also permit remote, on-line collaboration by premortem "home" teams that are physically separated from the on-site teams.

4.3.1.3. Scandinavian Star Ferry Fire

The Scandinavian Star was a European ferry that in 1990 experienced a disastrous arson-caused fire at sea resulting in 158 deaths. Many victims could not be visually identified because they were burned beyond recognition. A team of forensic investigators, including forensic odontologists, was called up to secure evidence for identification. In this case, the fire was so intense and long lasting that some remains were partly ashed, and even the teeth (that usually resist fire) had started to degrade. Because the remains were so fragile, it was crucially important that the odontologists were able to work on site in order to preserve the dental evidence (e.g., by spraying the remaining teeth with fixatives). Otherwise, as the evidence was recovered, documented, and packed for transportation it might well have been accidentally destroyed. The four forensic dental teams involved in the Scandinavian Star accident were based at Institute of Forensic Medicine at the University of Oslo in Norway. These teams used the Interpol DVI forms in their work and all victims were positively identified within 17 d. Dental identity was positively established in 107 cases (68% of the total victims) *(15)*. In cases such as these, dental identification has proven to be extremely effective and reliable.

4.3.2. Interpol's Role in Mass Disasters

Interpol is a global organization of 182 countries whose mission is to prevent and combat international crime and to assist in international mass disasters. I have interned at Interpol headquarters, located in Lyon, France. Interpol sets standards and also identifies, coordinates, and assists national and international forensic teams. The agency provides member countries with necessary resources such as the computerized Interpol DVI system. Interpol also sponsors symposia and meetings for DVI teams where the latest forensic techniques are presented. In summary, Interpol provides a support network for the forensic experts in different countries, so that they can work together more effectively.

In addition to its work assisting DVI teams, Interpol maintains and publishes databases that help governments find missing persons and identify unknown victims. Interpol also provides a network of secure computer databases that are accessible to member countries' law enforcement agencies. These databases include data concerning criminal intelligence information (e.g., trends in international crimes), the modus operandi of various criminal and terrorist networks, and information about variety of police support activities. Interpol's databases and reference collections also encompass comprehensive examples of genuine and fraudulent travel documents (i.e., passports) and currency forgery examples. Finally, Interpol provides a conduit to disseminate information about fugitives and missing persons. Interpol staff members are top-level experts in various areas of policing and forensic sciences. Forensic odontologists and forensic teams should take advantage of Interpol's resources, particularly in the case of disasters or crimes involving international participants. It is important that all law enforcement agencies, including forensic teams, work together in an effort to create a safer world.

5. POLICE CASES

Although mass disasters are prominent news stories, the daily work of forensic odontologists involves assisting in the solution of every day police cases. Suppose, for example, that an old person lives alone and one day his neighbor calls the police because he has not seen him for many days. Then the police and forensic pathologist would go to the house and perhaps find a partly decomposed body in bed. In this case the identity may still be in question, and then the forensic odontologist would be called to verify the old person's identity based on his dental records. This type of work is the bread and butter of forensic odontology. Although this might be termed an ordinary case, the forensic odontologist also becomes involved with fascinating and even notorious criminal cases.

5.1. The Case of an Ambitious Surgeon

In one case I participated in, a well-known female surgeon from a prestigious hospital was suspected of murder. She had an unambitious husband who had lost his job, was known to abuse alcohol, and was reportedly violent. One day she reported her husband was missing. Police started an intensive search. A black garbage bag was found near the victim's home that contained an upper human torso. Soon afterwards another bag was found containing the lower torso. Body parts kept turning up in a gruesome fashion: 1 wk later legs and arms were found and, finally, the head. These body parts were unusual in that they were precisely cut, as if in a medical amputation. In order to verify the victim's identity, the forensic odontologist examined the teeth and compared the findings to the missing man's dental record. Every detail matched, and the missing husband was therefore quickly identified. The wife was later found guilty in this case.

5.2. The Case of a Missing Teen

Sometimes an unusual dental injury or condition can provide the crucial clue needed to establish identity. For example, I participated in one case involving a missing teenage girl who had disappeared without a trace after a birthday party. One year later some skeletonized remains were found, but they were badly eroded because the remains were in a gravel pit. The teeth were the only remains in good condition because (as previously mentioned) they are the most resistant tissues in the human body. Some of these particular teeth were stained in a characteristic pattern—a horizontal, gray line in the enamel—consistent with childhood exposure to tetracycline, an antibiotic normally not given to children. Indeed, medical records showed that the missing girl had accidentally received tetracycline at about 7 yr of age. The stains in the skeletal teeth were in those permanent teeth that would have developed at about age 7. This case shows that teeth may have particular characteristics, such as discoloration owing to antibiotics, which provide relatively unique and important dental evidence that can solve the case.

5.3. The Case of the Pink Teeth

Another example of unusually colored teeth was the result of a postmortem cause, not premortem damage. This was the "case of the pink teeth." Some townspeople came across a set of teeth on a nice spring day when the sun was shining and the resulting snowmelt uncovered a corpse on the bank of a local river. Police were then called to the scene and uncovered a partially skeletonized body with shoes and jacket still on. The male corpse was brought to the morgue for autopsy, where it was found that one of the most remarkable features was that the teeth were pink. The jacket included a wallet and driver's license, indicating that the corpse was that of a taxi driver who had gone missing the previous fall. Therefore, although identification was not in question, the mechanism of death was. The body was partly skeletonized and there was no obvious bullet wound or trauma. However, the pink teeth strongly suggested a death by strangulation. The phenomenon of pink teeth is typically produced by engorgement of the pulp and dentin of the tooth with blood. This can occur when venous pressure in head is raised, such as during strangulation or choking. When this happens the erythrocytes (red blood cells) are released into the tooth's pulp and dentin. Development of this appearance takes a long time after death, as the erythrocytes must decay, and the decay process is aided by a wet environment. These factors were both present in this case *(16)*. The presence of the pink teeth led the forensic pathologist to more closely examine the hyoid bone ("Adam's apple"), which was fractured in a manner consistent with strangulation. The suspect—a late evening passenger—finally confessed that he had strangled the driver from behind in order to take the last of that day's fares.

6. INJURY ANALYSIS

Another cornerstone of forensic odontology is the analysis of injuries. These include bite marks on a victim or a suspect, facial injuries in criminal and civil cases, and malpractice cases. For example, who committed that sexual assault and bit the victim? Did the victim bite back, and, in that case, do the suspect's injuries match the victim's teeth? Was someone's dental injury really caused by that bar fight, or was it pre-existing? These are the sorts of injury questions forensic odontologists answer.

6.1. Bite Marks

One unique branch of forensic dentistry attempts to match a victim's bite mark to the unique dentition of a suspect. These cases are not uncommon. For example, one case involved a young woman who had just left a party and was on her way home. She matched the profile for being a good target: walking alone on a quiet street, distracted by using her cell phone, had long hair that was easy to grab, and was wearing high heels (making it hard to run away). She was later found sexually assaulted and murdered, and a severe and distinctive bite mark was found on one breast. The mark was particularly distinctive because it was an indented, three-dimensional mark. That showed that the bite had been inflicted at the time of death (postmortem) or even shortly after death. If the woman had been alive for even a short time afterwards, the normal reaction of live tissue would have caused the mark to become raised. The finding of the three-dimensional bite mark is significant because it tells us that the person who bit the woman was present and in physical contact with the woman at the time of her death and most likely also responsible for the death. In this case the forensic odontologist who examined this mark matched it to the unique misalignment of the suspect's teeth. The suspect was subsequently arrested, convicted, and sentenced to lifetime imprisonment.

6.2. Facial and Dental Injuries in Civil or Criminal Trauma

Dental injuries occur relatively frequently in family disputes, brawls, and gang fights. The forensic odontologist is sometimes called to determine how the dental injury happened (the trauma mechanism) and what damage was incurred. The forensic odontologist provides evidence that may show who is to blame for the injury, so that a court may subsequently rule who is to pay the costs of the treatment and suffering. For example, in one case I have seen, a man claimed that his front teeth were kicked out in a recent fight. He attempted to get compensation for his injuries from his alleged assailant. However, our examination showed that this "victim" had severe periodontal disease that likely explained the missing teeth, and dental X-rays showed that the bone around the teeth had long been healed. In this case the claim was clearly fraudulent, although that fact would not necessarily be obvious to a lay jury or even to a treating physician. Forensic odontologists are frequently called on to validate assault cases or civil lawsuits for trauma or injury, and they can often provide conclusive testimony.

6.3. Malpractice Cases

Forensic odontologists also take part in malpractice cases. These cases often involve some long-term treatment that has had a poor result. For example, an orthodontic treatment may result in undesirable alignment of the teeth. Malpractice cases can also result from a failure to diagnose. For example, the treating dentist may fail to recognize a cavity. If that cavity then gets bigger and reaches pulp chamber, the tooth often requires root canal treatment and an extensive crown, instead of just a simple filling. In these cases the patient may ask for compensation and the forensic odontologist may be asked to provide evidence.

6.4. Anthropology and Archaeology

Anthropology is also an important field in forensic odontology—and one with surprising applications to criminal cases as well. There was a news report indicating that three sets of fetal remains were discovered in an attic during remodeling. Were these children stillborn, or born alive and then murdered? The forensic odontologist may be called on to provide that answer, and they may do it using the same anthropological techniques used to assess the age and health status of ancient children.

Forensic odontologists may work in collaboration with archeologists to examine persons that are long dead, such as ancient peoples whose remains are uncovered in archeological digs. For example, I have been involved in several anthropological projects involving investigation of skeletal remains of the Middle Helladic period (approx 2000–1700 BCE). These projects involved ancient peoples from the Lerna and Asine areas of ancient Greece, nearby present day Nauplion, Greece. I worked closely with both archaeologists and anthropologists to estimate the age and health of ancient individuals based on their dental remains *(17)*. In the Asine and Lerna studies, the main focus was on children and even fetuses. The death rate was high among young children and infants in ancient Greece. In this study, a subject's health and nutritional status was estimated by examining the extent of dental enamel hypoplasias. Hypoplasias are visible both grossly (when severe) and microscopically. These lesions indicate a reduction in enamel growth, usually resulting from severe illness or malnutrition, which are conditions of great concern to anthropologists.

The anthropologist in this study also wished to determine whether the infant skeletons represented live births or stillbirths. Many infants in the Middle Helladic period were probably stillborn. I was able to estimate whether a fetus had been born alive or was stillborn by determining the presence or absence of the "neonatal line." The neonatal line is similar to an enamel hypoplasia, but represents the changes in dental growth that occur acutely at birth instead of changes related to illness later in childhood. Thus, infants who are stillborn lack the neonatal line because they have not undergone the birth process. The presence or absence of the line is determined by microscopic examination of a sectioned tooth. Such a technique has obvious applications in criminal cases, as indicated in the attic example.

7. How to Become a Forensic Odontologist

Few degree programs in forensic odontology exist, so formal education is not always easy to obtain. After obtaining my dental degree, I took a PhD in forensic medicine with a specialization in forensic odontology. The program, based at the University of Helsinki and University of Tartu, included a set of courses in forensic pathology, death investigation skills, causes of death, and other fields in addition to the dental forensic science. The dental forensic sciences studied included dental anthropology, embryology, and dental development. I also attended special seminars and courses, such as those offered by the United States Armed Forces Institute of Pathology in Maryland and the Karolinska Institute in Sweden. To some degree, forensic odontologists must often put together their own curriculum by combining courses and materials from different institutions. The aspiring forensic odontologist is also well advised to join the

American Academy of Forensic Sciences' Odontology Section and participate at the annual meetings and continuing education activities.

Of course, the very first step to become a forensic odontologist is to go to dental school and become a qualified dentist. Many forensic odontologists are part-time clinical dentists and, even if they eventually give up clinical practice, they will still need to have excellent clinical knowledge. Subsequent training may involve a formal program, but at a minimum has to include investigative skills and a thorough grounding in forensic pathology. The best way to achieve the investigation skills is to work on an active, multidisciplinary forensic team. Being involved in actual case work and training with criminalists, police investigators, and medical examiners is an essential activity. Because no forensic case is routine, the odontologist must be trained to a very high standard. In many cases someone's life is at stake when a forensic examination is performed: a suspect may be convicted or exonerated depending on the forensic evidence. For example, if the suspect's teeth could not have left the bite mark that was observed on the victim's skin, then the suspect could be exonerated. Likewise, based on neonatal line analysis, the forensic odontologist may find that a baby whose body was found discarded was in fact a murder victim, not an unfortunate stillbirth. Small and seemingly unimportant pieces of evidence are almost always worth investigating and so the forensic odontologist must be patient and painstaking in her work. Sometimes, as the first case in this chapter has indicated, even a small tooth fragment can provide the missing piece that unlocks a forensic puzzle.

The next step in becoming a forensic odontologist is to gain an advanced degree if possible and to pursue board eligibility in forensic odontology. As indicated previously, very few advanced degree programs are available. However, there are a number of continuing education courses and short courses that can prepare a forensic odontologist short of a full doctoral degree. For example, the laboratory of Dr. David Senn at the University of Texas at San Antonio offers several such courses. The American Board of Forensic Odontologists does board certification. However, the certification standard is very rigorous and maintaining currency is difficult for forensic odontologists who are not full time. This may explain why only a minority of forensic odontologists actually achieve board certification through the American Board of Forensic Odontologists. One recent study found that highly trained (not necessarily board certified, however), as opposed to medium- and low-trained forensic odontologists, achieved significantly higher identification accuracy *(18)*. This finding strongly emphasizes the critical role of training and recurrent education for forensic odontologists. One cannot emphasize enough how important it is to join a recognized, multidisciplinary forensic team to acquire this training and experience.

8. CONCLUSIONS

Forensic odontology is an exciting field that can combine one's interests in clinical dentistry and criminal investigation. In this exciting field, forensic odontologists may often have the chance to "pull the rabbit out of the hat" and supply the missing piece to a forensic puzzle by means of their detailed knowledge of dentistry, forensic medicine, and criminal investigation.

Forensic odontologists start as highly trained clinical dentists, familiar with tooth development, oral anatomy, disease pathology, and dental surgery and restoration. They combine this specialized clinical knowledge with additional criminal investigative skills in such areas as evidence recovery, documentation, and analysis. This unique combination of clinical and forensic skills makes them uniquely skilled to investigate criminal cases when dental evidence is relevant. Most forensic odontologists participate as part of a wider multidisciplinary forensic team that includes criminalists, police officers, forensic pathologists, and other specialists. Legal cases may quite often turn to the evidence that forensic odontologists are able to interpret. Forensic odontologists often investigate questions of identity in single cases, determine the age of unknown persons living and dead, and analyze facial and dental injury patterns. They almost always play a critical role in mass disaster victim identification, such as the September 11th tragedy. They even play essential roles in purely scientific work, such as forensic anthropology and archeology.

Someone who wants to become a forensic odontologist must first successfully complete dental school and then combine their clinical qualifications with an interest in forensic and criminal matters. Additional training required beyond dental school may consist of attending short-term courses or obtaining an advanced degree in forensic medicine. Most important, the forensic odontologist should join and actively participate in a multidisciplinary forensic team. This teamwork helps to train and keep the forensic odontologist sharp. In this exciting field, forensic odontologists often have the chance to supply the crucial missing piece of a criminal or forensic puzzle that has eluded others.

ACKNOWLEDGMENTS

I wish to kindly acknowledge all of my teachers in clinical dentistry and forensic odontology. I would like to especially thank Dr. Edvitar Leibur of the Faculty of Stomatology, Faculty of Medicine, at the University of Tartu, Estonia and Dr. Helena Ranta of the Department of Forensic Medicine at the University of Helsinki, Finland. I also thank Dr. Antti Pentilla, Professor and Chairman of the Department of Forensic Medicine at the University of Helsinki, who taught forensic pathology, Dr. Tarja Formisto, and Dr. Irena Dawidson (both of Sweden). I acknowledge and thank the Estonian DVI team and its team leader, the Director General of the Estonian Police, Mr. Robert Andropov. I thank the Danish DVI team for inviting me to participate in the Milan SAS crash disaster. My work has been supported in part by grants from the University of Tartu and the University of Helsinki Center for International Mobility. I also wish to thank my husband, Michael J. Lincoln, MD, for his continual support and proofreading.

Glossary

Antemortem:	Before death. Latin *ante* = before, *mortem* = death.
Anthropology:	The scientific study of the origin, the behavior, and the physical, social, and cultural development of humans.
Archaeology:	The systematic study of past human life and culture by the recovery and examination of remaining material evidence, such as graves, buildings, tools, and pottery.
BCE:	Before Common Era. Years are designated as before the Christ's birth.
Cementum:	A bonelike substance covering the root of a tooth.
Decomposed:	Broken down or disintegrated by rot.
Dentine:	The main, calcareous part of a tooth, beneath the enamel and surrounding the pulp chamber and root canals.
DVI:	Disaster victim identification.
Enamel:	The hard, calcareous substance covering the exposed portion of a tooth. It is the hardest substance of the human body.
Embryology:	The branch of biology that deals with the formation, early growth, and development of living organisms.
Hypoplasia:	A condition of arrested development in which an organ or part remains below the normal size or in an immature state.
Interpol:	International Criminal Police Organization. Interpol has 182 member countries and its headquarters are in Lyon, France.
Molar:	A tooth with a broad crown used to grind food, located behind the premolars.
Neonatal:	Relates to newborn infants.
Odontology:	A science dealing with the teeth, their structure and development, and their diseases. Greek *donti* = tooth.
Orthodontics:	The dental specialty and practice of preventing and correcting irregularities of the teeth, as by the use of braces.
Perimortem:	Around the time of death.
Periodontal disease:	A disease that attacks the gum and bone around the teeth.
Porcelain veneer:	Porcelain coating bonded to the surface of a cosmetically imperfect tooth.

Postmortem:	After death. Latin *post* = after, *mortem* = death.
Pulp:	The soft tissue forming the inner structure of a tooth and containing nerves and blood vessels.
X-ray:	A relatively high-energy photon with wavelength in the approximate range from 0.01 to 10 nanometers. A stream of such photons is used for their penetrating power in radiography, radiology, radiotherapy, and scientific research. Also called roentgen ray.

REFERENCES

1. Gustafson G. Age determination on teeth. J Am Dent Assoc 1950;41:45–54.
2. Johanson G. Age determinations from human teeth. Odontol Rev 1971;22 Suppl 21:1–126.
3. Bang G, Ramm E. Determination of age in humans from root dentin transparency. Acta Odontol Scand 1970;28:3–35.
4. Lamendin H, Baccino E, Humbert JF, Tavernier JC, Nossintchouk RM, Zerilli A. A simple technique for age estimation in adult corpses: the two criteria method. J Forensic Sci 1992;37:1373–1379.
5. Solheim T. A new method for dental age estimation in adults. Forensic Science Int 1993;59:137–147.
6. Kvaal S, Solheim T. A non-destructive dental method for age estimation. J Forensic Odonto-Stomatol 1994;12:6–11.
7. Soomer H, Ranta H, Lincoln MJ, Penttila A, and Leibur E. Reliability and validity of eight dental age estimation methods for adults. J Forensic Sci 2003;48(1): 149–152.
8. Pretty IA. The use of dental aging techniques in forensic odontological practice. J Forensic Sci 2003;48(5):1127–1132.
9. Sweet D. Is there a future for forensic odontology in identifying human remains in light of recent advances in DNA technology? Expert Forensic Odontology Workshop, International Committee of the Red Cross, July 14–16, 2003, Geneva, Switzerland.
10. Fallon M, Dobrin LA. OCME/DMORT Recovery Operations of 9/11 at the World Trade Center and Staten Island Landfill; Proceedings of the American Academy of Forensic Sciences annual meeting, February 17–22, 2003, Chicago, Illinois.
11. McGiveny J. WinID-Dental Identification System. http://www.winid.com. Last accessed July 14, 2005.
12. Rainio J, Lalu K, Penttila A. Independent forensic autopsies in an armed conflict: investigation of the victims from Racak, Kosovo. Forensic Sci Int 2001; 116(2–3):171–185.
13. Lunetta P, Ranta H, Cattaneo C, et al. International collaboration in mass disasters involving foreign nationals within the EU: medico-legal investigation of Finnish victims of the Milan Linate airport SAS SK 686 aircraft accident on 8 October 2001. Int J Legal Med 2003;117(4):204–210.

14. Soomer H, Ranta H, Penttila A. Identification of victims from the M/S Estonia. Int J Legal Med 2001;114:259–262.

15. Solheim T, Lorentsen M, Sundnes PK, Bang G, Bremnes L. The "Scandinavian Star" ferry disaster 1990—a challenge to forensic odontology. Int J Legal Med 1992;104(6):339–345.

16. Whittaker DK, Thomas VC, and Thomas RI. Post-mortem pigmentation of teeth. Br Dent J 1976;140:100–102.

17. Ingvarsson-Sundstrom A. Children lost and found. A bioarchaeological study of Middle Helladic children in Asine with a comparison Lerna, with an appendix by Helena Soomer. Uppsala, Sweden 2003. Dissertation available publicly at http://publications.uu. se/uu/fulltext/nbn_se_uu_diva-3289.pdf

18. Soomer H, Lincoln MJ, Ranta H, Penttila A, Leibur E. Dentists' qualifications affect the accuracy of radiographic identification. J Forensic Sci 2003;48(5):1121–1126.

Chapter 9

Forensic Pathology

Joye M. Carter, MD

1. INTRODUCTION

Forensic pathology is the medical component of the forensic sciences. It is also known as "forensic medicine" and often is referred to as "medical legal death investigation." Forensic pathologists are medical doctors who have specialized in pathology and have studied anatomical and clinical pathology as part of their postgraduate medical residency training and then have gone a step further to pursue forensic pathology as a subspecialty by doing a 1- or 2-yr fellowship. Therefore, forensic pathologists have specialized in death investigation.

The foundation of medicine is the study of pathology, which, in its most simple terms, means the study of disease. A physician must understand the process of normal vs abnormal function in all specialties of medicine. Pathology is one of the most important courses that a medical student will encounter in their second year of medical education. It is one of the few pre-clinical science courses that is also, in its own right, an individual medical specialty. After graduation from medical school, a student may choose to specialize in pathology, which means the student will spend a minimum of 6 yr studying the pathological basis of disease. In essence, they will learn all of the other medical specialties that deal with disease and curative processes.

The pathologist studies all organ systems to gain a background in the knowledge of what causes disease and organ failure, as well as learns to diagnose diseases in order to assist the clinicians who are treating living patients. The basis of clinical pathology is to make a diagnosis of disease by examining and testing small pieces of tissue and body fluids in a laboratory.

From: *The Forensic Laboratory Handbook: Procedures and Practice*
Edited by: A. Mozayani and C. Noziglia © Humana Press Inc., Totowa, NJ

Clinical pathologists assist in the treatment of the patient by evaluating the body's response to therapy and by determining blood levels of prescribed drugs in order to assist the attending physician in keeping those drugs within the therapeutic range. Most hospital laboratories are supervised by clinical pathologists.

The basis of *anatomical pathology* is assisting the attending physician in diagnosing diseases in the living patient by biopsy, gross and microscopic evaluation of tissue, cytological (cellular) examination, or in the recently dead patient by the performance of postmortem examination in the hospital setting. There are distinct differences between the hospital and forensic postmortem procedures, which will be discussed later in this chapter.

Most pathology residency programs combine the study of anatomical and clinical pathology so that a well-rounded pathologist is produced who may then choose one or more subspecialties in the pathology field.

Forensic pathology is usually studied in medical examiner's offices. These are government-funded agencies that investigate unnatural deaths in accordance with local law enforcement and public health agencies. The length of a forensic fellowship is generally 1 yr, but it may be extended to 2 yr. It is more of an apprenticeship performed by a doctor who has completed all of the prerequisites in anatomical and clinical pathology. The reason for this format is to ensure that the pathologist has a broad foundation in determining what causes disease and death in order to provide a basis on which to expand with medical legal concepts. During the year of the forensic pathology fellowship, the pathologist learns how to conduct the forensic style of autopsy, work alongside law enforcement officers, and interact with attorneys and grieving families. It is through this type of supervised hands-on work that the novice pathologist begins to embrace the meaning of medical legal death investigation. Forensic pathology is a blend of medical knowledge, an understanding of the legal process in both civil and criminal terms, the development of a sense of investigation, grief counseling, and dealing with the litany of questions from insurance companies and the media. Part of the forensic training is to endow the fellow with the ability to handle the gigantic amounts of paperwork that will accompany each case with which he becomes involved.

The most ominous and distinguishing fact about becoming a forensic pathologist is the need for the doctor to confront his beliefs about death and face his fears before he is confronted with the reality of death investigation. No other forensic science professional is as closely associated with the death and dying process as the forensic pathologist.

2. FORENSIC PATHOLOGISTS, MEDICAL EXAMINERS, AND CORONERS

Forensic pathology is one of the few nonhospital based medical specialties. Forensic pathologists are employed by city, county, or state organizations to investigate deaths of citizens in those jurisdictions and perform their work from medical examiner's offices. When the pathologist is employed by the government, his title is medical examiner. In some states, the term *medical examiner* is sometimes used by state licensing boards to describe those physicians who perform insurance physicals, leading to some potential confusion. The medical examiner carries out postmortem examinations and death investigations in accordance with local public laws, some of which may be unique to that particular government. Within the law, the medical examiner is charged with determining the cause and manner of death, producing a written autopsy report, maintaining the vital records of death for the region, and testifying as a neutral entity in court.

There are other government agencies that may be confused with the medical examiner's office and their unique functions. The public often equates the title of coroner with medical examiner. Coroners are elected officials who, as part of their routine duty, may be called on to certify a death that occurs in their jurisdiction. Coroners may also hold inquests to try to determine how a person died. Coroners are not usually physicians and they generally hire pathologists to conduct the autopsies. The pathologist sends a report of the results of the postmortem examination to the coroner or uses some other means of communication to inform the coroner of his findings so that the elected official can complete the death certificate.

In some jurisdictions there is another elected official with functions similar to the coroner, the justice of the peace (JP). Both JPs and coroners are elected by popular vote and have constituencies to respond to. Certifying deaths is a small part of what these government officials do on a daily basis for the public. Frequently, the elected official has only a whirlwind introductory course in rudimentary death investigation after they are elected to their positions. The best systems are where the coroner and medical examiner coexist in the same place or the coroner contracts with properly trained forensic pathologists to perform the postmortem examinations, who then notify the JP or coroner as to the results of the autopsy. Then the official may complete the death certificate using the proper medical terms.

In contrast to the elected official, medical examiners are appointed by the governing body in their local jurisdiction and they have no constituents to answer to. This enables the medical examiner to make the sometimes unpopular decisions that are required in the field of death investigation without concern for re-election. Medical examiners are meant to be neutral. For this reason the medical examiner will be able to provide professional services to the criminal justice system by working with both prosecutors and defense attorneys in an effort to achieve a more balanced criminal justice system.

3. DIFFERENCES BETWEEN THE HOSPITAL AND FORENSIC AUTOPSY

It is important to understand the differences between the approach to an autopsy performed in the hospital and the forensic autopsy performed in the medical examiner's office. In the hospital an autopsy is not automatically done unless the family gives consent. The family may also limit what areas of their loved one's body are examined or they may deny the autopsy procedure completely. The hospital autopsy is performed on a known individual and not on a deceased patient who is unidentified. In the hospital setting, an autopsy is done to evaluate prior medical treatment or a known disease entity. The hospital pathologist conducts the postmortem examination and then communicates the results to the treating physician, who then completes the death certificate. The hospital autopsy report is the last entry on the patient's medical chart and is protected by medical record laws.

In contrast, the forensic autopsy is conducted in a government facility in accordance with public law and consent is not sought from the next of kin. This is because the law requires that the postmortem examination be done to satisfy the citizen's need to know why this particular death occurred and when certain conditions existed which may have contributed to or resulted in that death. Those conditions may include unnatural situations, such as homicides, suicides, drug overdoses, accidents, child abuse, unidentified persons who have received medical treatment, deaths of persons that happened in public spaces (e.g., sudden death on the sidewalk, bus, or airplane), deaths that have occurred in police custody, cases where allegations of medical malpractice exist, or cases that threaten the general public health. The code of criminal proceedings of most jurisdictions contains a list of what types of deaths require the intervention of the medical examiner. The forensic autopsy is considered confirmatory and evidentiary and the written report is a legal document, not a medical record. The forensic autopsy report is available under public information requests in most jurisdictions.

The forensic autopsy is a complete examination of the entire body. This means all body cavities and organs will be opened and examined, microscopically sampled, and described. In contrast to the hospital autopsy, in a forensic autopsy it is important to determine if a person who was shot numerous times also had evidence of cardiac disease. It may be a factor in understanding why and how certain individuals survive and others succumb to fatal injuries. The forensic autopsy is considered confirmatory because it helps the forensic pathologist and law enforcement officials understand the relationship of the dead body to other evidence recovered at the scene of death. The forensic autopsy may be conducted for reasons other than determination of a disease or injury, for example the identification of the victims in mass transportation accidents. Therefore the forensic autopsy is a documentation procedure that is not duplicated by the hospital procedure. The documentation aspect of the forensic approach is multitiered, where diagrams are drawn, photographs are taken, and hand-written notes may be used. All of the associated written documents become part of the permanent record file, which may then be subpoenaed as part of the medical examiner case folder.

During the forensic autopsy small amounts of body fluid and tissue are usually retained for additional laboratory tests in order to assist in answering the question of what, if any, drug or poison played a role in the person's death. Toxicology is not a part of the hospital autopsy procedure. Any suspicion of a drug-induced death in the hospital must be reported to the local medical examiner or coroner office. Although both hospital and forensic autopsies are performed by pathologists, the hospital pathologist may not have all of the training required to perform a complete forensic case.

Compared with other medical specialties, there are relatively few forensically trained and board-certified pathologists. Currently, there are approx 500 certified forensic pathologists with the American Board of Medical Specialties, a division of the American Medical Association. Because of the nature of medical legal death investigation and its being outside the scope of the hospital system, many pathology-training programs send their residents to their nearby medical examiner facility to gain some autopsy experience and a proper introduction to the world of forensics.

It is important to understand the volume of forensic cases in the medical examiner's office as compared to that of the hospital. A hospital may have a request for an autopsy once a week or less. The medical examiner faces countless autopsies on a daily basis. Large metropolitan medical examiner's offices perform thousands of postmortem examinations annually.

In general, the hospital autopsy procedure is reserved for hospital patients who have died after receiving care in the facility and whose medical history is known to the health care institution. Hospital autopsies involve natural deaths of patients with known identity and medical history. The forensic autopsy encompasses a broader array of categories of deaths and is a much more thorough examination.

4. RESPONSIBILITIES OF THE MEDICAL EXAMINER

The medical examiner is responsible for the performance of the autopsy on the deceased, for the certification of that death by completing the vital death certificate record, and for giving expert testimony in court. These are only a few of the responsibilities familiar to the layperson.

The medical examiner is responsible for the body when it is recovered from the scene of death. The medical examiner does not automatically respond to a scene when a call comes over the police radio. The pathologist must be invited to the scene by law enforcement, who are in charge of the scene with the exception of the dead body. One of the most common misconceptions portrayed by the media is that the stereotypical forensic pathologist needs only a brief encounter with a corpse at the scene of a homicide before relaying a huge volume of information to the lead police officer. This television medical examiner has determined the extent of mortal injury without ever having even turned the body over. In reality, the forensic pathologist gives scant and preliminary information at the scene followed by a thorough examination in the proper setting, the morgue.

The medical examiner is also responsible for maintaining the records of the forensic death investigation. These records are kept in the course of ordinary business and are part of the vital records. Unlike health care institutions, the medical examiner records cannot be destroyed and must be archived and easily retrieved when called for. This requires extensive record storage systems in these offices. Because there is no statute of limitations in medicine, any case may be reopened at any time. One of the biggest sources of frustration in the medical records section of the medical examiner's office is the retrieval of ancient records that were developed prior to the age of the computer and have been damaged by age, humidity, and critters. Seldom is the medical examiner budget increased to assist in record management.

The medical examiner has the unique responsibility to help the grieving family understand what has happened to their loved one. Unlike the rest of the forensic science field, one must remember that forensic medicine is not an exact science. The medical examiner will have direct interaction with the family members, who are trying to comprehend the tragic death of their loved one. The comforting of these people seldom has as much to do with scientific logic as it does with the pathologist's ability to be a sympathetic listener.

The forensic pathologist's role in the courtroom is also unique among forensic scientists. The medical examiner is expected to be a neutral source of information to both the prosecuting attorney and the defense attorney. The medical examiner testifies as an expert on the factual nature of the case, as well as expounds on the medical possibilities through hypothetical questions posed by both attorneys. In a perfect world, there would only need to be one forensic pathologist involved in a single trial. However, the adversarial nature of our criminal justice system often pits medical examiners and other forensic pathologists against one another in the quest for an outcome in favor of a particular side. Although many opinions of forensic scientists are supported by their scientific reports, the medical examiner often bases his opinion of the cause or manner of death on his experience, training, peer review, or literature search to support his findings. There have been instances where so many expert medical witnesses were paraded in front of the juries that the jury members became thoroughly confused, defeating the purpose of forensic testimony whose sole purpose is educating the jury.

Probably the most overlooked responsibility of the medical examiner is the promotion of social change. The forensic death investigation process provides a tremendous amount of information. Without sharing that information, lives would be lost. There is a need for the forensic pathologist to share what he has learned from the autopsy so that other people may benefit from his work. Medical examiners are responsible for educating those physicians involved in direct patient care of the advances in disease detection and the effectiveness of the therapy that their patients had received. Although the information is not going to bring the deceased person back to life, it may help the next person. Most forensic pathologists feel as though they are contributing to the improvement of society by fulfilling their duties in the courtroom.

Few people realize how important a role the medical examiner plays in the safety of consumer products. Medical examiners and coroners report any product associated with the death of a person to the National Consumer Products Safety Commission in Washington, DC. This assists in the removal or modification of unsafe items and runs the gamut from toys to washing machines to pajamas. Many forensic pathologists gain satisfaction from engaging in primary research or lecturing to medical groups and the public on some of the preventable causes of death in our communities.

5. DETERMINING THE CAUSE AND MANNER OF DEATH

The determination of the cause and manner of death is the best example of the forensic pathologist's departure from the hard and fast rules of basic science, where scientific determinations should be able to be duplicated using a similar set of calculations. The cause and manner of death are opinions made by the medical examiner based on all of the available information for each death that is certified. That opinion may be influenced by the doctor's training, experience, and information provided by law enforcement investigators.

The cause of death is generally defined as the disease or injury that resulted in the death of the person. *Immediate* causes of death are those situations in which there is a short interim period between the onset of disease of injury and the death of the individual. Examples of immediate causes of death are a person who dies from a heart attack, a person who dies shortly after sustaining severe blunt trauma injuries in an automobile accident, or a person who dies from gunshot wounds while undergoing surgery.

In contrast, a *proximate* cause of death is defined as those situations in which there has been a delay between the initiating disease or injury and the ultimate death of the person. Determining the proximate cause of death is often much more problematic and should include a series of foreseeable events that may be tied to the initiating injury or disease process. Examples of proximate causes of death would be a stab wound victim who dies several weeks after the injury because of infection attributed to the complications of the stab wound. Another example would be a case where there was documented exposure to asbestos fibers that resulted in the development of mesothelioma after several years. Often the ruling of a proximate cause of death creates more work for law enforcement. When the victim of a gunshot wound dies 20 yr after the original event, the death may be ruled a homicide. This type of ruling causes the police to undertake an investigation where the alleged perpetrator may already have died, as well as alter that year's statistics on violent crime. There will be a homicide ruling by the medical examiner, but no charges will be filed because there are statutes of limitation with the law but not with medicine. This is one of the factors that needs to be examined when the number of violent crimes investigated by medical examiner's offices is not in agreement with the number reflected in the statistics of law enforcement agencies.

The distinctions between immediate and proximate causes of death are important because of the legal ramifications for civil and criminal proceedings. There is a need for the medical examiner to obtain as much information about the decedent as possible before rendering an opinion on the cause of death. When new or relevant information becomes available, those involved in forensic science must understand that any case may be reopened and reviewed.

The manner of death is an expressed opinion by the medical examiner as to how the death occurred. This opinion is based on all available knowledge of the circumstances of the death. The autopsy by itself does not determine the manner of death.

The general designations for manner of death are natural, accident, homicide, suicide, and undetermined. In some regions there may be a listing on the death certificate of *pending*. Pending means that the cause and/or manner of death have not been determined and there is a need for further information. The classification of "undetermined" means that the medical examiner has exhausted all of his sources of information or is unable to determine what caused the person's death. There are a variety of examples, but the best one is actually based on a fictitious television character.

Several years ago, the television series *Quincy* featured a show about a single bone found on a development site during construction. Quincy succeeded in determining exactly who that bone belonged to and the person's whole life story, without the aid of DNA. In real life, a single bone found without any physical clues and without running any standardized laboratory tests would most likely result in an undetermined manner of death.

In general, the classification of manner of death reflects a totality of the information that has been gathered in the death investigation, which includes the autopsy findings, police report, medical records, witness statements, social background, and any other available and reliable data. This information may change depending on laboratory results or further investigation. Sometimes, another medical professional decides that the classification should be changed after a review of a particular case. Sometimes new information comes to light that leads to the re-examination of the facts and a change in the manner or cause of death. The forensic pathologist must sometimes face situations where his work has caused an innocent person to be imprisoned or worse. All that the medical professional can do is his best every day.

The real value of defining the cause and manner of death outside of the criminal justice system is for statistical reasons. The certifier, on the death certificate, is supposed to have the best knowledge of what events may have occurred to cause the death of the individual. This information is gathered as part of the local vital records bureau and is formulated into data that can then be shared with nonmedical people who make decisions about the needs of their populations, e.g., politicians who pass laws about when to fund preventative health care programs or state transportation departments who place stop signs at intersections where there have been several fatal traffic accidents.

Certification of death may be very complex when dealing with violent deaths, insurance companies, and the legal system. The medical examiner must be well versed in his medical training and experienced in forensic pathology, as well as have the ability to form sound opinions based on the available information. The situation may arise where pressure is brought to bear on the certifying official because his opinion is in contrast to another's. This means that the forensic pathologist must be able to voice his findings in an atmosphere free of external pressure, such as politics or media speculation.

6. Scene Investigation

The forensic autopsy cannot be performed in a vacuum. There must be interaction with those who are investigating the incident from a law enforcement standpoint and those who are testing the evidence from a scientific viewpoint. This calls for team investigation and excellent communication between the different entities. Scene investigation is the beginning of the forensic involvement in the crime. Generally, the police investigate the scene of death and the medical examiner is invited onto the scene to examine the dead body. At the time of notification that a dead body has been found, the medical examiner takes charge of the corpse. The forensic examination at the scene is a cursory one where limited information is given to the police to assist them in their investigation. This allows for a more thorough examination in the proper setting, the morgue. There are often physical hazards at the scene that may hamper the collection of evidence. Unlike our media counterparts, who can determine the exact injury without disrobing the dead body and can direct the police to which exact weapon to search for, the release of limited information at the scene is best undisclosed until the complete autopsy has been performed. The main reason for the medical examiner to visit the scene is to be able to correlate the findings from the scene and make meaningful interpretations of the autopsy results. Many forensic pathologists believe that the "autopsy begins at the scene."

Of course it is not always possible for the medical examiner to visit the scene of death because of the location, time of the event, or manpower shortages. The pathologist may need to rely on police information or have trained investigators respond to scene on the medical examiner's behalf.

Currently, there are national certifying examinations and training programs for medical examiner death investigators. Death investigators are usually nonmedical people who have varied backgrounds in law enforcement, emergency response, or a criminal justice education, are trained in basic forensics to document the crime scene and relate their findings to the medical examiner. There is also a relatively recent medical specialty, forensic nursing, that fills the void when there are not enough death investigators to perform scene investigation. Forensic nurses, in addition to having formal nursing degrees, have been trained in the basic forensic principals of scene documentation, medical record review, and sexual assault examination.

7. ESTABLISHING A MEDICAL EXAMINER'S OFFICE

The establishment of a medical examiner's office can be an expensive proposition. Medical examiner facilities are funded by the taxpayer and their size is limited by the size of the population and the amount of forensic work in the immediate vicinity. The expense comes from the need for special architecture, plumbing, security requirements, sewage treatment, specialized equipment, vehicles, and highly trained staff. To the average politician, the needs of the dead come second to the needs of the living. It is often when a heinous crime is committed or some problem results in a miscarriage of justice that proper funding is given to the death investigators. It seems to be widely practiced to ignore what goes on in a medical examiner building until it involves a personal loss.

The function of a medical examiner's office would never be accomplished if not for a small army of dedicated employees, each doing his or her part for the good of the community. There is a lot of attention placed upon the shoulders of the chief medical examiner, but there is a tendency to overlook the other staff that makes the whole office responsive to the requirements of thorough death investigation. The chief medical examiner is the head of the agency and he is usually appointed to that position. Literally, the buck stops with him. All of the problems and complaints go to the chief. This physician not only must be well trained, experienced, and board certified in forensic pathology, but also must exhibit firm resolve and a vision to continue the improvement of death investigation for the community. Like the head of any company, the other employees look to their chief for leadership.

Next to the chief medical examiner, there should be one or more deputy chief medical examiners who assist in the overall day-to-day case management of the forensic investigations. These physicians should also be board certified in all areas of pathology and should be able to serve as a stand in for the chief in his absence.

Next in line come several assistant medical examiners who perform the daily examinations and confer with the senior medical examiners. These physicians should be board certified in forensic pathology or be eligible to obtain board certification. The most important thing that the senior medical examiner staff can do for the assistant medical examiners is to ensure that these physicians do not become overwhelmed with the workload. The paperwork and court testimony seem to accumulate so fast with the individual cases that the junior staff may suffer from burnout and become derelict in their daily function. One of the most daunting problems with staffing a medical examiner's office is the low numbers of pathologists who are interested in performing forensic examinations. There never seems to be enough forensic pathologists to serve the needs of the medical examiner's office or the community. One reason is that these physicians, employed by the local government, do not make a salary comparable to the private sector. That factor takes on greater importance when these doctors have families to support and student loans to repay, for example.

To assist the limited number of available certified medical examiners, there will need to be several investigators who are certified in forensic investigation. There is now a national examination for these employees, which helps them to focus on the forensic aspects of crime scene investigation from the medical examiner's perspective. In the past, the forensic investigator received on-the-job training, but as forensic science has become more sophisticated in its procedures, so has the need to have more formally trained death investigators. Today there are criminal justice programs and forensic nursing curricula that instill the forensic principles of investigation into these helpful assistants.

Often overlooked is the absolute need for excellent transcriptionists, either as in-house clerical staff or as employees of private companies that have signed confidentiality agreements and who are connected to the medical examiner's office electronically. Many offices choose to maintain an in-house system to protect the sensitive nature of the cases and are afraid of the newer electronic pirating techniques that endanger the confidentiality or security of the case file. It is unfortunate that the long-term effects of the descriptions of the violence and wounds on the transcriptionists are often overlooked. It is recommended that these staff have the opportunity to debrief when particularly vile cases are examined in the office.

The autopsy assistant is a person who assists the doctor in the perfor- mance of the autopsy. Although these individuals are sometimes referred to as "dieners," the term is considered offensive and should not be used. These men and women are extremely important to the smooth functioning of the morgue area in the medical examiner's office. The autopsy assistants have many responsibilities outside of the autopsy suite as well. They often are utilized to pick up the corpses from the scene of death or health care institutions. The assistants may find themselves in perilous conditions when trying to remove a corpse from a precarious position. The autopsy assistants are also involved with the release of the body to the authorized funeral director. They are involved with the intake of the dead body when it arrives at the morgue. The autopsy assistants play an integral role in the training of "green" forensic pathology fellows, as the doctor gets used to the atmosphere of the morgue. The assistants often help the doctor fine tune his or her autopsy skills, as well as teach him or her the secrets of difficult dissections. The autopsy assistants usually have received on-the-job training and may have some background in mortuary science. These individuals must be trustworthy and must be treated like the valuable members of the team that they are. It would be extremely difficult for any medical examiner's office to run without autopsy assistants.

The forensic photographer has become an important part of the medical examiner's office and is much more sophisticated than the casual photographer of the past. These people are formally trained photographers with backgrounds in computer images, videography, and criminal justice. It is a relatively new specialization, but, as the knowledge progresses in forensic science, so does the need for accurate documentation. The forensic photographer interns in a medical examiner's office so that he gains experience in filming the dead body and forensic evidence and develops expertise in crime scene photography. The photographers are another way in which the medical examiner's office can maintain its autonomy from law enforcement in the crime scene investigation process. It is better to have a completely independent view of a crime scene than to rely on another investigative entity. The forensic photographer has become an invaluable member of the crime lab as well as an integral part of the trace evidence team. Although expensive to maintain, no well-run medical examiner's office can afford to go back to using amateur photographers when the stakes of proper forensic investigation are so high.

Modern medical examiner's offices need business offices to handle the medical records, collection of fees, case requests from the attorneys, courts, and insurance companies, and to assist the bereaved family members. The business section usually has a few administrators to handle the clerical issues, benefits of the employees, and record management. Because the medical examiner records may never be destroyed, there is an urgent need for those skilled in this administrative area. The business office is often overlooked when the issue of budget is on the table, but becomes a glaring issue when medical examiner records are unable to be located.

Because the medical examiner may encounter almost any type of death investigation, it is important to maintain a small number of vital consultants whose individual specialties help make the medical examiner's job less difficult. The most commonly requested consultants are forensically trained dentists (forensic odontologists), cardiovascular pathologists, neuropathologists (specialists in the brain and central nervous system), forensic anthropologists, and pediatric pathologists. These individuals are highly specialized and may be available on a regional basis depending on the location of the medical examiner's office.

Many medical examiner's offices stand alone as autonomous government agencies, but most offices now have a forensic toxicology laboratory as part of their facility to conduct on-site drug testing on the autopsy victims. Several large medical examiner departments now have their own forensic science laboratories to conduct the forensic examination of evidence recovered from the body at the time of autopsy or recovered from the crime scene. This system enables the direct establishment of chain of custody for handling forensic evidence. The relationship of the medical examiner to the crime laboratory also underscores the need for the team approach to death investigation. The medical examiner relies on the nuances and updates in the realm of forensic science to assist with solving forensic problems. The crime laboratory relies on forensic questions to explore new and more scientific means of testing evidence and furthering the quest for knowledge. Because forensic medicine is not purely based on scientific data, the mix of the two specialties is a win–win situation for both and the criminal justice system.

8. CONCLUSION: "REEL" FORENSICS MUST NOT REPLACE "REAL" FORENSICS

Unfortunately, the specialty fields of forensic science must compete with the media and public fascination with popular stereotypical characters that seem to grace our television screens on a nightly basis. First there was the character of "Quincy, M.E.," who was a medical examiner from the 1970s era. Dr. Quincy in television reality was a surgeon who became a forensic pathologist after his wife died and he was unable to save her utilizing his surgical skills. According to the story line, he decided to go into the completely different medical specialty of forensic pathology, but the story line never explained if he went back and studied for an additional 5 yr to learn forensic pathology. Dr. Quincy was known for defying all medical and scientific reason by doing the impossible and solving all of his cases, often by last minute laboratory procedures that were developed overnight, in many cases by his faithful assistant, Sam. Sam was the brains behind the fictionalized Dr. Quincy character. The show certainly should be given credit for bringing the world of forensic science to the attention of the television viewing public. However, the ideas of real forensic science and procedures were blurred in the show and in the minds of many people who watched as crimes were solved and questions answered week after week. To this day, there are many who believe that if the science is shown in the media then it must be real. That concept is, unfortunately, applied when jurors are asked to render decisions based upon scientific evidence presented in a courtroom. How many times did the laboratory assistant Sam developed an untested procedure in the nick of time to help Quincy solve a case? There are many professionals today who still believe that the medical examiner always knows the exact time of death, down to the minute. There have been instances where I have explained to a jury panel that the only way for me to tell them the exact time of death would be if I had committed the crime. Repetitive procedures shown in the visual media format have a way of seeming true to the viewing public.

In the 1990s, the emphasis in the media portrayal of death investigation was coupled with the police investigation, almost to the exclusion of the defense team being a part of any meaningful discussion in the administration of justice. The medical examiner was often depicted as a female (in inappropriate dress) who was able to determine the exact time of death and describe the exact weapon used by the alleged assailant to police to aid their investigation. Seldom, if ever, was the medical examiner shown in conference discussing the case in a neutral manner with the defense attorney. Indeed, the medical examiner was always closely associated with the district attorney and police officers. The crime laboratory became more important in its supporting role, as the science of DNA became more widely accepted in the court. The crime laboratory personnel were portrayed as having close association with the prosecution team. Both of these characterizations have been detrimental to the actual relationships between forensic scientists and real life attorneys.

In the new millennium, the focus has been directed to television crime scene investigation with fabulous studio laboratories that hardly live up to the local medical examiner and crime laboratories, which are begging continuously for funding to carry out the standard level of scientific analysis that is demanded in today's modern court proceedings. With the emphasis on ultra modern laboratories and use of new methods of working evidence, the need for the police detective has been relegated to improper intrapersonal relationships. The crime scene investigator is doing all of the investigation, questioning of suspects, and often arresting the presumably guilty party. The crime laboratory is more akin to a museum of modern art than a governmental agency funded by the taxpayer. Now the emphasis is placed on the sexy crime scene investigator and the savory way that evidence is processed. Again the roles of the medical examiner and crime laboratory personnel are tightly linked to the prosecutorial component of the criminal case. There seems to be little room for the accurate portrayal of neutrality in the actions of the forensic scientist, thus leading to the adversarial relationships in the courtroom drama that seems to spill over into real life. The question becomes: Which is imitating the other, art or life?

The bottom line is that forensic science is a wonderful and diverse field that, through old and new laboratory techniques, is able to assist in the investigation of criminal acts and help the victims through the gathering of information and the presentation of such data in a neutral manner that lends itself to the administration of justice. Forensic pathology is but one part of the forensic puzzle that comes together in unison, while maintaining the necessary but separate existences in order to achieve the lofty goal of balanced criminal justice. The fact that a medical doctor can participate in the criminal justice system in this manner is exciting and meaningful to the process of death investigation as we learn more and more about this topic. The pursuit of an education in forensic pathology is a noble idea that is not mentioned enough. There exists a need for more well-trained forensic pathologists across this country and beyond its borders, as the subject of death investigation takes on global significance. Perhaps this information will help enlighten those who looking for a means to contribute to the science and investigation of forensics.

GLOSSARY

Anatomical Pathology:	Pathology study directed at detecting diseases and treatment modalities in the patient by examining the tissue of the human body.
Clinical Pathology:	Pathology study directed at the detection of disease through examination of body fluids and cells and includes laboratory identification of metabolic abnormalities and microbiological organisms.
Coroner:	An elected official who has the duty to investigate deaths of the citizens in his local jurisdiction, often hiring pathologist to perform post mortem examinations.
Forensic Pathologist:	Medical doctors who specialize in the study of diseases and injuries that lead to death and conduct medicolegal investigations.
Forensic Pathology Fellowship:	Postgraduate medical study conducted in a medical examiner office after pathology residency.
Medical Examiner:	A forensically trained pathologist who is employed by a goverment entity to investigate death of citizens under criteria established by the state, county or local ordinances.

SUGGESTED READING

DiMaio DJ and DiMaio VJM. Forensic Pathology, 2nd ed. New York: Elsevier, 2001.

Froede RC, ed. Handbook of Forensic Pathology. Northfield, IL: College of American Pathologists, 1990.

Spitz WU, ed. Medicolegal Investigation of Death: Guidelines for the Application of Pathology to Crime Investigation. Springfield, IL: Charles C. Thomas, 1993.

Chapter 10

Assuring Quality in the Crime Laboratory

William J. Tilstone, PhD

1. GETTING IT RIGHT

At the time of writing this chapter, forensic science is under considerable pressure from scientific peers, the legal community, and the public for what they regard as poor standards of practice. The reality is much different. Laboratories process hundreds of thousands of cases each year in a timely manner and without errors of fact or interpretation. This is achieved in laboratories because of the application of resources and personal commitment to quality assurance. The aim of this chapter is to give the nonforensic scientist an insight into what is involved in assuring quality in the crime laboratory.

1.1. Quality Assurance Standards

Quality assurance (QA) standards have never been higher than they are currently. There are two main reasons why: (1) the resources that laboratories are devoting to QA and (2) the recognition that although analysts all have a personal responsibility for the quality of their work, the best assurance comes from implementation of effective systems.

QA can add as much as 25% to the direct costs of running a laboratory. Even today some laboratory administrations and analysts balk at the cost and try to minimize the resources given to the area. Here is an example of the argument against QA costs that usually ensues: the laboratory employs capable and experienced staff who know what they are doing; their job is to apply their

From: *The Forensic Laboratory Handbook: Procedures and Practice*
Edited by: A. Mozayani and C. Noziglia © Humana Press Inc., Totowa, NJ

judgment and practical skills to each case, and everything will be fine. This is the *personal standards* approach to quality. Unfortunately, experience shows that the personal expert approach is not effective. Equally unfortunate are the errors that are made. The expectations that the public and the justice system place on forensic science are so high that these have been headline grabbers. Most of them share a common thread: errors result from misjudgment made by an individual analyst working independently of a quality system. In other words, the personal expert approach does not provide a sufficient assurance of quality. Not only that, but the cost of the resulting quality failure is greater than the cost of the alternative *quality systems standards* approach. Judicial reviews, resources diverted to review of errors, compensation payments to and erroneous incarceration of wrongly convicted individuals, and the disruption of response to the need for improvement all are very expensive in dollars. Effective QA in forensic science is not only a necessity, but also is a worthwhile investment.

2. How to Get It Right

The goal of every forensic scientist is to get the right answer every time. The expectation of every user is that all testing is error free. In the context of testing, "right" means the correct identification in qualitative analyses and the correct amount in quantitative analyses. This is reasonably straightforward, but incomplete. "Right" in forensic science means making a correct interpretation of results in the context of the case. The circumstances of the case also become factors when deciding what is the "right" test or range of tests to apply to which sample or samples. Nobody knows what really happened in the case. The forensic scientist is expected to seek the truth in the middle of an extremely partisan contest. One side, the prosecution, believes it has found the perpetrator and is trying to wring out every piece of evidence to support its case. Meanwhile, the other side, the defense, has a responsibility to represent the interest of the defendant and seeks to minimize the impact of the laboratory testing by any means it can. "Right" can become contextually dependent when the case circumstances are to be considered. The approach of this chapter is to concentrate on those objective areas that are within the control of the analyst. The more subjective case-dependent issues are legitimate and must be addressed by the laboratory through effective case management, but that is another topic.

2.1. Variation in Testing

One of the first things that an analyst learns is that there is intrinsic variability in all testing, especially quantitative analyses. How then can we add "every time" to "right?" The answer is that if we understand, identify, and measure the sources of variation and their consequences, we can make meaningful decisions about the reliability of our testing and show that it is producing results that are sufficiently reliable to meet the "right every time" requirement.

Therefore, the *objectives* of QA are to:

- Identify the sources of variation.
- Measure them.
- Minimize and control them.

The process of *quality management* is identifying, measuring, minimizing, and controlling variation in order to produce reliable results fit for the intended purpose. I will now discuss the sources and control of variation in testing, and identify how the QA system in the laboratory can minimize variation to an acceptable level.

2.2. Sources of Variation in Testing

The first area to be considered is how variation can arise. There are three main sources of variation in testing: the physical environment, variation in sampling, and factors resulting from the testing itself.

2.2.1. Physical Environment

The physical environment contributes variation in many ways. At a micro-environmental level, temperature control can affect the stability of materials. Accreditation standards generally require that the laboratory provide storage facilities that will protect against degradation. These standards are typically aimed at temperature control through cold rooms and local refrigerators or freezers. Humidity control is also important. Poor climate control at the room temperature level has been shown to introduce variability in DNA testing using capillary electrophoresis units. Poor lighting—low levels or the wrong color temperature is unacceptable in many areas of forensic science testing, such as searching of evidence, comparison of colors, and document examination.

Physical accommodation has a substantial indirect influence on the reliability of testing. A forensic science laboratory needs to have a design that prevents contamination. The relative layout of work areas must be designed to ensure separation of processing of known and unknown, as well as separation of storage of evidence from victim and accused, and separation of testing of trace drug levels in toxicology from bulk levels in controlled substance examination. The area of space available for work also contributes at least the potential for contamination. There are various guidelines but in practice the minimum realistic target should be in the range of 500–750 square feet per analyst, with an absolute minimum acceptable level of 400.

2.2.2. Sampling

Sampling is generally accepted as the main source of variation in testing. Some authorities estimate that collection can account for two-thirds of total variation in testing, and preparation of samples for analysis can contribute a further 20%. Sampling in forensic science repeatedly arises as a significant factor. In toxicology, the concentration of drug in a postmortem blood sample can vary depending on the site from which it was taken. On the other hand, multiple-site sampling is recommended for alcohol analysis where postmortem ethanol production may be a factor. In controlled substance cases, sampling from a bulk seizure of powder or taking a representative sample of plants from a cannabis plantation present sampling challenges to the analyst. In biology, there is always a sampling issue whenever there are multiple blood stains at a scene or on clothing.

In all cases, the rule is to take all reasonable steps to ensure that the results obtained from the testing give a sufficiently accurate and reliable account of the true value. Tools, such as coning and quartering for powders, sample sizes of the square root of the number of original items, and statistically based random sampling, can be used. One thing to avoid is basing estimates of variation on replicate testing of a composite, as valuable data regarding variation between samples will be lost.

2.2.3. Test Procedures

Test procedures are the third source of variation. The method used, the correct calibration and functioning of the test equipment, and the competency of the analyst all contribute to the reliability of the actual testing.

There are many sources of methods. In general there is a hierarchy of reliability. Official and consensus-based standard methods, such as those published by American Society of Testing Materials (ASTM), are best. Use of methods developed in house is acceptable provided that they have been thoroughly validated. The typical matrix encountered, and the expected range of analyte in it, influence the selection and performance of the method. The laboratory should be able to demonstrate that the methods it uses satisfy the user requirements for variation. It can do this by simple verification of performance for official published methods or by more extensive performance checks for in house ones.

Validations should include the use of certified reference materials (if they exist) and some form of interlaboratory check, such as external proficiency samples. Analyst competency goes hand in hand with validation. The laboratory should have records that demonstrate that the analysts using the technique are trained and have successfully completed some form of competency test.

2.3. Measuring Variation

The performance of each quantitative test can be described in terms of its accuracy and precision. *Accuracy* is how close the test answer is to the true concentration of analyte in the sample. *Precision* is a measure of the dispersion of repeat analyses. Accuracy and precision come together in situations, such as:

- Quantitation of controlled substance in a seized sample in a jurisdiction where sentencing depends on the amount of drug,
- Measurement of serum concentrations of drug in toxicology and reference to published data on therapeutic, toxic, and lethal levels, and
- In blood or breath alcohol testing where the offense is defined by the concentration of ethanol in the biological sample.

In the first and third examples, the test must be capable of producing an accuracy and precision such that the legal decisions based on it are dependable beyond reasonable doubt. In the case of the toxicology assay, both the legal demands and the actual capability of the test are less stringent.

Accuracy is typically measured by spiking blank matrix and analyzing the product. It is also addressed thorough comparison of results in interlaboratory collaborative trials and comparison of results to those obtained by a reference method of known performance. Precision is measured by comparing the spread of repeat analyses. The repetitions can cover different analysts working on different equipment sets on different days.

Accuracy is usually expressed in terms of the mean of several test results compared to the known or target concentration in the samples tested. Precision is measured by the variance of the set of results about that mean. Variance has a valuable property in QA, in that the total variance of testing is the sum of the variances contributed by each step. In practice, the spread of results is often expressed as the standard deviation, which is the square root of the variance. Sometimes the standard deviation is reported as a percentage of the mean, which is called the coefficient of variation. These various statistical parameters can be used to answer questions of reliability, for example approximately two-thirds of all results will lie within the mean plus or minus 1 standard deviation. The reliability of the estimate of the mean can be described from its standard error and tables of the *t*-statistic. The advantage of this approach is that it permits an estimate of the effect of repeats on the validity of the mean.

Qualitative testing is more straightforward. The basic principles of standard methods, validation, use of reference materials, effect of matrix, analyst competency, and participation in collaborative trials are the same. However, the only variable to be considered is that of incidence of false identifications, either false-positive or false-negative.

2.4. Uncertainty of Measurement

Variation in testing is a complex and specialized discipline in itself. Practitioners make use of the term "uncertainty of measurement" (UM) to describe the intrinsic and inevitable variation that exists in any test procedure. The tools described previously, such as direct measurement of the standard deviation from repeat tests, are used to quantify UM. The goal is that the UM of a test is known and can be compared to the variation that is acceptable to the user in the application of the test results. Thus, the UM for a blood alcohol test, where the result not only can determine guilt or innocence, but also can affect someone's livelihood, has to be sufficiently small in order that the court be confident that a reported level above the statutory limit is indeed valid. In contrast, the UM for a low blood level of a sedative drug found at an autopsy of someone who has died of a heroin overdose can (and will) be considerable. The law has tried to address the same issue, for example the Supreme Court decision in *Daubert v. Merrell Dow Pharmaceuticals, Inc.*, (*Daubert v. Merrell Dow* 509 US 579) requires something it calls "error rate" to be considered as a factor in determining the admissibility of scientific evidence in federal courts. The factor that the court intended to be considered is UM. The use of the expression "error rate" is extremely misleading, implying that the variability arises from mistakes and failing to appreciate that the variability is intrinsic.

3. CONTROLLING VARIATION

Now that the context of QA in forensic science has been set, we can consider how to make QA happen. A description of the essential elements of a QA system is discussed in the following sections.

3.1. The Quality System

A *quality system* is the organizational structure, procedures, processes, and resources needed to implement quality management. There is a hierarchy within the quality system. The highest level consists of the quality manual, which describes the quality system. Next, are procedures, which are the activities needed to implement the elements detailed in the quality manual. Last, the laboratory will have documented instructions, which are detailed work documents.

Quality assurance is all the planned and systematic actions necessary to provide adequate confidence that a product or service will satisfy given requirements for quality. The planned and systematic actions are specified in the laboratory *quality manual* and standard operating procedures. The quality manual is the formal document that describes the organization's quality system. The manual documents all policies, systems, programs, procedures, and instructions to the extent necessary to assure the quality of the test results.

Quality control is the operational techniques and activities that are used to fulfill requirements for quality.

3.2. The Quality Manual

The purpose of the quality manual is straightforward. However, many laboratories embarking on documentation of their quality system for the first time find it extremely difficult to actually write the manual. There are some easy-to-follow guidelines that will ensure success.

First, the stimulus is often preparation for accreditation. The accreditation program should detail what it requires to be in the manual. It is a good idea to use the specified areas as section titles. Even if you are not preparing for accreditation, the requirements from a program can still be used as a template. Using the clauses in International Organization for Standardization 17025 in this way would result in a manual with 25 main sections, as shown in Table 1.

This then would be the skeleton of the manual. How do we put flesh on its bones? There are three simple rules for a quality system and its documentation:

- If you do it, write it.
- If you write it, do it.
- If it isn't written, it didn't happen.

Every laboratory will have a way of doing things that work, more or less. The main problem is that the way is often enshrined in oral or informal traditions that depend on personnel knowing, retaining, and implementing the traditions. The best way to begin preparing a quality manual is to capture what actually happens; take the time to record the actual daily activities. Then they can be edited into a suitable format and reviewed for compliance with the requirements of the agency or accreditation program. This is a much more effective way than borrowing the quality manual from another agency, writing in your own name in place of the original, and expecting effective implementation.

Once you have a manual, you must follow it. If you do not, you will not achieve accreditation because you will be out of compliance. You will have wasted the time it took to prepare the manual and will have denied yourself a valuable tool. It is vital to understand at the outset that the manual is a living document. If it turns out that there is a better way to do something than detailed in the manual, change the manual.

The only way to collect objective information about the performance of the quality system is to record events. If an assay depends on the temperature when

Table 1
Quality Manual Structure

Chapter	Title
1	Organizational Structure Roles and Responsibilities
2	Policies and Procedures to Establish, Implement, and Maintain the Quality System
3	Document Control
4	Review of Requests, Tenders, and Contracts
5	Subcontracting
6	Purchasing Services and Supplies
7	Service to Client
8	Complaints
9	Control of Nonconforming Work
10	Corrective Action
11	Preventative Action
12	Control of Records
13	Internal Audits
14	Management Reviews
15	Competency of Personnel
16	Accommodation and Environmental Conditions
17	Method Validation
18	Uncertainty of Measurement
19	Control of Data
20	Equipment
21	Measurement Traceability
22	Sampling
23	Handling of Test Items
24	Assuring Quality
25	Reporting the Results

a critical step is conducted, that should be specified in the relevant part of the quality system documentation. Having identified the critical factor, it makes sense to measure it and show that the assay conditions are within the acceptable limits when the testing was conducted. If you consistently find that conditions are not being met, then you know to proceed to improve the reliability of the control. This cannot be done without records.

The format of each section should address these factors:

- Policy or reference to policy, which defines the governing requirement.
- Purpose and scope, i.e., why, what for, area covered, and exclusions.
- Responsibility.

- Actions and methods in the form of a step-by-step list of what needs to be done.
- Documentation and references, including a listing of any documents or forms required.
- Identification of what records are generated using the procedure and description of their retention.

3.3. Accreditation

As mentioned previously, accreditation should be used as guidance for preparing the quality manual. Accreditation is a powerful QA tool because it is the step that ensures that standards are in fact put into practice.

First, accreditation requires defined standards of performance, competence, and professionalism. These may be consensus practitioner standards, e.g., those developed for DNA and controlled substance testing through the Scientific Working Group on DNA Analysis Methods and the Scientific Working Group for forensic drug testing methods, respectively. They may be more broad-based peer programs, such as the American Society of Crime Laboratory Directors/Laboratory accreditation program, or they may be formal international consensus standards, such as International Organization for Standardization/IEC 17025 "General requirements for the competence of testing and calibration laboratories."

Second, accreditation requires that the laboratory demonstrates compliance with the standards through a third party review of its performance—self assessment is not acceptable. The value of the external review is strengthened by the requirement that it is conducted by an impartial and competent authority.

3.4. Objective Tests

The International Laboratory Accreditation Cooperation Guide (ILAC) 19 introduces a powerful concept in regard to the reliability of testing in forensic science, namely the *objective test*. An objective test has been documented and validated and is under control so that it can be demonstrated that all appropriately trained staff will obtain the same results within defined limits. Objective tests are controlled by:

- Documentation of the test.
- Validation of the test.
- Training and authorization of staff.
- Maintenance of equipment.
- Calibration of equipment.
- Use of appropriate reference materials.
- Provision of guidance for interpretation.
- Checking of results.
- Testing of staff proficiency.
- Recording of equipment/test performance.

This list will closely resemble any chapter on QA in forensic science. It provides a road map for ensuring quality and it is one that can be applied to all areas of the discipline: from toxicology to document examination and from the crime laboratory to the environmental testing one.

GLOSSARY

Accreditation:	The formal assessment and recognition by an impartial competent authority that a laboratory is capable of meeting and maintaining defined standards of performance, competence, and professionalism.
Accuracy:	The closeness of a test measurement to the true value. Sometimes represented by the Greek character μ.
Calibrate:	To standardize by determining the deviation from standard, especially so as to ascertain the proper correction factors.
Competency:	The quality or state of being functionally adequate or of having sufficient knowledge, judgment, skill, or strength.
Competency test:	A test to establish the sufficiency of knowledge, judgment, or skill of an analyst in a specified field.
Contamination:	The action by something external to an object which, by entering into or coming in contact with the object, destroys its purity.
Error rates:	The term used (erroneously) by the Supreme Court in Daubert for uncertainty of measurement.
IEC:	International Electrotechnical Commission. *See* ISO.
ILAC:	The International Laboratory Accreditation Cooperation. A voluntary organization representing stakeholders with an interest in accreditation. Among other things, ILAC prepares consensus guides assisting implementation of International Standards in accreditation for testing and calibration laboratories. ILAC Guide 19 refers to forensic testing.
ISO:	The International Organization for Standardization. ISO publishes Standards and Guides covering a wide range of topics, including the accreditation of testing and calibration laboratories.
Nonstandard:	A method that has not been adopted as a consensus standard method through evaluation and publication by a reputable standards body, such as the ASTM.
Objective test:	A test which, having been documented and validated, is under control so that it can be demonstrated in order for all appropriately trained staff to obtain the same results within defined limits.

Precision: The agreement or repeatability of a set of replicate results among themselves or the agreement among repeated observations made under the same conditions.

Proficiency test: The use of interlaboratory comparisons of results from a number of laboratories to determine laboratory testing performance.

Quality assurance (QA): All the planned and systematic actions necessary to provide adequate confidence that a product or service will satisfy given requirements for quality.

Quality control (QC): The operational techniques and activities that are used to fulfill requirements for quality.

Quality manual: A written document or documents that identify the policy, organization, objectives, functional activities, and specific quality assurance activities designed to achieve the quality goals set for the operation of the laboratory.

Quality system: The organizational structure, procedures, processes, and resources needed to implement quality management.

Reference: A material or substance, one or more properties of which are
Material (RM): sufficiently well established for it to be used for the calibration of an apparatus, the assessment of a measuring method, or for assigning values to materials. A Certified Reference Material (CRM) is a reference material of the highest metrological quality available that has values certified by a technically valid procedure, accompanied by or traceable to a certificate issued by the certifying body.

Sample: A sample is a set of data obtained from a population.

Standard deviation (SD): The square root of the sample variance.

Standard methods: Standard consensus methods are those developed by recognized organizations using collaborative studies involving a number of laboratories and then published.

Technical records: Accumulation of data and information which result from the performing of tests and/or calibrations and which indicate whether specified quality or process parameters are achieved.

Test report: An accurate and unambiguous presentation of test results and all relevant information in a format agreed upon by the laboratory and its clients.

Uncertainty of: A parameter associated with the result of a measurement that measurement (UM): characterizes the dispersion of values that could reasonably be attributed to the measurand.

Validation: The determination of the statistical parameters of a method to demonstrate that it is fit for a specified purpose.

Variance: The sum of the squares of the differences between individual values of a set and the arithmetic mean of the set, divided by one less than the number of values.

SUGGESTED READING

Wenclawiak BW, Koch M, Hadjicostas E, Hadjicostas E, eds. Quality Assurance in Analytical Chemistry: Training and Teaching. Berlin, Heidelberg: Springer Verlag, 2004.

Dux JP. Handbook of Quality Assurance for the Analytical Chemistry Laboratory, 2nd Edition. New York, NY: Van Nostrand Reinhold, 1998.

Garfield FM, Klesta E, and Hirsch J. Quality Assurance Principles for Analytical Laboratories, 3rd Edition. Gaithersburg, MD, AOAC International, 2000.

Chapter 11

Introduction to Forensic Document Examination

William L. Leaver, BS, D-ABFDE

1. INTRODUCTION

Picture this scenario: the patrolman notices an abandoned automobile in the parking lot of a Las Vegas store. It matches the description of a missing person's vehicle. The detectives respond and question the store manager about the missing victim. Checking the previous week's videotape of the in-store camera covering the slot machines, they notice the missing female is on camera during the early morning hours. On the next sweep of the slot machines, the woman has disappeared. The store manager wonders if the message scrawled on the women's restroom wall may have something to do with the case. The message, thought at first to be a rude joke, had been scrubbed off the metal stall wall. He recalled the message said something about murdering women.

The crime scene analysts respond to the scene. The analysts at the crime scene telephone the questioned document unit to determine what, if anything, can be done to visualize the message that has been removed. The crime scene analysts dismantle the metal dividing wall and take the evidence to the forensic laboratory.

Experience enables the forensic document examiner to determine that the two methods most likely to produce results will be infrared luminescence or luminescence using the alternate light source (ALS) (laser). Using the ALS and filtration, the writing that has been washed from the wall "magically" appears, allowing the examiners to photograph the writing, preserving the handwritten message as evidence *(1)*.

From: *The Forensic Laboratory Handbook: Procedures and Practice*
Edited by: A. Mozayani and C. Noziglia © Humana Press Inc., Totowa, NJ

Evidence that may be of interest to a document examiner is not only found on paper; writing left on walls, mirrors, windows, plumbing pipes, the side of automobiles, or even on the bodies of victims are submitted to the Questioned Document Section for examination. Plain paper or tablets that do not appear to have any writing on them are also examined for indentations of writing. Though the majority of work performed by the forensic document examiner is the examination and comparison of handwriting and hand printing, other examinations include the deciphering of obliterations and erasures, typewriting, printing processes, computer printing, machine printing, machine impressions, office machine copies, fraudulent credit card manufacture/alteration, identification cards, ink, paper, and, in some agencies, footwear impressions. This chapter will discuss, without going into specific detail, the examinations performed by forensic document examiners. Examinations within the field of questioned documents cover a wide range and specialization within the field is becoming necessary. An entire book could be written regarding handwriting comparison alone. The purpose of this chapter is to explain what evidence can reveal and, perhaps, what evidence cannot inform the analyst, the investigator, and the litigators.

2. HANDWRITING

Most people learn handwriting from a system, such as Palmer, Zaner-Bloser, or the newer D'Nealian style. We usually learn to hand print and eventually graduate to a cursive handwriting style. This is referred to as "Copybook Style" because, in the past, the handwriting system was copied from a book of instruction and then repeatedly practiced. The copybook is a thing of the past, but many of us can recall the strip at the top of the chalkboard and the mimeographed sheets containing the alphabet that were the model of handwriting taught in the schoolroom. It now may be rare to find the same emphasis in practicing penmanship in the schoolroom as in the past. In recent years, wide assortments of handwriting systems are taught in schools (2).

As we learn to write and practice this writing, we develop our own individual handwriting habits and characteristics. Some people may stay mainly with a hand printed style, whereas others write completely in a cursive style. However, some others may combine a hand printed style with a cursive style sometimes referred to as script. Of course, some writers are more skilled than other writers based on their motor coordination and the amount of practice in penmanship they endure. This repeated exercise of handwriting formulates a person's handwriting habit usually by the completion of adolescence. Some writers are capable of improving their writing through practice after this time, but usually a person is unable to write above their skill level. The writing habit becomes so ingrained and automatic that the writer is unaware of how uniquely individual the handwriting habit has become.

Can the handwriting of two different persons look the same? Handwriting must look sufficiently similar to be recognized as letters that make up words and sentences. There may be class characteristics that make some person's handwriting look similar to another person's. There may even be enough similarity that some characters or letters may have a striking resemblance, but the intricate details of construction, beginning and ending strokes, connecting strokes, height and spacing proportions, and relationship to the baseline will be different when comparing entire words and groups of words. The identity of a person's handwriting is not based on one or two characteristics, but is based on a sufficient combination of significant characteristics in agreement between a questioned and known writing. The basis of identification will be discussed later in this chapter (*See* Subheading 2.2.).

There are certain things that cannot be determined from handwriting. With very few exceptions, the following cannot be determined based on handwriting: the gender of the person writing, which hand was used to write, or the age of the writer. Rounded writing having a straight up slant (no slant) that many people may stereotypically associate with the writing of a junior high school-aged girl could instead be the writing of a middle-aged left-hander or the writing of a right-handed executive, male or female.

Another question sometimes posed to the examiner concerns the state of mind or condition of the writer when the writing was executed. Conditions, such as stress, mental incapacity, illness, medication, nervousness, infirmity, inebriation, injury, substance abuse, or fatigue, can all certainly affect the appearance of handwriting. However, there are no characteristics that an examiner can specifically identify as a manifestation of a particular stimulus or problem affecting writing in a certain way. The uncontrolled trailing off of a writing stroke could be because of a number of different factors or a combination of factors. It would not be accurate to identify that type of writing characteristic as invariably being a result of inebriation. However, if evidence is produced to show that someone's writing was influenced by some condition or outside stimulus, it can be stated that these influences can affect the writing so that it appears differently than the writing would under normal circumstances.

Certain things *can* be determined from the appearance of the writing. Speed of execution and fluency of the line quality are usually evident in the written line. The line quality is the condition of the written line of ink left by the stroke of the writing instrument. The general rule is that the slower a person writes, the more tremor is introduced in the pen stroke or line. Conversely, writing executed at a normal speed shows fluency or smoothness in the written line. The fluency or smooth flow of the writing line can indicate the authenticity of the writing. The lack of smooth line quality with tremor, pen stops, hesitations, and blunt beginnings and endings can indicate that a tracing or simulation of a signature or writing has occurred. But tremulous line quality, natural to an aged or ill person, may also be indicative of authentic writing for that aged or ill writer.

A tracing is self-explanatory. It is simply drawing over the top of a signature or writing. This can be accomplished in several different ways. A model signature can be placed onto another paper, then the lines of the model signature are drawn over leaving an indented impression on the paper underneath. The indentations can be followed with a writing instrument producing a close duplicate of the model signature. To accurately follow the line indentations, the drawing must be done slowly leaving evidence of tremor and slowness and sometimes hesitation, pen stops, pen lifts, restarts, blunt beginnings and endings, and retouching. Rarely can this be accomplished using flying starts and finishes.

Using a variation of this method, a carbon or no carbon required (NCR) sheet can be placed in between the model signature and the paper to which the signature is being traced. This will produce an image of the traced signature that can be written over with a pen to make the signature appear original. Rarely can the lines of the tracing be followed so accurately that remnants of the carbon or NCR will not show. Even the best attempt will leave remnants that can be observed under a microscope or good magnification and proper lighting.

A fiber-tip pen can be used to cover the carbon lines. An advantage is that the tip and subsequent ink line are broad enough to skillfully cover the carbon line. However, with proper lighting, the different reflectivity of the ink and carbon is apparent. Another method of exposing this type of tracing is examination under infrared absorption or infrared luminescence. In addition, the examiner may find that the indentations of the traced line do not match up with the ink line.

Figure 1 shows the slow tremulous line quality and blunt beginning and ending strokes that are found in tracings. Oblique lighting reveals the indented lines from the model signature that are obviously missed by the tracer as indicated by the arrows.

Figure 2 demonstrates the use of a fiber-tipped marker overwriting the guidelines of a tracing. Infrared luminescence shows the hand-drawn guidelines under the wider marker ink. The wider ink line of the marker was employed to cover the guidelines to give the signature an original appearance and less shaky line quality when observed with the unaided eye.

Another tracing method is the use of transmitted light. A paper is placed over the model signature and is then backlit using a light table. A glass table with the light placed under the table to transmit the light through the documents or

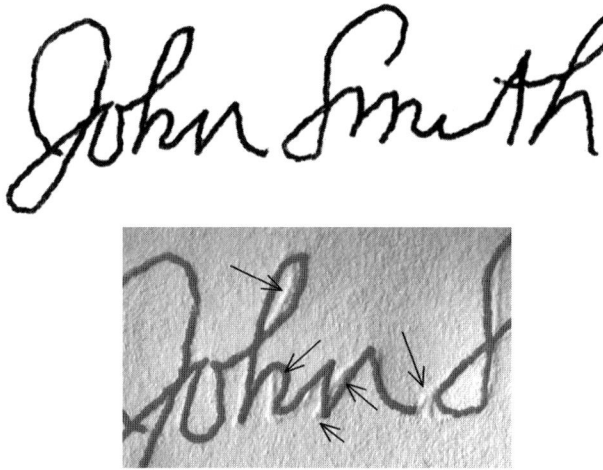

Fig. 1. The pen strokes miss the indented guidelines of the traced signature.

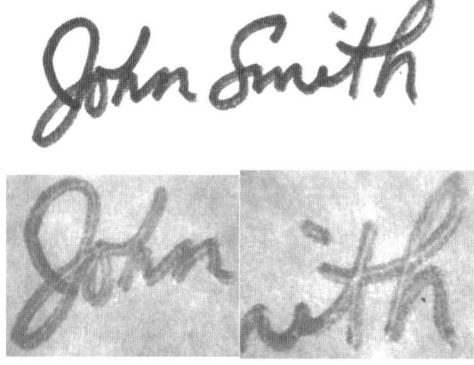

Fig. 2. A fiber tipped pen is used to hide the telltale guidelines of a traced signature.

simply placing the documents on a window so daylight transmits through are simple methods to accomplish the visualization of the model signature. This signature is then traced onto the paper placed above it. However, the same faulty line quality characteristics are apparent in this type of tracing also.

A simulation of a signature is the simple drawing of a model signature. Again, to attempt reproduction of the model signature, the simulator must slowly draw the signature to insure accuracy. The same line quality problems are introduced into the simulation giving an unnatural appearance to the drawn signature.

Fig. 3. An example of variation in the construction of the letter "t."

Writings that have slow tremulous line quality or constructions that appear to be disguised can be authentic writings. Such is the case in the distinctive appearance of the writing of the blind. It has a square construction and follows a ruler-like baseline. Also the writing of some aged and impaired persons display tremor and hesitation in the writing line that is normal for their writing and condition.

2.1. Variation

Every writer has natural variation in his/her writing. Just as some writers show more control or higher skill than other writers, some writers have more or less variation in their writing depending on the skill level and circumstances under which the writing is executed. Because we are not machines, we cannot exactly replicate our writing each time we write. Though it may seem so with highly skilled writers, a person's signatures are not exact duplicates each time the name is signed. There will be slight variation in each signature. A letter or character may even vary whether it is written at the first of a word, the middle of the word, or the end of the word. Figure 3 shows an example of this in the letter "t." The construction is different with this particular writer depending on whether the word begins or ends with the "t." A less conspicuous example of variation is the letter "r" in Fig. 3. The "r" in "first" has a sharper peak and is slightly narrower than the "r" in "thirty." However, the finishing stroke of each "r" is lower on the baseline than the beginning stroke and the right shoulder of each "r" has the same rounded construction to show the similarity between the "r" in both words.

Variation is very important in identifying a writer. On examination of a sufficient amount of writing, the variations a writer includes in his/her writing becomes a significant factor, not *the* single factor, but *a* significant factor on which, when combined with other significant agreement between characteristics, an identity can be based.

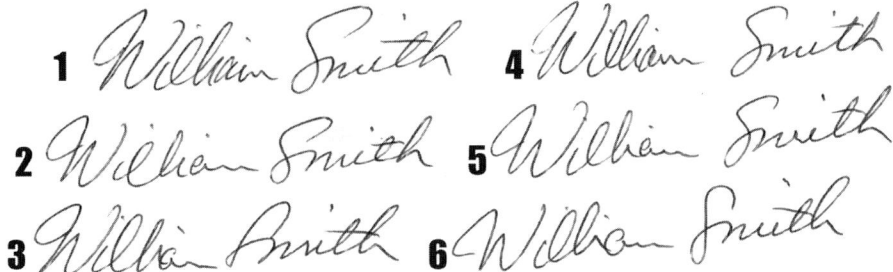

Fig. 4. Variations in construction among several signatures.

Figure 4 demonstrates how some variations in characteristics come into consideration to assist the examiner in coming to a conclusion concerning the authorship of a writing. This writer varies certain features from signature to signature, but will incorporate the different variations in the total number of signatures so when cross-comparing the signatures, those variations can be accounted for in the signatures. Note that the "W" in signatures 1, 3, and 4 share a similar beginning loop, whereas signatures 2 and 5 share similar beginning loops as 1, 3, and 4, but the line begins to the right of the down stroke. Yet the beginning stroke of the "W" in signature 6 is separated from the down stroke, whereas the v-shaped first bowl of the "W" with its narrow pointed vortex at the base is similar to the first bowl of the "W" in signatures 1, 2, and 3. The "ia" combination in signatures 3 and 6 are similar to each other and the same combination in signatures 2 and 5 are similar to each other, but slightly more varied than in signatures 3 and 6. The middle portion of the "m" in "Smith" on signatures 3, 5, and 6 forms a "v" that is similar. All the signatures have an uphill baseline where the bottom of the "S" dips below that baseline except for signature 3. The "m" in "William" in signatures 1 and 4 has three peaks; however, in signatures 2, 5, and 6, the "m" has consistent double peaks. The signature 3 "m" in "William" has essentially one peak, whereas the stroke between the "a" and "m" is the same in signatures 2, 3, 5, and 6. The intermixing of these variations lends authenticity to the conclusion that they were written by the same person. A forger would not be aware of these features and their significance, nor be able to replicate them with any speed of execution.

External factors, such as the writing surface, pen position, writer position, type of writing instrument, hot and cold temperatures, may introduce variation into handwriting. These factors may introduce varying degrees of temporary changes in handwriting depending on the intensity of the stimulus and the skill level of the writer. Other factors affecting handwriting and variation, some of which were already discussed in the section on handwriting, are advanced age, medications, or substance abuse, poor health, nervousness, stress, or fatigue. These factors may manifest as a deterioration of the writing and less attention to detail. Prolonged substance abuse may produce a gradual deterioration of the writer's skill.

Poor health and problems associated with advanced age result in tremor, wandering baseline, and loss of control of the pen. The symptoms of drug or alcohol abuse may produce similar effects on handwriting. Depending on the present condition of the writer, these internal and external factors may affect the handwriting for better or worse depending upon the presence or absence of the stimuli or factors. This can introduce temporary or permanent variation into a person's handwriting.

2.2. Basis of Identification

Does everyone's handwriting look the same? It has to look sufficiently the same in order to be recognizable for communication. Most people can generally tell the difference between two different person's handwritings and can usually recognize the writing of relatives and friends. Lay witnesses are sometimes enlisted to identify the handwriting of someone with whom they are familiar. However, the untrained person makes a far greater number of misidentifications *(3–5)*. These errant opinions are usually based on pictorial appearance. Similar writers can be mistakenly misidentified if the intricate details of the writings are not analyzed thoroughly. Basic differences in handwriting habit cannot be ignored or passed off as variation. Otherwise, the writing of two different persons that appear similar can be misidentified as the writing of the same person. The identification of handwriting goes beyond the general appearance. Identification is based on writings having a sufficient number of unique, identifying, individual features, or characteristics in the handwriting that are in agreement with no unexplainable differences.

To begin identification, the known writing is examined for naturalness in execution and for repeated consistent features that determine the established habit of the writer. The questioned writing is examined to establish the naturalness in the writing. Then the questioned and known writings are compared with each other. Some examiners begin an examination by formulating the hypothesis that the questioned writing is not written by the writer of the exemplar writing and attempt to prove the hypothesis. If the hypothesis cannot be proven based on the evidence, then the examiner can begin again using the hypothesis that the same person wrote both the questioned and exemplar writings. Some begin at a completely neutral point and weigh the similarities and differences between the writings and make a determination based on the significance of the characteristics, whether the features are generally similar, belonging to a general group, or if the characteristics are individual characteristics. Instead of class and individual characteristics, some examiners prefer to use the terms "more common" and "less common." Observations concerning the significance of varied characteristics are decisions based on the training, background, and experience of the examiner.

Earlier in this section, it was stated that the identity of a person's handwriting is not based on one or two characteristics, but rather on a sufficient combination of significant characteristics in agreement between a questioned and known writing. The questioned and known writings must contain characteristics that are repeated, consistent natural features of the writing. There must be a sufficient quantity of these individualized characteristics in agreement between the questioned writing and exemplar writing and an absence of unexplainable variations to effect the identification of the writer *(6)*. To make the determination whether dissimilarities between two writings are the variations of one or more writers, the examiner will need to evaluate a sufficient volume of exemplar writing. This exemplar writing should contain a sufficient volume of writing, both request and nonrequest "normal course of business," that shows repeated patterns/characteristics or the lack thereof to distinguish whether variation is the cause of the dissimilarities or if a different writer is involved. The conditions under which the separate writings were produced may not be that which can be duplicated, resulting in the inability to resolve the question of authorship.

To prove that two sets of writing are indicative of two different writers, a dissimilarity must be found that is fundamental to the structure of the handwriting, has no reasonable explanation for its presence, and must be consistent in addition to being a natural feature of the writing *(7)*. Consequently, a feature that appears to be a variation must be evaluated for its naturalness, its significance to the writing and its consistency in the writing. The dissimilarity could be what Harrison refers to as an accidental *(7)*, but not every deviation can be passed off as an accidental. It must be determined whether a nonagreeing characteristic is a basic fundamental difference that cannot be accounted for by a logical common sense explanation *(8)*.

Handwriting is identifiable to an individual writer *(9)*. Several treatises have been devoted to proving this fact. Whereas DNA cannot distinguish between identical twins, the examination of their handwriting can identify them individually. Studies by Boot *(10)*, Gamble *(11)*, and Beacom *(12)* have established that identical twins who were raised in the same family, attended the same schools, and were taught to write under the same handwriting systems do not have identical handwriting. Quite the contrary, these twins have individually identifiable handwriting characteristics that distinguish them one from the other. Just like everyone else, these twins have handwriting that is unique and identifiable to them individually.

3. ORIGINAL DOCUMENTS VS COPIES

The original document is always the best evidence for examination by a forensic document examiner. Only on original documents can examination by magnification and microscopy reveal evidentiary features such as direction of stroke, sequence of strokes, skillful retouching, pen lifts, pen stops, pressure of strokes, variation in pressure and rhythm, shading, and intricate construction detail. Infrared and ultraviolet examination, specular reflection, detection of erasures, and the deciphering of obliterations are examinations that also can only be performed on original documents.

The examination of copies limits the examiner's ability to discern certain significant details in the writing. Features in handwriting that are apparent in an original writing cannot be accurately evaluated in a copy. Copies can be easily manipulated by various methods. Evidence of cut-and-paste, simulation, tracing, and computer manipulation may be undetectable on a copy. The detection of these flaws is further complicated by the attempt to examine multiple generation copies, microfilm copies, and facsimiles.

Copies of tracings skillfully overwritten by a fiber-tip instrument may not show the telltale characteristics associated with such forgeries. Photocopy transfer of signatures, if skillfully done, may go undetected when the original document is "lost." There have been high-quality copies submitted as original documents where the recipients were not able to distinguish the copy from the original. Color copies showing what appears to be original blue ink signatures have been accepted as original documents only to be discovered by a forensic document examiner to be color photocopies, not originals.

For the document examiner to provide a meaningful conclusion, original documents need to be examined. Otherwise, the examiner is not afforded the best opportunity to examine all the aspects of the documents in question and thus render the optimum conclusion based on those examinations. If the case is important, then it is important enough to acquire the original documents for submission for examination. Does that mean that one should not even bother to submit copies of documents if the originals are destroyed or unavailable? No, submit the documents to a qualified forensic document examiner. Examination can be conducted on copies, just be prepared for a qualified opinion. The competent document examiner should be well aware of the dangers involved in the examination of copies. Kelly's research *(13)* on modern facsimile machines suggests even though there is sufficient quality to show tapering in strokes in a fax copy, subtle characteristics that are needed for examination are lost, which is confirmed by the research of several other reliable document examiners. The provenance of the document may give some presumption of authenticity or lead to its lack of consideration in an examination. One should not expect any opinion other than a qualified opinion—no identifications—when the questioned document being examined is a facsimile copy.

The range of opinions given by documents examiners usually fall within the following standard categories:

- Identification: The exemplar writer wrote the questioned writing.
- Strong probability: There is a virtual certainty that the exemplar writer wrote the questioned items, but there is a feature missing that prevents an identity.
- Probable: The evidence is very strong that the exemplar writing and the questioned writing are written by the same person, but it is less than a virtual certainty.
- Indications: There is significant evidence to indicate that the same person wrote the questioned and known writings, but there are differences that preclude a more definite conclusion.
- No conclusion: No determination can be made whether the exemplar writer did or did not write the questioned items.
- Indications did not: There are sufficient differences between the questioned and the known writings, but a few similarities prevent elimination of the writer.
- Probable did not: There evidence is very strong that the questioned and exemplar writing is not written by the same person.
- Highly probable did not: There are overwhelming differences that virtually eliminate the exemplar writer, however some feature prevents absolute elimination.
- Elimination: The writer of the exemplars did not write the questioned items.

Some examiners vary the range of opinions slightly. Some will not make a distinction between highly probable and probable, believing that there is too fine a line between these categories. This widens the range for the probable category. Other examiners are more comfortable with a range of opinions that include identification, probably did, inconclusive, probably did not, and elimination. This broadens each of the categories, especially the inconclusive range, to include a portion of the indications category.

4. FACTORS LIMITING OPINIONS

Can document examiners always give conclusive opinions regarding examinations? There are limiting factors that sometimes preclude absolute identifications and eliminations of a writer. The basic reasons that an examiner may render an inconclusive or qualified conclusion include, but are not limited to: the examination of copies, insufficient or incomplete exemplar writing, limited writing, the lack of naturally executed writing either questioned or known, the lack of comparable writing, or the lack of individuality.

One of the major factors restricting an opinion is the examination of copies. This has already been referred to in the previous section of this chapter.

Sometimes a copy is the only evidence available, but that does not change the quality of the copy. It should not be assumed that simply because a copy is the only evidence available that the limitations placed on the examination of a copy can now be disregarded. It is doubtful that any absolute opinion can or will be rendered. Other than in extraordinary circumstances, once the expert is required to examine a copy the submitter should expect nothing more than a qualified opinion based on the limitations imposed by the quality of the copy.

Generally, the submission of original questioned documents and a sufficient amount of naturally executed known writing, both exemplar writing and normal course of business writing, give the examiner the best opportunity to render a meaningful conclusion. Known writing should contain naturally executed handwriting exemplar forms having a varied selection of hand printing, handwriting, and numerals, along with exact text dictated writing, referred to as exemplar writing or request writing. These writings should be accompanied by documents written and signed in the normal course of business, sometimes referred to as nonrequest writing. An examiner may request known writing from the same time period as the questioned documents to determine if there have been changes in the person's writing over time. The examiner may also request the same type of known documents as are in question, such as cancelled checks or legal documents.

Even when an original document is submitted, the examiner may not be able to clearly identify or eliminate a writer. A limited amount of text, unnatural execution of writing, or the lack of individuality may prevent a definite conclusion no matter how much known or exemplar documentation is provided.

It is not possible to compare hand printing with cursive writing. The characteristics differ too much between the different styles of writing to expect any features to be in common. Figure 5 shows the same word written in hand printing and handwriting. The top word is written in all block letter, the second row is written in lower case hand printing, and the bottom row is written in cursive. There is literally nothing in common among the characteristics of each of these different styles of writing to permit a meaningful comparison. The examiner needs to compare block letters to block letters, upper and lower case combinations with upper and lower case combinations, and cursive writing with cursive writing. Hand printing cannot be compared with cursive writing. The characteristics of each are grossly different from one another.

A questioned writing that is not written naturally is sometimes referred to as disguised. Many document examiners prefer to consider text not written with the normal writing habit as simply unnatural writing, whether intentionally or unintentionally written in an unnatural manner. Comparing unnatural questioned writing to a large volume of same text known writing will not be helpful. If the questioned writing is written unnaturally, then the natural writing

Fig. 5. Different styles of writing cannot be accurately compared.

habits on which identification is based are absent. No amount of additional exemplar writing will change the condition of the questioned writing. Unnatural writing cannot be compared to other unnatural writing because there are no natural writing habits to compare. Identification must be based on the agreement between consistent natural writing characteristics.

Naturally executed writing usually contains smooth, fluent line quality in the stroke of the writing. It will manifest tapering in the beginning and end strokes, sometimes referred to as "flying starts" and "flying finishes," meaning the stroke was performed with a reasonable speed of execution. Scribbled writing, though in some instances may be natural, can also be an indication of a person writing faster than normal in an attempt to produce unnatural writing and elude indentification of their writing. A person attempting to produce an unnatural writing generally changes the size, slant, speed, and style of their writing, and may also include awkward or bizarre forms of letters to avoid their natural writing from being associated with the unnatural or disguised writing.

The lack of common text, such as comparing "Glenn Jones" with "William Smith," even if written dozens of times, leaves the examiner with little in common to compare. Again, no matter how many times the writing is repeated, if it does not contain letters and letter combinations common to the questioned writing, there is nothing on which to base an opinion or conclusion. "Bob" cannot be compared to "Jack" because there are no letters in common.

Some signatures lack individuality. The characters are so general and so lacking in significant features so as to make the writing unidentifiable. This type of writing usually consists of a few pen movements with indistinct or simple forms that would be easy to duplicate. Figure 6 shows examples of such signatures. These signatures may appear individualized, but it would not require much practice for a semiskilled penman to duplicate any of these signatures. The more complex and precise the characteristics are in a signature, the more difficult it is for another writer to successfully imitate the signature. Caution should be exercised because this theory is predicated upon the assumption that the complex characteristics are consistent and precise from signature to signature and executed with skill. A complex signature containing wild variations

Fig. 6. Signatures lacking complex characteristics may be easily forged.

from signature to signature leaves too much leeway for the person imitating the signature to produce something with characteristics within the range of variation of the signature being imitated.

5. EQUIPMENT

The basic equipment for a document examiner to begin with is a variety of magnifiers, a good quality stereoscopic microscope, and various light sources including a light table, photographic filters, and dichroic filters. Also included in this basic equipment should be a good quality camera. It could be a standard 35 mm with a normal lens and a macro lens, but a good digital camera may be better owing to modern computers. Images can be downloaded into photo software for recording, storing, titling, and enhancement of captured images. A scanner can also be used to import images and record them for use. A lightweight scanner can be taken on scene for the collection of images as easily as a camera. This of course implies that a computer should be part of the equipment along with a good quality printer. The advent of all these impressive capturing and storage devices still does not preclude the need for examining the original document under various lighting techniques.

The type of examinations that can be performed in a document laboratory would be limited with only the previously mentioned equipment. A complete document laboratory should include and electrostatic detection apparatus (ESDA) and a video spectral analyzer (VSC) or similar equipment. The ESDA and similar

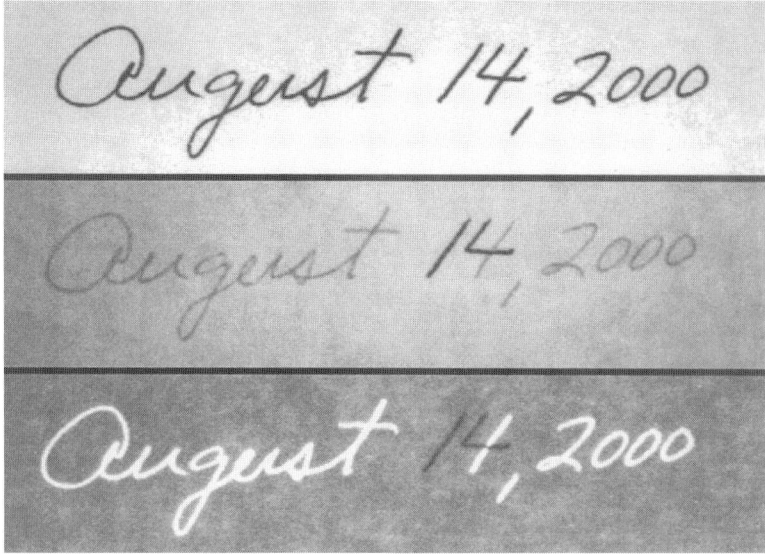

Fig. 7. The altered date (top), infrared absorption showing the alteration (middle), and infrared luminescence showing the alteration (bottom).

equipment, such as the kinderprint indentation materializer (IMEDD), allow an examiner to perform nondestructive examinations for indentations on documents. Indented writing on a document can be visualized and preserved utilizing this or similar piece equipment. The advantage of using this type of equipment is that latent indented images that cannot be visualized by oblique lighting can be detected and preserved. A new technique using gelatin lifts of indented writing indicates that on some types of paper this method may be more effective than electrostatic methods *(14)*. The VSC allows the examiner to do nondestructive ink differentiation. The VSC comes in a variety of portable and desktop models. Less expensive systems that differentiate ink can be purchased or even constructed using a charge-coupled device camera, filters, and a light tight box, such as the Richards Camera *(15)*. Different systems have improved features enabling the examiner to perform a variety of examinations limited only by his equipment and his expertise in the use of the equipment.

All the systems perform the examination of inks by infrared absorption and infrared luminescence. This may allow the examiner to determine if different inks were used to prepare a document, alter a document, and decipher obliterations. Figure 7 shows a photograph of infrared reflectance, absorption, and luminescence reactions where a different ink was used to change a date. The top portion shows the date as it appears to the unaided eye. The middle section of the photograph depicts the date under infrared filtration showing the portions of the ink appearing lighter to be partially reflecting infrared and the darker portion to be absorbing infrared. The bottom section of the photo shows the luminescence of one ink and the absorption (darker) of infrared by the ink used for altering the date. These particular inks display significantly different reactions. Caution should be exercised when only slightly different reactions occur. Reactions that differ slightly may be caused by the same ink applied at different density, i.e., one portion of the same ink applied with more writing pressure.

Some laboratories do not see many typewriter cases, but a set of typewriter templates and a typewriter classification system should be available.

6. INK AND PAPER

The examination of ink by the forensic document examiner is usually accomplished by the nondestructive examination of ink. This would include examination of ink using dichroic filters, ALSs, equipment to observe the reaction of ink under infrared absorption, infrared reflectance, and infrared luminescence and ultraviolet light.

These examinations will reveal whether different inks may have been used to write or alter portions of a document, but will not make a determination that two or more inks are the same. To determine if two inks are the same, a qualified ink chemist should perform the testing. A few forensic document examiners are also qualified as forensic ink chemists.

The procedures used to chemically distinguish inks are destructive to the document. Samples of the ink and paper are removed from the document for testing. The ink differentiation performed by most document examiners is nondestructive, but may not be conclusive. The nondestructive examination may separate inks as being different but cannot determine if the inks are the same. Additionally, nondestructive testing may not distinguish between two inks that are indeed different but do not react differently under testing.

Many criminalists and ink chemists have been examining and testing other methods of ink examination and differentiation using methods, such as Raman scattering spectroscopy with microscope attachment, Fourier transform infrared spectroscopy (FTIR), scanning electron microscope/X-ray fluorescence spectroscopy, surface-enhanced resonance Raman spectrometry (SERRS), attenuated total reflection (ATR), and FTIR-micro transmission spectra.

The type of examinations performed on paper include thickness, weight, color, opacity, fluorescence, physical characteristics, watermarks (date of changes and dating codes), fiber content, pulping process, the relative proportion of different fibers and origin of those fibers, and chemical analysis for trace elements. The Technical Association of the Pulp and Paper Industry and the American Society of Testing Materials have standard methods for examining paper. Edge cut characteristics from cutting equipment on commercially produced paper can result in matching a page to adjacent pages *(16)*. Other physical characteristics, such as creases, crinkling, indentations, and defects, can be used to source pages to a common source.

6.1. Obliterations

Obliterations made by ink may best be examined by infrared examination or ALS. The obliterated ink and the obliterating ink may have different infrared absorption or luminescent properties. The obliterating ink may "disappear" under infrared absorption, but if not, the obliterated ink may luminescence through the obliterating ink or through the paper from the reverse side of the paper. Other methods that may reveal the obliteration are oblique lighting, computer image enhancement, and examining reverse side embossing. Something as simple as specular reflectance may work when all the other methods do not.

Some of the same methods may be used on opaquing substance and correction fluid obliterations. Transmitted light passed through the document may reveal the original writing/markings. Substances that temporarily render the correction fluid translucent may allow the examiner to decipher the markings underneath.

6.2. Erasures

Oblique lighting and infrared examination have been the standard methods to decipher erasures and determine the content of the erasure. Computer image enhancement has been advantageous in visualizing the erased text. Recently, it has been demonstrated that certain scanning software may reveal the erased text *(17)*. When scanned into a computer, writing that has been completely erased, at least that is no longer visible to the naked eye, can sometimes be visible on the scanned image.

6.3. Sequence of Writing

Examination of writing strokes to determine which stroke is over the top of the other can be done using standard methods of stereoscopic examination, lifting techniques, and scanning electron microscopy, all having a varying range of certainty. Research has been done with three-dimensional laser profilometry *(18)* to determine line sequencing. Different writing pressures and different surfaces were studied with a claimed 60% accuracy in determining line intersections

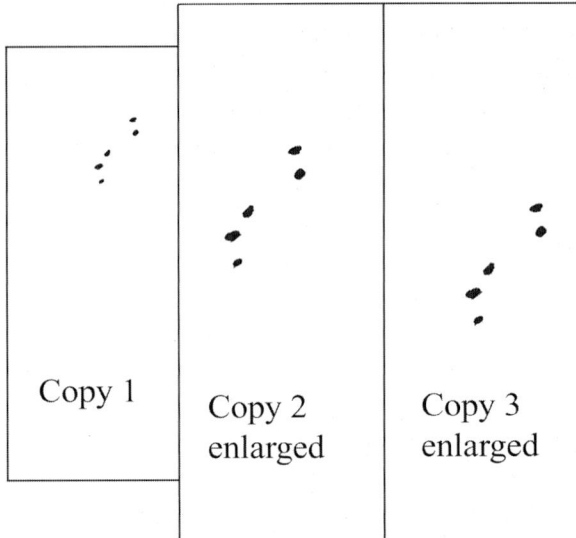

Fig. 8. Repeated patterns of photocopier trash marks transferred to subsequent copies.

and no false determinations. Additional study is being performed with a LumenIQ Inc. computer software program called measurement of internal consistencies software, but no conclusions have come forth yet. This system basically examines the density of the lines.

7. OFFICE MACHINES

7.1. Copiers

Photocopy machines can be identified by "trash marks." Trash marks are small marks on the copy from marks that were on the document being copied or from extraneous toner fused onto the copy. Any copies made from that document thereafter will bear those trash marks. Figure 8 shows a pattern of trash marks repeated on subsequent copies. Trash marks can also be made by flaws or damage on the drum, scratches on the glass platen, or marks from the lid if the paper does not cover the entire imaging area. These marks from defects can be traced back to the machine producing the defective marks. Owing to maintenance and repair and even cleaning the glass platen, these marks can be transitory. Using the time frame when the marks were present on other copies made by the machine, suspect documents can be dated relative to the time that the marks first appeared and the repair or cleaning was performed.

Manipulation of documents by photocopier began and still may be done by the cut-and-paste method. On older machines, the outlining of the cutouts were frequently obvious. Darkness and lightness adjustments can be made to minimize the cutout marks. Newer machines can use the central processing unit to eliminate areas on the intended copy. As early as 1985, photocopiers were introduced where two documents could be placed in juxtaposition on the platen and the signature on one document transferred to the other without a trace of alteration.

Defects in the transport system, rollers, fusers, and drum that impart individual markings to the document can be of identifying value. Gas chromatograph/mass spectrometer analysis of the toner may serve to identify a class characteristic feature such as the manufacturer.

Color copy machines produce a pattern that can be examined microscopically. This pattern is a set algorithmic pattern that can be traced back to a specific machine *(19,20)*. So all color copies made on a machine have this pattern imprinted on each copy identifying the source.

Analysis of the toners may be a significant factor in identifying machines *(21)*. There is also evidence that some aging determination can be made on photocopy toners *(22)*.

7.2. Fax Machines

Fax machines produce a transmitting terminal identifier (TTI) that is a line of data (sending number, date, and time) across the top or the bottom of the facsimile copy, if the information is properly programmed into the machine. This is generated by the sending machine in the transmitting terminal and thus will have a different font than the text of the fax document. This may become significant if the fax copy is manipulated to appear as if it were sent from another machine, such as a "cut-and-paste" method. Some receiving machines will override the sending machine's font style for the TTI and use their own font. The American Society of Questioned Document Examiners has produced a collection of fax machine fonts to identify font styles with models and machines. Analysis of toners may be a significant factor for tracing the source of a fax.

7.3. Typewriters

Typewriters can be traced to manufacturer and model by examining the font. There are search systems and computer programs that assist in tracing type fonts to classes of machines. The degree of certainty of this type of search results in grouping the typing into a general category. Depending on the extent/volume of the typing, a determination of the manufacturer can be made and sometimes the model of typewriter. However, there is more than one company that manufactured daisy wheels for other companies' machines. This type of determination is completely different than identifying the actual machine that did the typing. The narrowed down category could be a large group of machines that fit into the same classification. If there is a limited amount of typing, less than a full strike up, then the determination may not be narrowed down very far unless there is some very unique character in the questioned typing.

Single element typewriter identification is a more unique identification problem than the typebar machine. The ball fonts and daisy wheels are interchangeable from machine to machine of the same manufacturer. The identification is dependent on both the typing element defects and defects in the function of the machine unit on which the element is mounted. Thus, a change in either the single element or the typing unit can affect the identification. Specific damage/defects to the typeface of the element can be used to identify the specific element. Defects caused by wear and malfunction of the typing unit remain consistent within the machine and can be used to identify the actual machine. These defects do not change when a different element is interchanged. This is true with ball element typewriters and daisy wheel machines. Character alignment, spacing, and mechanical malfunctions are features of the machine and would not be modified by interchanging the single elements. Figure 9 shows two different daisy wheel elements that fit the same machine. Note the obvious differences in the shape and angles of the serifs of the "d" and the shape of the top of the "f." The bottom serif of the "f" in the questioned letter is wedge shaped and the questioned "o" is more oval in shape in addition to the wear to the left side of the letter.

A combination of factors or features are involved in the identification of typebar machines. Type size and type style lead to a general category of machine. Particular defects in a typewriter are the factors that individualize a machine. Damage or defects in the actual typeface can identify a particular machine. Alignment defects, such as a character typing "off its feet," vertically misaligned, horizontally misaligned, or twisted on its axis, are individual features of a typebar typewriter that can be used to identify a particular machine. Other mechanical problems of a machine such as paper slippage, skipping spaces, and improper indexing of the ribbon also can be used to identify a particular machine. These defects and mechanical failures in the same combinations between a questioned typing and what a machine produces are the features upon which identification depends. Any differences in these combinations of defects preclude an identification. It must be born in mind that some defects are transitory depending on repair and service intervals or additional damage to a machine.

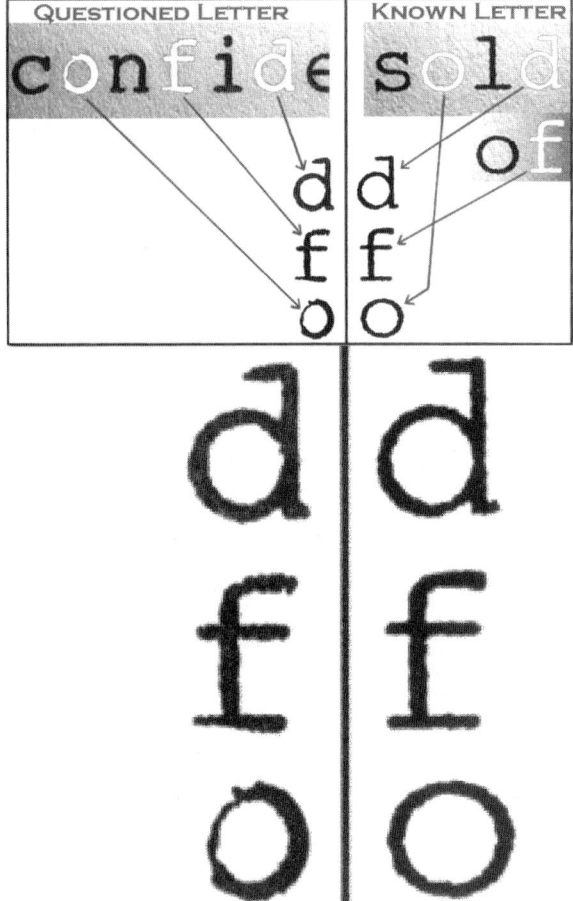

Fig. 9. A different daisy wheel was used to type the questioned document.

8. PRINTING PROCESSES

Through microscopic examination, the document examiner can easily distinguish the differences between printing processes. Offset lithography, letterpress, screen-printing, intaglio, thermal, or laser printed processes all have distinguishable characteristics that identify the process used to produce the document. Each of these processes has identifiable characteristics that can be distinguished under microscopic examination. Defects in these processes can be traced back to the source; a flaw in an offset plate can be traced to that plate just as a fingerprint can be linked to a person. If defects on the plate were removed, identifying marks from these corrections, absence of background, or remnants of something from the original image not completely removed from the plate would be features for which to look.

9. COMPUTER-GENERATED DOCUMENTS

Xerographic or laser printed processes, dye sublimation, dot matrix, and ink jet all have distinguishable characteristics that identify the process used to produce the document. Each of these processes also has identifiable characteristics that can be distinguished under microscopic examination. Defects in these processes can also be traced to a source; a bent pin in a dot matrix printer or damaged/clogged jets in an inkjet will leave identifiable characteristics on the printout that can be traced to that machine. Bent and nonfunctioning pins and jets that leave a repeated pattern on the document would be of identifying value. The pin and jet configuration can be a class characteristic, identifying a brand of machine or even a model. Drum defects on a laser printer that appear on the prints can identify the products from that particular machine. Maintenance, repair, and cleaning can make these defects transitory. This, however, can serve to date a document coming from a machine by comparing the defects in prints produced on relative dates before, during, or after maintenance. Trash marks on documents resulting from defects in the machine can be traced back to the machine.

Defects in the transport system, rollers, fusers, and drum that impart individual markings to the document can be of identifying value. Analysis of the toners and ink jet inks may serve to identify a class characteristic feature indicating the manufacture and model of a printer. Color ink jet ink can be traced and even dated based on analysis of the ink. By sampling the ink from an ink jet printed document, that document can be associated with the make and model of printer producing the document *(23)*. Some analysis of the ink can be accomplished by nondestructive means without taking samples from the documents *(24)*.

Photocopy manipulations of a signature use model signatures that can be identified to the exact model signature if available. A computer manipulation will also use a model signature, but computer software can be used to add variation to the manipulated signature and thus foil the attempt to identify the exact model signature. When examining the original document, there will be no indentation of the writing instrument coinciding with the ink line. Also, through microscopic examination an original ink can easily be distinguished from fused toner as found in the copy process and laser printed documents. The ink jet process will also be revealed under microscopic examination if that type of printer was used in the manipulation.

Another manipulation by computer is the problem of reinsertions. Lines of text can be added to a legitimate document by typing text into the computer, reinserting the document into the printer, and printing the new text onto a blank portion of the document. It is not impossible, but highly unlikely, that the added text will fit the document at exactly the same line spacing and margins that already exist on the document. The added text may appear to fit on casual inspection, but magnification and measurement reveal the reinsertion.

10. Summary

This chapter is intended to introduce the reader to the field of forensic document examination. To treat some of the topics in detail would require a separate book. Some specific determinations can be made when examining documents, but there are also limitations depending on the type of evidence and the limitations of that evidence. There is a need for ethical conclusions regarding forensic document examinations. The competent examiner is willing to admit that an opinion cannot always be given concerning some evidence. Those who have limited, introductory, incomplete, or spurious training should not pretend to be experts in the field. The examiner should be aware of the limitations of some types of evidence, should not be influenced by the circumstances of the case, and should not render any subjective conclusions not supported by the evidence. There are numerous well-qualified document examiners advising investigators and litigators and testifying in courts. There are some, however, that have been allowed to testify that should not.

Forensic document examination is an interesting and diverse field of study. The different areas in which examiners become involved continue to expand. This requires vigilant continued education keeping abreast of new developments and technology.

Glossary

ALS:	Alternate light source.
Cut-and-paste:	Method of cutting signatures from one document, pasting them onto another document, and then photocopying the pasted document to create a false document to be presented as an authentic document.
Copybook style:	Handwriting that is copied from a handwriting system book to practice penmanship exercises following the design of model characters of the system in the copybook.
Dichroic filters:	Color separation filters.
Goop:	A blob of ink on or adjacent to the writing line transferred to the gooping: paper from the writing instrument when an excessive amount of ink has built up on the ball point housing of the pen.

Handwriting:	A system or style of writing, such as Zaner-Bloser or Palmer system: that contain specific forms or models of handwritten letters.
Imitation:	The attempt to imitate the design or pictorial appearance of a signature, see simulation.
Interlineation:	The addition or insertion of a word(s) into an existing text or writing.
Line quality:	The condition of the written line of ink left by the stroke of the writing instrument, ranging from rapid, smooth and fluent to slow and tremulous.
Luminescence:	Florescence (glow) of components of ink when exposed to the electromagnetic spectrum.
Nondestructive:	Testing or examination of documents using methods that do not change, alter, or damage the original document.
Obliteration:	The condition when writing (or some marking, stamp impression, typing, etc.) is scribbled over or marked over with ink or some other substance to obscure a writing on a document.
Oblique lighting:	Light directed onto a document from an angle nearly parallel with the surface of the document, sometimes referred to as side lighting.
Simulation:	The attempt to freehand draw a signature capturing the design or pictorial appearance of that signature or writing.
Specular: reflection:	The reflection of an ink when light is directed perpendicular to the document. Some inks, such as ballpoint inks, are more "shiny" than other inks, such as fiber tip markers. This is sometimes useful in examining obliterations.
Tracing:	Closely following the outline of a genuine signature by various methods to produce a signature resembling the original.
Tremor:	Shakiness in the line of a writing lacking smoothness and fluency in the execution of the writing line.
Transmitted: lighting:	Light directed from the back of a document so the light shines-"through" the document.

REFERENCES

1. Leaver WL, Smith JW. Using an alternate light source to restore writing. J Forensic Sci 1999;44:653–655.
2. Huber RA, Headrick AM. Handwriting Identification: Facts and Fundamentals. Boca Raton, FL, CRC Press, 1999, p. 29.
3. Kam M, Gummadidala K, Fielding G, Conn R. Signature authentication by forensic document examiners. J Forensic Sci 2001;46:884–888.
4. Sita J, Found B, Rogers DK. Forensic handwriting examiners' f signature comparison. J Forensic Sci 2002;47:117–1124.
5. Kam M, Lin E. Writer identification using hand-printed and non-hand-printed questioned documents. J Forensic Sci 2003;48:1–5.
6. Homewood SL, Oleksow DL, Leaver WL. Questioned Document Evidence. California Lawyers 1998:VIII-4.

7. Harrison WR. Suspect Documents; Their Scientific Examination. Chicago: Nelson-Hall Inc., 1981.
8. Hilton O. Scientific Examination of Documents. Chicago: Callaghan & Company, 1956.
9. Srihari SN, Cha S-H, Arora H, Lee S. Individuality of handwriting. J Forensic Sci 2002;47:856–872.
10. Boot D. An Investigation into the degree of similarity in the handwriting of identical and fraternal twins in New Zealand. J ASQDE 1998;1:70–81.
11. Gamble DJ. The handwriting of identical twins. Can Forensic Sci J 1980;13:11–30.
12. Beacom MS. A study of handwriting by twins and other persons of multiple births. J Forensic Sci 1960;5:121–131.
13. Kelly JS. Facsimile documents: feasibility for comparison purposes. J Forensic Sci 1992;37:1600–1609.
14. de Koeijer JA. Gelatin Lifting: A Novel Technique For The Examination of Indented Writing. ASQDE Meeting, San Diego, CA, August 2002.
15. Richards GB. The application of electronic video techniques to infrared and ultraviolet examinations. J Forensic Sci 1977;27:53–60.
16. Bodziak WJ. Edge Characteristics of Commercially Produced Paper Stock. J ASQDE 1998;1:57–66
17. Herbertson G. Detection of Erasure by Canon Scanner. Southwestern Association of Forensic Document Examiners meeting, Anaheim, CA, April 2003.
18. Berx V, De Kinder J. The Application of 3-D Profilometry in the Analysis of the "Crossing Lines" Problem. ASQDE Meeting, San Diego, CA, August 2002.
19. Tweedy JS. Class Characteristics of counterfeit protection system codes of color laser copiers. J ASQDE. 2001;4:53–66.
20. Li CK, Leung SC. The identification of color copiers: a case study. J ASQDE. 1998;1:8–11.
21. Chopra G, Sehgal VN. Applications of Energy Dispersive X-Ray Microanalysis to Toner Materials From Photocopiers. ASQDE Meeting, San Diego, CA, August 2002.
22. Lyter AH. Characteristics of Photocopier Toners by X-Ray Photoelectron Spectroscopy (XPS): How They Change With Age. ASQDE Meeting, San Diego, CA, August 2002.
23. Doherty P. Classification of Ink Jet Printers and Inks. J ASQDE. 1997;1:88–106.
24. Mazzella WD. Diode Array Micro Spectrometry of Colour Ink-Jet Printers. J ASQDE. 1999;2:65–73.

SUGGESTED READING

Conway TVP. Evidential Documents. Thomas. 1978.
Ellen D. The Scientific Examination of Documents; Methods amd Techniques. Taylor & Francis, 1997.
Harrison WR. Suspect Documents; Their Scientific Examination. Chicago: Nelson-Hall Inc, 1981.

Herbertson G. Rubber Stamp Examinations: A Guide for Forensic Document Examiners. Wide Line Pub, 1997.

Hilton O. The Scientific Examination of Questioned Documents. Elsevier. 1982.

Huber RA, Headrick AM. Handwriting Identification: Facts and Fundamentals. CRC Press, 1999.

Kelly JS. Forensic Examination of Rubber Stamps; A Practical Guide. Thomas, 2002.

New Zealand Police Document Examination Section. Printing Processes Manual. Office of the Commissioner New Zealand Police, 2003.

Osborn AS. Questioned Documents. 2nd Ed. Nelson-Hall, 1929.

Osborn AS. The Problem of Proof. 2nd Ed. Nelson-Hall, 1975.

Rochester Institute of Technology. Printing Process Identification and Image Analysis for Forensic Document Examiners. RIT, 2004.

Chapter 12

Toxicology in the Crime Laboratory

Ashraf Mozayani, PharmD, PhD, D-ABFT

1. INTRODUCTION

Toxicology is the science of poisons and their effect on the human body. To paraphrase Paracelsus (1493–1541), all substances are poisons. The only difference between a remedy and a poison is the size of the dose. Toxicologists, therefore, deal with those substances that may cause bodily harm if taken in sufficient quantity. They deal with substances ranging from illicit street drugs to rat poison to prescription drugs, and everything in between.

Poisons rarely leave unique marks on the body. When searching for a cause of death, the medical examiner cannot determine from an autopsy whether or not drugs were involved. Samples of body fluids are collected and sent to the toxicology laboratory for study by the toxicology staff.

Similarly, erratic driving may be caused by any number of medical conditions, as well as drugs or alcohol. Although police officers are well trained in evaluating individuals in these situations, only the toxicology exam can tell for sure whether a drug is involved.

Most of the work of toxicologists involves the identification and quantitation of poisons in biological fluids and tissues, e.g., blood, urine, and liver. It is the toxicologist who measures the amount of drug or poison in the blood and determines if that amount was sufficient to cause death or impairment.

The scope of the toxicology aspect of a modern crime laboratory largely depends on the organization of the local criminal investigation apparatus. Traditionally, the crime laboratory has been a function of the police department

From: *The Forensic Laboratory Handbook: Procedures and Practice*
Edited by: A. Mozayani and C. Noziglia © Humana Press Inc., Totowa, NJ

and the investigations undertaken by the crime laboratory have focused on crime scene investigation, firearms, tool marks, trace evidence, arson investigation, fingerprints, questioned documents, and similar fields. Most of these traditional crime laboratories also have a forensic chemistry section, the function of which is to identify unknown chemical substances in bulk form, e.g., powders, liquids, pills, and plant material. Toxicology in these laboratories is usually restricted to blood alcohol determinations and the investigation of "under the influence" situations.

In these traditional organizations, investigations involving death fall under the jurisdiction of the medical examiner's office, and any toxicological investigation in these cases is performed by a toxicology laboratory selected by the coroner or medical examiner (ME). In most large cities, the toxicology laboratory is located in the ME's facility and is a permanent fixture of that office. In smaller jurisdictions, there is little need for a full-time toxicology laboratory (or ME for that matter) so any toxicology work is sent to an off-site reference laboratory.

As a result, the toxicology laboratory in many crime laboratories is a rather small unit with limited capabilities. Because many deaths involve criminal activity or criminal investigations, the toxicology aspect requires close coordination between the crime scene investigators, the medical investigators from the ME's office, the investigating police officers, and the ME. Because these entities are generally located at different sites, proper coordination can sometimes be difficult.

Several large jurisdictions in the United States (e.g., Bexar County [San Antonio] and Harris County [Houston] in Texas and Sedgwick County [Wichita] in Kansas) have addressed this problem by creating centralized forensic science centers. These centers contain most of the laboratories involved in criminal investigations thereby allowing consolidation of physical plant requirements, as well as the regular close interaction of the personnel investigating the crime. Thus, in a death case involving drugs or poisons, the autopsy, the firearms examination, the trace evidence from the body, and the toxicology can all be performed in a central location with minimization of chain of custody requirements and the chance for evidence to be lost or mishandled.

No matter which type of organizational structure is in place, the toxicological aspect of the crime laboratory involves two fundamental types of investigation: antemortem and postmortem. Depending on the organization, drug identification may also be performed in the toxicology laboratory, but this is generally not good practice because the possibility of contamination is always present.

In toxicology, as in every other aspect of forensics, a good rule that must always be remembered is that *every time a forensic examination is performed, no matter how simple, someone's life is at stake.*

2. INSTRUMENTATION

As any viewer of the popular television series CSI knows, the modern crime laboratory is packed with highly complex instruments. In toxicology, the primary function of these instruments is twofold: first, to separate the drugs and poisons from blood or tissue and from each other and, second, to identify those drugs and poisons.

2.1. Separation Technology

Modern toxicology laboratories rely extensively on the technique of chromatography and most of the analytical instrumentation found in the laboratory is based, at least in part, on this principal. Chromatography is a separation technique capable of separating minute quantities of chemicals from similar substances. Gas chromatography is performed on a gas chromatograph (GC), employing a tube (column) up to 30 m (100 ft) or more in length. The tube has a very small diameter and the entire 100 ft can fit into an oven the size of a shoebox. The GC is attached to an injector for the introduction of the sample and a detector for the identification of the components of the sample after separation by the column. The sample is dissolved in an organic solvent like hexane or methanol and injected into the GC injector with a small syringe. The injector is quite hot and the solvent and sample are immediately vaporized. The sample is carried through the column by a stream of gas, usually helium, and by the time it reaches the end of the column the components of the sample are separated from each other. Using identical conditions for each injection, the time required for a compound to move through the GC (called the retention time) should be the same each time. Modern GCs are capable of reproducing retention times within a few hundredths of a second. Figure 1 is a chromatogram from an actual urine specimen. The largest peak was identified as metoprolol, a heart medication.

The second most common type of chromatography seen in the toxicology laboratory is high-performance liquid chromatography (HPLC, or sometimes just LC). The principles are the same as for GC, except in HPLC the column is much shorter (usually about 15–30 cm in length), the separation takes place at much lower temperatures (usually employs at least some water as a solvent), and it does not require vaporization of the sample. This low temperature separation is used for compounds that decompose under the high temperature injections of GC or for compounds that dissolve in water but not in organic solvents (e.g., sugars).

Some toxicology laboratories still use thin layer chromatography (TLC), although it is not seen as frequently today as it once was. TLC is similar to HPLC except that instead of a column, a glass plate coated with silica is used. Separation is less efficient than with GC or HPLC and sensitivities are lower.

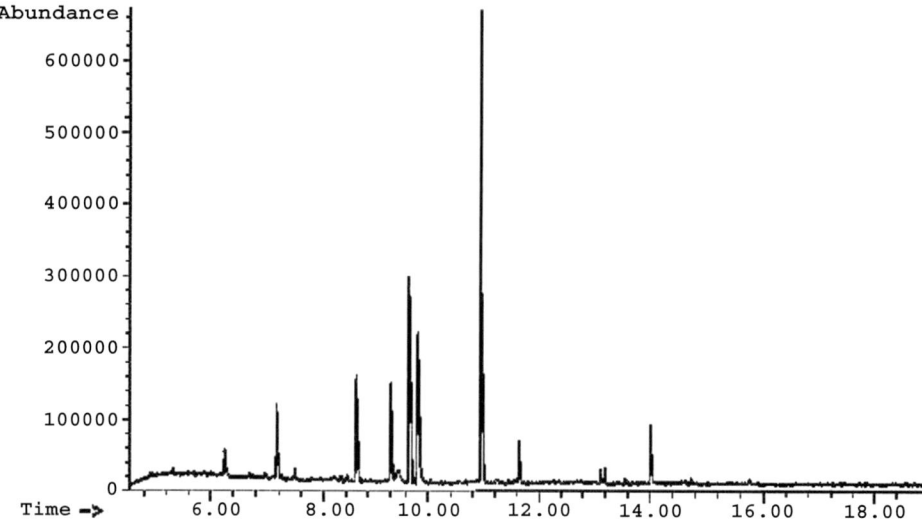

Fig. 1. Gas chromatogram of urine sample containing metoprolol.

2.2. Detectors

No matter which chromatographic technique is used, once the separation is complete, the components must be identified. This identification may be accomplished by a number of different techniques, all of which have their strengths and weaknesses. In principle, any detector may be attached to any chromatographic device. The pairing is usually identified by combining the acronym for each technique employed. The combination of a GC (separation device) and a mass spectrometer (MS, detector) is referred to as a GC/MS or GC-MS. An HPLC using an MS detector is called HPLC/MS or an LC/MS.

Detectors commonly seen in the toxicology laboratory include the flame ionization detector (FID), the nitrogen-phosphorus detector (NPD), the Ultraviolet detector (UV) and the MS. The FID and NPD are used on the GC to provide GC/FID and GC/NPD techniques, whereas the UV detector is employed on the HPLC to give HPLC/UV. The MS detector is seen on both the GC (GC/MS) and the HPLC (LC/MS) instruments. It is even possible to "piggyback" detectors to create hybrids like LC/MS/MS or GC/MS/MS.

The FID responds only to substances that burn. The NPD responds only to substances containing either phosphorus or nitrogen. The MS is the most versatile of the three, providing a "mass spectrum" containing a wealth of information about the unknown substance. As practiced in most toxicology laboratories, the mass spectrum is compared (by computer) to a vast library containing the known mass spectra of hundreds of thousands of substances and identification is made based on that comparison.

Most toxicology laboratories use the GC/FID for the determination of blood alcohol. There are only a few substances that may be present in the human body that are vapors and that burn, so the GC/FID is a good choice for routine samples. Methanol, ethanol, isopropanol, and acetone (the most commonly encountered "volatiles" in the human body) are easily detected and quantified using this technique. GC/FID can also be used to detect organic solvents such as toluene and xylene.

The major drawback of the GC/FID is the fact that the only information it imparts is that the detected substance burns. The presence of unusual substances has caused laboratories to erroneously report the presence of ethylene glycol *(1,2)*. Although this can lead to inappropriate legal action being taken against the individual, a false identification also may cause a delay in seeking medical help if the misidentified substance is a toxin or an indicator of a metabolic disorder.

Because the vast majority of drugs and poisons contain either nitrogen or phosphorus, the GC/NPD is a good choice for the general screening of toxicological samples. The NPD has excellent sensitivity down to the nanogram level (billionths of a gram), the range in which most drugs and poisons are found in the body.

The disadvantages of the NPD are (1) that it is restricted to compounds containing nitrogen or phosphorus, so it will not detect substances like aspirin or tetrahydrocannabinol (THC, the active ingredient in marijuana) and (2) that there are many nondrug substances that contain nitrogen that may make correct identification difficult. For this reason, GC/NPD is widely used as a "screening" instrument and any identification made by NPD is confirmed by a more precise method.

MSs are the best all-around detectors available today. The amount of information available from a mass spectrum is at least 10 times greater than with any other detector. In routine operation by a trained operator, an MS is capable of definitively identifying thousands of drugs, poisons, and other substances. A good mass spectroscopist can extend that capability multifold and can frequently identify a new, unknown substance even though it has never been seen before. Figure 2 is the mass spectrum of the largest peak visible in Fig. 1. The sample has been treated with a chemical (a derivatizing agent) to enhance its detectability, so the mass spectrum is of the methaneboronate of metoprolol.

Chromatographs, both GC and LC, can handle only one sample at a time. A typical run time for a single sample is on the order of 10–30 min (note that the run time in Fig. 1 is about 19 min) not including sample preparation time which,

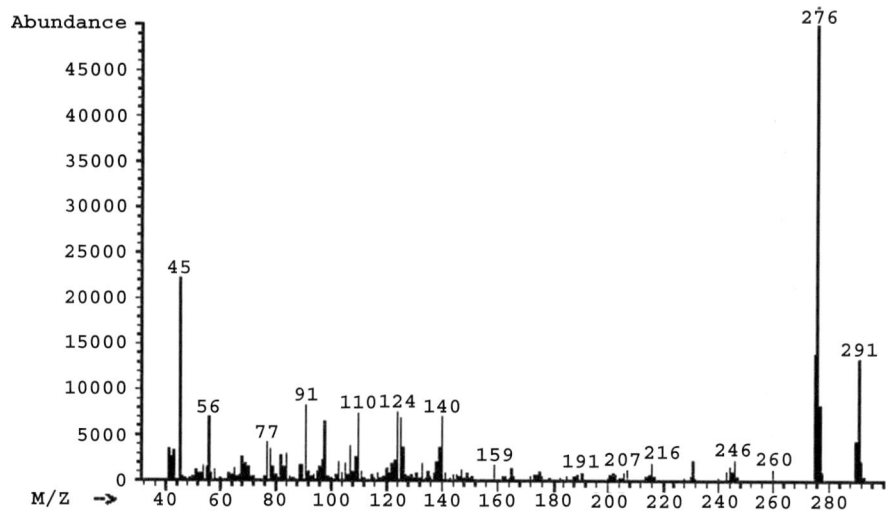

Fig. 2. Mass spectrum of metoprolol methaneboronate.

coupled with interpretation and data analysis, may add several more hours to the analysis. We are not yet to the Star Trek "tricorder" stage, where answers are instantaneously available. As good as the technology and instrumentation is, it must also be remembered that quality control, interpretation, and common sense all play a critical role in the final outcome of a toxicological analysis.

3. ANALYTICAL PROCEDURES

One of the fundamental principles of toxicology is that the identification of a drug or poison should be by two separate techniques in order to minimize the chance of error. A common means of accomplishing this is to perform a *screening* test and a *confirmatory* test. A screening test is generally designed to allow rapid, inexpensive testing of large numbers of samples for the *probable* presence of drugs or toxins. Confirmatory testing focuses on those samples which the screening test identified as probables (called *presumptive positives*) and uses an analytical procedure based on a different chemical principle and that is more specific than the screening test.

3.1. Screening Tests

There are two fundamental types of screening test widely used in modern forensic toxicology labs. The first is a chromatographic method utilizing GC/NPD (described under Section 2). The GC/NPD is useful as a broad spectrum screen, detecting substances that contain phosphorus or nitrogen atoms, including most drugs and poisons.

The second widely utilized screening test is based on the principle of *immunoassay* (IA). Immunoassay tests are based on the antibody–antigen reaction. Basically, the kit contains an antibody to the drug(s) in question and an indicator. If the sample contains the drug, the indicator will change. Some manufacturers use an indicator that results in a color change, others a change in the UV range, and still others use a radioactive tracer. The basic principle is the same in all IAs. IA kits are commercially available for most of the common drugs, such as amphetamines, opiates, barbiturates, benzodiazepines, cocaine, marijuana, phencyclidine (PCP), methadone, fentanyl, LSD, and many more.

One major drawback to IA kits is that they only detect the targeted drugs or drug classes and the sensitivity to specific drugs in a given class varies considerably. For instance, the Syva EMIT (a brand name) opiate assay detects morphine and codeine quite well, but is some 50 times less sensitive to oxycodone (Oxycontin®) even though all three drugs are opiates.

Another potential problem with immunoassays is that the antibodies are not 100% specific. The antibody will frequently detect substances that have similar chemical structures to the target compound. The amphetamine assays sometimes detect pseudoephedrine (Sudafed®) and similar drugs. The PCP assay sometimes reacts to large amounts of dextromethorphan, a cough suppressant.

Overall, because of the cost effectiveness and the ease of automation, IAs are a mainstay in the toxicology laboratory. Owing to the limitations cited previously, it is standard practice that all IA results are verified by GC/MS or a similar specific technique.

4. PREMORTEM TOXICOLOGY

Premortem toxicology in the forensic toxicology laboratories is focused on three general areas:

1. Driving under the influence (DUI) of alcohol or of other substances (driving under the influence of drugs [DUID]).
2. Erratic or unusual behavior in nondrivers.
3. Drug testing in probation and pretrial cases.

4.1. Driving Under the Influence

The most frequently performed tests in the modern crime laboratory toxicology department are breath alcohol or blood alcohol concentration (BAC) determinations. Most states have a legal BAC limit for driving of 0.080 g%.

Years of research have shown that there is a good correlation between the amount of alcohol in breath and the BAC. When a Breathalyzer® or similar instrument is used, the instrument automatically converts the breath alcohol level to BAC.

Breathalyzer examinations must conform to specific standard operating procedures, including a 15-min wait prior to the analysis, removal of dentures and other objects in the mouth, certification of the operators and regular calibration of the instrument. The Breathalyzer exams are routinely administered by trained personnel outside of a laboratory with the procedure being fully documented or videotaped.

When blood is used to determine BAC, the toxicology laboratory performs the analysis. There are several techniques used for this analysis, but the most common and one of the most reliable when properly performed is GC/FID.

The proper determination of a BAC begins at the collection site. The individual responsible for drawing the blood must sterilize the venipuncture site with a nonalcohol-containing substance such as iodine or Betadine®. The blood must be collected in a tube containing fluoride preservative. The commercially available gray top Vacutainers® used in many hospitals are appropriate for BAC blood collections. The blood should be stored in a refrigerator after collection with only minimal time at room temperature.

After arrival at the laboratory, storage should again be in a refrigerator until analysis. At that time, a small amount of blood is taken from the tube and placed in a vial, which is then sealed. A small amount of the vapor above the blood is then introduced into the GC. The volatile components are separated from each other and the ethanol identified by the FID and quantitated.

Quality control for DUI analyses should include a minimum of the following:

1. A standard containing all of the common volatiles (methanol, ethanol, isopropanol, and acetone) should be run to show that the instrument is capable of distinguishing between them.
2. A standard curve should be constructed by injecting ethanol standards of known concentration to show that accurate BACs can be determined by the method.
3. A blank should be run to show that the instrument can distinguish between no alcohol and alcohol and also to show that no alcohol was introduced into the samples during preparation.
4. A proper control should be injected to monitor the analysis.

4.2. Driving Under the Influence of Drugs

This analysis is generally performed only when the arresting officer suspects the presence of a substance other than alcohol or when alcohol is suspected but the

GC/FID analysis fails to detect any alcohol. The procedures followed are a simplified version of those employed by the ME's office when investigating the cause of death. In short, the specimen may be analyzed by IA. Alternatively, the blood or urine is subjected to an extraction procedure that removes any drugs from the blood into an organic solvent. The resulting solution is then analyzed by GC/NPD or GC/MS.

If the analysis is by GC/NPD or IA, the sample should be reanalyzed by GC/MS to provide definitive identification of any suspected substances. Once the substance is identified, a known sample of that drug should then be injected to verify that the proper identification was made.

Quality control for DUID analyses is similar to that for DUI cases:

1. A standard containing several common drugs should be injected to show that the instrument is capable of separating the components.
2. A standard curve should be constructed by injecting drug standards of known concentration to show that accurate concentrations can be determined by the method.
3. A blank should be run to show that no drug was introduced into the samples during preparation.
4. It is good laboratory practice to run positive samples in duplicate to show that no errors were made during the measurement of the sample.
5. A proper control should be injected to monitor the analysis.

It must be remembered that many prescription or over-the-counter (OTC) drugs may cause erratic behavior in some situations and any quality analysis will search for and identify those drugs, as well as the common drugs of abuse. For instance, the common OTC allergy medication diphenhydramine (Benadryl®) may cause drowsiness in moderate doses and hallucinations in excessive doses. In some cases, it may be necessary to search for the *absence* of a drug. An individual with epilepsy may have permission to drive when taking the proper medication. Erratic driving or accidents may result from seizures owing to the absence of the appropriate medication.

4.3. Nondriving Situations

A number of situations involving erratic behavior but not involving driving may require toxicological examination. Many jurisdictions have laws against public intoxication or being "under the influence" of drugs. Frequently a crime will involve the use of a drug to incapacitate a victim. The classic example of this is the old "Mickey Finn" used to Shanghai sailors in the 1800s and has evolved to "trick rolls," where wealthy individuals are rendered helpless by the addition of drugs to a drink so that they can be robbed. Drug-facilitated sexual assault uses the same approach with the purpose being rape rather than robbery.

All of these situations require the analysis of blood and/or other body fluids for the presence of drugs. The procedures used are identical to those used in DUID cases.

4.4. Other Premortem Situations

Poisoning by other substances, such as household products, rodenticides, or insecticides, intentional poisoning by prescription medications, and similar situations are investigated by law enforcement officials, but the actual analysis is rarely performed by a crime laboratory. In many cases, the point of first contact is with the emergency department at the hospital and the initial toxicology is done at the hospital laboratory. These hospital laboratories are generally not equipped to perform full forensic toxicology screens, so it is conceivable that many potential poisonings are misdiagnosed. Unfortunately, in many cases the best samples for full-screen toxicological testing from the initial hospital admission are either of insufficient quantity, are destroyed, or are never collected by hospital personnel, so follow-up testing is difficult.

4.5. Interpretation of Results

In any situation involving toxicological analysis, interpretation is critical. The information available from a toxicological analysis depends to some extent on the sample. Blood samples provide more information about which drugs might currently be affecting the individual, whereas urine samples are better at revealing what drugs the individual has been exposed to in the past several days. When interpreted by a forensic toxicologist, blood levels of drugs can be instrumental in determining impairment or even cause of death.

5. POSTMORTEM TOXICOLOGY

As a general rule, the most thorough toxicological analyses are performed by toxicology laboratories involved in the investigation of death. The *cause* of death may be almost anything, e.g., blunt trauma, gunshot wound, or heart attack. The *manner* of death may only be natural, homicide, suicide, accidental, or undetermined. Because the purpose of a postmortem examination is to determine the cause and manner of death, the contribution of foreign agents must be evaluated.

Autopsies are performed by forensic pathologists in an effort to unravel the circumstances surrounding a death. During the autopsy, specimens are collected for toxicological analysis. Because of the untidy nature of death, the type of specimens that are available may vary from case to case, so the toxicologist must be able to adapt the analysis to the available specimens. Routinely, the autopsy team will collect vitreous fluid (from inside the eyeball), liver, heart blood, femoral blood (from the femoral artery in the upper leg), gastric (stomach) contents, and urine. In some cases other tissue specimens are also collected, including kidney and brain.

The specimens collected at autopsy are processed in the laboratory using a variety of extraction procedures designed to separate the drugs and poisons from the body fluids. Once the extractions are complete, any drugs are contained in a relatively clean solution that can be analyzed by one of the methods outlined previously in this chapter. Rare or unusual poisons (ricin, aconitine, tetrodotoxin) or new illegal synthetic drugs may be more difficult to detect and may require specialized methods or instrumentation.

The presence or absence of drugs or poisons can never be determined without performing a complete toxicology screen. The purpose of the screen is to determine whether the death was caused by drug overdose or whether a particular drug was present (or absent, in some cases) in sufficient amounts to alter behavior and thereby contribute to the death. A few examples will help to make the possibilities more clear.

5.1. Example Cases

The cases outlined in the next few paragraphs are fictionalized accounts of the type of situations encountered by forensic toxicologists.

5.1.1. Case 1

A deceased 23-yr-old male is found in a tenement with a tourniquet around his left arm and a syringe in his right hand. Toxicological analysis finds that his blood contains morphine and 6-monoacetylmorphine, both metabolites of heroin. Based on these results coupled with the autopsy findings, the medical examiner determines:

Cause of death:	Drug overdose
Manner of death:	Accidental, suicide or homicide, depending on the remainder of the investigation

5.1.2. Case 2

A fight between two construction workers results in one of the men being killed by blunt trauma to the head by a piece of lumber. Toxicological analysis reveals a significant amount of PCP in the blood of the deceased man. Further investigation reveals that the victim was behaving in a bizarre, aggressive manner and attacked the other man, who defended himself. Based on these results coupled with the autopsy findings the medical examiner determines:

Cause of death:	Blunt trauma of the head
Manner of death:	Accidental

5.1.3. Case 3

A 43-yr-old female with a history of epilepsy is involved in a fatal single car accident, with the automobile hitting a tree. Toxicological analysis reveals no drugs in the blood even though the victim's physician reports that she is supposed to be taking daily doses of phenytoin and carbamazepine to control her seizures. Based on these results coupled with the autopsy findings the medical examiner determines:

Cause of death: Blunt trauma
Manner of death: Accidental

5.2. Limits on Interpretation

Forensic toxicology is not an exact science. The techniques used to detect and quantitate drugs are often accurate, but the exact meaning of those findings is subject to the experience and interpretation of the forensic toxicologist. For many drugs, the amount of drug seen in the blood in one person when the substance is taken as prescribed may be the same as the level in another who suffers severe toxicity or even death. For example, in 13 individuals who were determined to have died from methamphetamine overdose, the blood levels ranged from 90–18,000 ng/mL. However, when methamphetamine is taken for the treatment of obesity, blood levels in 10 volunteers ranged from 62–291 ng/mL *(3)*. An example of a task faced by the toxicologist is the determination of whether a level of 200 ng/mL is lethal or not because it falls in the ranges seen in therapeutic use and in reported fatal overdoses.

Another example of the interpretation of results is seen in the extrapolation of BACs. Almost a century of research on blood alcohol levels has established several well-founded principles. Alcohol is absorbed from the gut in about 0.5–2.0 h. One standard drink will raise the blood alcohol about 0.017 g% (the legal limit for driving in most states is 0.080 g%). The average human will eliminate alcohol from the blood at a rate of about 0.017 g% every hour.

Because these principles are so well established, it is not uncommon for the toxicologist to be asked to extrapolate results.

5.2.1. Case 4

An individual is arrested at the scene of an automobile accident 30 mi from the nearest hospital. The officer responding to the scene suspects that the individual is intoxicated, so he requests that blood be drawn at the hospital for a blood alcohol determination. The accident occurred at 1:00 AM, the officer arrived at 1:45 AM, the ambulance arrived at 1:55 AM, and the individual arrived at the hospital at 2:45 AM. The individual was stabilized and blood was drawn for the alcohol determination at 3:00 AM. The BAC on the 3:00 AM sample was 0.070 g%. The toxicologist is asked to estimate the BAC at 1:00 AM based on established alcohol metabolic parameters.

The forensic toxicologist uses his or her knowledge of the principles of alcohol metabolism to determine that the BAC was near 0.104 g% and, thus, the individual was probably driving with a BAC above the legal limit. The toxicologist also considers other parameters that may affect that interpretation such as:

- Is the individual average?
- Does he/she absorb and eliminate alcohol at the average rate?
- Was there food in the stomach?

Interpretation of toxicology results is a complex problem. The true meaning of those results should be taken in context with all of the other information obtained from a thorough investigation and should be interpreted only by a competent, trained forensic toxicologist.

6. CONCLUSION

As demonstrated by the cases outlined in this chapter, toxicology is a complex science even in the simple cases. Each case must be approached with a trained, experienced eye. The forensic toxicologist must look at all possibilities, examine each piece of evidence with objectivity, "stand on the shoulders of the giants" who have provided the mountains of pertinent research and to process the bulk of the findings into a logical, coherent explanation. The process is an arduous one, but the search for the truth is never easy and is always fulfilling.

GLOSSARY

BAC: Blood alcohol concentration. Usually reported in gram percent (g%). The legal limit for driving in most states is 0.080 g%.

DUI: Driving under the influence, usually restricted to situations involving driving under the influence of alcohol.

DUID: Driving under the influence of drugs. Usually used for situations involving driving under the influence of any drug other than alcohol.

FID: Flame ionization detector. A device used to detect compounds that have been isolated by a gas chromatograph. An FID essentially detects anything that burns.

GC: Gas chromatography. A separation technique that is used to separate mixtures of chemical compounds. A GC is usually run at relatively high temperatures (100–300°C) and uses helium to help move the unknown compounds through the system. A GC is coupled to any one of a number of different detectors, including NPD, FID, and MS detectors.

GC/MS: A GC coupled to an MS detector.

HPLC: High-pressure (or high-performance) liquid chromatography. A separation technique that is used to separate mixtures of chemical compounds. An HPLC is usually run at relatively low temperatures and frequently uses aqueous solutions so that the analysis of temperature sensitive and water-soluble substances may be detected. An HPLC is coupled to any one of a number of different detectors, including UV and MS detectors.

IA: Immunoassay. A detection technique relying on the interaction of an antibody with a drug or poison.

LC/MS: Also called HPLC/MS. An HPLC coupled to an MS detector.

ME: Medical examiner.

MS: Mass spectrometer. A device used to detect compounds which have been isolated by a gas chromatograph, a liquid chromatograph (HPLC), or can be used alone to identify pure substances. A mass spectrometer provides a great deal of information to help identify unknown substances, information which may include the molecular weight, a unique mass spectral fingerprint, presence of nitrogen or other halogens, and some information on how the molecule is structured.

NPD: Nitrogen-phosphorus detector. A device used to detect compounds that have been isolated by a gas chromatograph. An NPD essentially detects anything that contains nitrogen or phosphorus and is useful for detecting drugs, poisons, and explosives.

OTC: Over the counter. Drugs that are available without a prescription.

Toxicology: The science of poisons.

UV: Ultraviolet detector. A device used to detect compounds that have been isolated by a liquid chromatograph. A UV detector detects anything that absorbs ultraviolet light.

REFERENCES

1. Shoemaker J.D, Lynch RE, Hoffmann JW, and Sly WS. Misidentification of propionic acid as ethylene glycol in a patient with methylmalonic acidemia. J Pediat 1992;120:417–421.
2. Woolf AD, Wynshaw-Boris A, Rinaldo P, and Levy HL. Intentional infantile ethylene glycol poisoning presenting as an inherited metabolic disorder. J Pediat 1992;120: 421–424.
3. Baselt RC, ed. Disposition of Toxic Drugs and Chemicals in Man, 7th Edition. Biomedical Publications, Foster City, CA, 2004.

SUGGESTED READING

LeBeau M and Quenzer C. Succinylmonocholine identified in negative control tissues. J Ana Tox 2003;27:600–601.

Levine, B. Principles of Forensic Toxicology.

Fenton J, Fenton JJ. Toxicology: A Case-Oriented Approach.

Harris J. Criminal Poisoning: Investigational Guide for Law Enforcement, Toxicologists, Forensic Scientists, and Attorneys. III Trestrail.

Drummer O, et al. The Forensic Pharmacology of Drugs of Abuse.

Karch SB. Karch's Pathology of Drug Abuse, Third Edition.

Klaassen CD, Watkins JB. Casarett & Doull's Essentials of Toxicology.

Chapter 13

Trace Evidence in the Real Crime Laboratory

Richard E. Bisbing, BS

1. INTRODUCTION TO TRACE EVIDENCE

Trace evidence includes all the small bits and pieces of material that can be used to assist with the investigation of crimes and accidents. Trace evidence originates from the accumulation of material fragments left behind at the scenes of crimes or accidents that serve as reminders of someone or something that was present there during the crime or accident. The traces are often microscopic in size and, therefore, are not noticed right away, particularly by the perpetrators of crime. Fortunately for the police, the criminal is usually too busy to realize that his hairs and clothing fibers were left behind or that he took away fragments of glass on his clothing.

1.1. The Locard Exchange Principle

Material traces are left behind when someone touches something or when things rub together because, whenever any two objects come in contact, they transfer material from one to the other. The more violent the contact, the more likely the transfer will occur. Edmond Locard described these transfers in the early part of the 20th century. Dr. Locard was director of the crime laboratory in Lyon, France, between about 1910 and 1940. Since the earliest crime laboratories, forensic scientists have explained these transfers as a result of the Locard Exchange Principle. Locard explained that the microscopic debris that covers our clothing and bodies actually are silent witnesses of all our contacts.

From: *The Forensic Laboratory Handbook: Procedures and Practice*
Edited by: A. Mozayani and C. Noziglia © Humana Press Inc., Totowa, NJ

Thereafter, forensic scientists all over the world soon recognized that the principle applies to all criminals because wherever they step, whatever they touch, or whatever they leave behind, traces will serve as evidence against them. Not only their fingerprints or their DNA, but their hair, the lint from their clothes, the paint they scratch, the glass they break, and the dirt on their shoes will be there as evidence of the encounter.

1.2. Collecting Trace Evidence

Locard recommended that traces that can be seen with a magnifier should be collected directly using needles and tweezers and placed into folded paper packets. Many crime laboratories also collect trace evidence by shaking or scraping garments over clean paper on the laboratory bench. In the middle of the 20th Century, Dr. Max Frei-Sulzer, of the Zurich Police Department Crime Laboratory, first recommended collecting trace evidence completely invisible to the naked eye by pressing transparent tape to the surface where microtraces were suspected to be present, lifting the traces and placing the tape on a transparent plastic card. Today, tape is routinely used in the crime laboratory to collect hairs and fibers.

Gun shot residue (GSR) particles are also collected using tape, but of a different kind. GSR analysis using scanning electron microscopy (SEM) depends on finding traces of small particles left as a residue on the shooter after a gun is fired. The particles are collected from hands and clothing using double-sided tape placed on a metal disk for the SEM. Just as with fibers, areas on a suspect's clothing, such as a pocket where a gun was placed after it was fired, can be targeted with the tape lift.

1.3. Associative Evidence

Linking a suspect to the crime scene or linking a victim to a suspect is the essence of solving crimes. The term associative evidence was defined by James Osterburg, along with the New York City crime laboratory, and signifies that some connection or association has been established between crime scene and criminal. Fingerprints are used to associate a person with a place or object, such as a bank vault or a gun. Blood on a suspect's clothing is used to associate the victim with the suspect. Likewise, traces of hairs, fibers, paint, glass, and soil are used in the same way to prove that a person came in contact with an object, a place, or another person.

For example, the trace evidence left behind as a result of a hit and run accident, where a pedestrian is struck and injured, is a good example of associative evidence. As the car strikes the pedestrian, blood, hair, and clothing fibers are transferred from the victim to the car; and at the same time, paint and headlight glass are transferred from the car to the victim's clothing. Car parts, such as pieces of headlights, turn-signal lenses, and grill, are left behind after the car leaves the scene. When the suspect car is found, with all this evidence it is usually a relatively simple matter to associate the victim with the car, the car with the victim, and the car with the scene of the accident. In higher speed crashes where the driver and passenger bounce around inside the car, the driver is associated with the car by saliva and makeup on the airbag if it deployed, by trouser fibers on the dash, or by shirt fibers on the seatbelts. The passenger's blood and hair may be caught in the broken windshield.

1.4. TYPES OF TRACE EVIDENCE

Different groups of associative evidence are usually dealt with by different crime laboratory specialists. For example, impressions, such as fingerprints and footprints and those on bullets and cartridge casings or broken objects, are examined by the identification specialist and firearms examiner, respectively. Genetic markers from blood, semen, and saliva are identified in the DNA laboratory. Although the types of materials that might be used as trace evidence are nearly unlimited, hairs, fibers, paint, glass, and soil are the most common types analyzed in the microscopy laboratory.

Hairs are useful as trace evidence because they originate directly from the body. They are associated with the victim or suspect by comparing the questioned hairs found in the trace evidence with known samples collected later from animals or persons suspected of leaving the hairs. They are either associated by comparison of microscopic features or by analysis of DNA in the hairs.

Fibers, paint, and glass differ from hairs in many ways and are therefore analyzed in a different way. These microtraces are all minute portions of manufactured products. Fibers are manufactured in large quantities and distributed throughout the world to be made into the textile products (clothing, carpet, upholstery, etc.) we use in our everyday lives. Likewise, paint and glass are made in large batches and then used in cars and homes. They are identified and compared through microscopic materials analysis. All are characterized by their size, shape, and construction (morphology), by their optical and physical properties (color, refractive index, birefringence, density), and by their chemical composition. But seldom can any of these analyses determine that a particular microscopic portion originated from the suspected source (sweater, carpet, window sill, car, window) to the exclusion of identical materials that may be used elsewhere in the same product. Unlike fingerprints, footprints, and broken fragments, which can be matched to a single individual or object, fibers, paint, and glass cannot. Nevertheless, in many cases, these manufactured traces assist immensely with the investigation and determining their likely source by comparison often helps solve crimes of all types.

Many natural samples (soil, pollen, leaves), originating from the ecological environment, are also useful as associative evidence. These materials are either compared directly with known samples from the site where the questioned samples likely originated; or, in some cases, the identification of these natural samples provides leads to the location of the crime scene. A model case was described recently by Schierenbeck *(1)*. A botanist was given some leaves collected from the clothing of a missing child, apparently left behind by the murderer. After determining the plant species and predicting where the species would be found, the botanist and the detective visited the site where the clothing was found. They drove further up the mountain and visited several sites where the species of interest were found. At the fifth site, as the detective took global positioning system readings, the botanist climbed down a hill to examine the leaf litter. Just as she noticed that the leaves matched in every detail to the leaves from the clothing, she noted the strong odor of decay and a blanket near a log. The missing child's body was then discovered.

2. FORENSIC MICROSCOPY

Traces are usually very small and, therefore, must be analyzed microscopically. As many questions can be answered quickly and inexpensively with a microscope, it is the beginning point in nearly all trace evidence cases. The basic tools for forensic microscopy are a stereomicroscope, a polarizing light microscope, and a transmitted light comparison microscope. Where necessary to complete a comparison, light microscopy is used to prepare samples for infrared or electron microscopy.

2.1. Stereomicroscopy

The stereomicroscope, also known as a dissecting microscope, is the starting point of virtually every analysis. The main difference between the stereomicroscope and the more common compound microscope is that the compound microscope views the sample from a single direction, whereas the stereomicroscope views the object from two slightly different angles, just like our normal vision. There is also plenty of room under the microscope lens to handle evidence while observing its appearance and preparing samples. The stereoscopic microscope, however, views objects mainly by means of reflected light and its power, typically ranging from 5 to 50× magnification, is much less than the compound microscope. Nevertheless, the lower power has advantages because what you see with the naked eye compared to what you see through the stereoscopic microscope are similar, making it easy to use.

2.2. Polarized Light Microscopy

Polarized light microscopes are built on the higher power (1000× magnification possible) compound microscopes by adding two rotating polarizing filters in the light path, one before the specimen (polarizer) and one after the specimen (analyzer), in order to control the planes of vibration of the light used to view the sample. By manipulating the polarizing microscope and using appropriate attachments, a number of fundamental optical characteristics used to identify and compare trace evidence can be measured including refractive index and birefringence. Polarized light microscopy (PLM) is the principal means to identify fibers and soil minerals, for example. Polaroid®, 35 mm, digital, or video cameras can be added to the microscope to take pictures of the trace evidence. Nearly every trace evidence sample finds its way to the polarizing microscope.

2.3. Fluorescence Microscopy

Through the use of special filters and lights on a compound light microscope, the fluorescence of materials may be observed, allowing microtraces that are similar in normal or polarized light to be distinguished simply by their fluorescent colors, in the same way that a "black light" is used to create the unusual colors of some Halloween costumes. Dyed fibers are compared in this way.

2.4. Comparison Microscopy

The final step in most comparisons is to use two microscopes side-by-side, connected with an optical bridge, to view the questioned and known samples at the same time. The comparison microscope contains an arrangement of prisms whereby half the field of view from each microscope is viewed simultaneously in the eyepieces, with the left half of the image from the left microscope and the right half from the other. Two matching polarizing microscopes or two matching fluorescence microscopes are ideal for the comparison of hairs, fibers, paint layers, or any evidence requiring detailed comparison of microscopic features.

2.5. Infrared Microscopy

Infrared spectroscopy (IR) is the study of a substance's interaction with infrared light and is frequently used in crime laboratories to identify drugs, plastics, paint, fibers, and explosives. Fourier transform infrared spectrometers (FTIRs) are more sensitive and can be used in combination with a microscope to identify the small microtraces found in trace evidence.

2.6. Electron Microscopy

Electron microscopes use electrons instead of light to view trace evidence. For example, in the SEM, samples are bombarded with a focused beam of electrons instead of light, which produces more electrons and X-rays. These backscattered and secondary electrons produce high resolution images at magnifications 100 times greater than a light microscope with extreme depth of field making them appear almost three-dimensional.

X-rays generated by the electron beam striking the sample surface are captured with an energy dispersive spectrometer (EDS) and are used to determine the chemical elements in the sample. The EDS gives a quantitative measurement for virtually all the elements on the periodic table from carbon through uranium. Modern instruments can analyze thousands of particles automatically, such as particles collected from GSRs. (*See* ref. *2* for additional information on electron microscopy.)

2.7. Duct Tape

To illustrate how all of these microscopes might be used together, consider the case where ordinary duct tape found on a bomb package might be compared with a partial roll of tape in the suspect's workshop. First, the tape from the package is inspected for fingerprints and hairs, fibers, or other microtraces that might be adhering to the adhesive. The tape readily picks up traces from the bomb-maker's environment. Second, if the tape from the bomb and workshop look similar in size and color, the cut or torn ends are inspected to determine whether an irregular torn end from the package can be matched with an end from the roll, like a jig-saw puzzle. When possible matches are found, they are confirmed using a stereomicroscope and proven with photography. If a fracture match does not prove that the tapes are from the same roll, a materials analysis is next. Duct tape is comprised of an adhesive layer usually containing a filler (such as calcium carbonate), a cloth reinforcing material, and a polymer backing with a colored coating. Each of these materials is compared, in turn, and each must coincide before it can be concluded that the tape on the package could have originated from the roll from the workshop.

Each sample is compared visually and with a stereomicroscope for color, texture, structure and constituent parts. The adhesive is identified by infrared microspectroscopy (FTIR) and the filler is analyzed by PLM and SEM-EDS. The cloth weave is studied with a stereomicroscope. The reinforcing fibers are identified by PLM and FTIR, and any coatings on the fibers are analyzed by FTIR and SEM-EDS. The backing is identified by FTIR and melting point. The colored coating is compared with alternate light sources and microspectrophotometry (MSP) and its composition is determined by PLM, FTIR, and SEM-EDS. After the tape comparison is complete, it would be time for the crime laboratory to begin comparing the hairs, fibers, paint, glass, soil, and other microtraces trapped in the adhesive with samples from the suspect and workshop.

3. HAIRS

Human hairs are the most often used microscopic trace evidence. Hairs are readily shed and unwittingly left behind; they are relatively easy to discover; and they are not easily destroyed. The violence of homicidal and sexual assaults tends to result in the transfer of hairs from one person to another, to the crime scene, and to weapons. One of the earliest hair cases was the murder of Fanny Sébastiani, the Duchesse of Praslin, in her bedroom at the Hôtel Sébastiani, 55 rue du Faubourg, St. Honoré, Paris, on August 18, 1847. The Duke could not explain how his loaded pistol, found under the body, had bits of the victim's skin and hair adhering to the handle indicating that the Duchesse had been violently struck with it during the struggle. He died in prison.

Human head and pubic hairs are most often used as trace evidence, but animal hairs from domesticated animals (pets and farm animals) and from textiles (furs) are found occasionally. For example, clothing brought to a dry-cleaners by a robber and subsequently left on the counter when the robber fled was covered with dog hairs which were later compared with the suspect's pet. In cases of sexual assault, pubic hairs are sometimes transferred between victim and assailant, which is why the victim's pubic hair is combed during the medical examination. Consequently, hairs are often found and need to be compared with possible sources. The only disadvantage of hairs is that their origin cannot always be matched with sufficient certainty to the suspect.

3.1. Hair Comparison

The principal means for determining the source of a hair is by microscopic comparison between the questioned hairs and hairs collected from individuals who are possible sources. For human hairs, these characteristics can be broadly grouped into color, structure, and treatment. The structure of hair can be likened to an ordinary lead pencil consisting of an outer skin called the cuticle (like the paint), a shaft (like the wood), and an inner medulla (like the graphite). As with pencils, color is probably the most useful characteristic for distinguishing hairs from different sources. In addition, the tip ends may be freshly cut, split, or singed. The shape of the root (eraser end) may indicate whether the hair had been pulled. Bleached or dyed hair can usually be identified by a distinct demarcation line seen when the hairs grows out revealing the untreated "roots."

If all the features of two hairs are alike after comparisons using a stereo-microscope, polarizing microscope, and comparison microscope, then a conclusion that the hairs are similar in all respects (a match) is justified and the samples could have originated from the same individual. Conversely, if two samples of hairs are not alike, then it is logical to conclude that they did not originate from the same individual. The crime laboratory can often state that two hairs originated from different sources, but when two hairs appear similar they can only say, without DNA analysis, that they *could* have originated from the same source.

3.2. DNA Analysis

Following a microscopic comparison and an assessment of the root characteristics, hairs are selected for DNA analysis. Genomic DNA is found in the nucleated cells of the root tissue attached to the hair when pulled from the skin and, if sufficient DNA is recovered, the origin of the hair can be determined to a virtual certainty, in the same way the donor of blood and semen can be determined. In addition, the entire hair shaft contains mitochondrial DNA (mtDNA) that can be amplified and typed using PCR technologies. Although mtDNA is not as useful as genomic DNA for identifying the donor because the mtDNA is always the same as the person's mother, it is very stable, provides exclusions, and enhances the value of any microscopic associations. In summation, the combination of microscopic analysis and DNA analysis of hair can provide extraordinary trace evidence often associating victims with assailants.

4. FIBERS

Textile fibers are a good illustration of the Locard Exchange Principle. Whenever two people come together during an assault, there is often a cross transfer of fibers where the victim's clothing fibers transfer to the assailant's clothing and vice versa. Likewise, if someone rolls around on a carpet, carpet fibers will transfer to the person's clothing, as best illustrated by the case of the Atlanta Child Murders where many of the victims' bodies contained carpet fibers from Wayne Williams' bedroom and cars.

Fabrics and carpets are made from fine individual fibers formed into yarns or tufts used to construct the textile. There are many different natural and man-made fibers, many different ways to produce them, many different colors, and many more ways to make them into textiles. Therefore, each fiber and finished product is made to exacting specifications depending on the designed end use. The microscopist in the crime laboratory is tasked to first identify the fiber and then compare them with possible sources.

The fibers are recovered and compared in the crime laboratory using a variety of microscopic techniques that will identify, characterize, and compare the material composition of the fibers. If, after microscopic and chemical comparison, the questioned and known fibers cannot be distinguished, a match is proclaimed and the forensic scientist can conclude that the fibers could have a common origin. The match is not certain because there are thousands of pounds of fibers made the same and hundreds of garments or carpets made from the same fibers. The value of the fiber evidence depends on the circumstances of the case and on the likelihood that similar fibers will be found in the victim's or assailant's environment, that is, how common the fibers are. Fibers smashed on the car hood that hit a pedestrian are good evidence the car was involved, even if the fibers are a common cotton/polyester blend. Some judgment regarding the commonness can be made simply by looking around, such as in a shopping center, and observing how many people are wearing the same item of clothing.

4.1. Fiber Comparison

Once in the laboratory, fibers are first examined with a stereomicroscope. If the sample contains fragments of fabric, the construction (weave, knit) is also compared and the possibility of physically refitting the fabric with its source is considered. PLM is used to identify the generic class of individual fiber fragments, i.e., whether the fiber is cotton, wool, silk, rayon, polyester, nylon, acrylic, glass, etc., by considering the fiber size and shape and measuring two fundamental optical characteristics, refractive index, and birefringence. The fibers are contrasted further by comparing their fluorescence, their melting point, chemical composition, and dyes.

4.1.1. Refractive Index

PLM is used to determine refractive index, the primary means to identify the different types of fibers. The same methods are used for glass comparisons and for the identification of soil minerals. The refractive index of a transparent material (whether ice, glass, fiber, or gem) is equal to the ratio of the speed of light in a vacuum to the speed of light passing through the material. The difference in the speed causes the light to bend as it passes into and out of the material, just as when looking at a swizzle stick in a martini. In addition, all transparent fibers other than fiberglass display two refractive indices, one for light polarized parallel to the long axis of the fiber and one for light polarized perpendicular to the fiber.

The relative refractive index is determined by observing whether the fiber is higher or lower in refractive index than the liquid it is in, using the Becke line test. By changing the immersion liquid of which the refractive index is known (refractive index liquid), the absolute value can be determined when the object disappears in the right liquid. At that point, the liquid and the fiber have the same refractive index.

4.1.1.1. Becke Line

The edge of a small transparent object immersed in a liquid, such as a fiber or glass fragment immersed in a refractive index liquid, acts as a lens deviating the beam of light coming up through the microscope either toward or away from the object. As the focus is changed by moving the microscope stage up and down, a bright band of light, known as the Becke line, can be seen moving back and forth across the edge. On increasing the distance between objective lens and stage (lowering the stage), the Becke line moves toward the medium with the higher refractive index; conversely, on lowering the objective lens (raising the stage), the Becke line moves toward the medium with the lower refractive index. In this way, the microscopist always knows, with an easy turn of the focusing knob, whether the fiber has a refractive index higher or lower than the liquid, the refractive index of which should always be known. This helps to rapidly identify polyester fibers. For example, if the liquid has a refractive index of 1.66, only polyester fibers will have a refractive index greater than the liquid in one orientation with respect to the polarizer and lesser in the other orientation.

4.1.2. Birefringence

Most fibers have two refractive indices: one for each orientation of the polarizer. The birefringence is defined as the difference between the refractive index parallel and the index perpendicular to the plane of the polarized light. Absolute birefringence is determined by measuring both refractive indices by the Becke line test. The interference colors of the fiber as seen with a polarizing microscope are dependent on the fiber thickness and birefringence based on the formula: Retardation (nm)/Birefringence = 1000× Thickness (mm). The retardation causing the interference colors can be estimated by comparing the colors with a Michel-Lévy chart. The birefringence is then calculated from the formula or estimated from the chart. For a birefringent fiber, the sign of elongation is negative when the parallel index is less than the perpendicular index. Only acrylic fibers have negative signs of elongation.

4.1.3. Fluorescence

Fiber fluorescence usually results from the dyes—there are thousands of dyes. Even fibers similar in color may fluoresce differently when compared using various combinations of filters and a comparison microscope.

4.1.4. Infrared Spectroscopy

FTIR microscopy assists with the identification of man-made fibers because each of the different types has different chemical compositions. Polyester is made from polyethyleneterphthalate, acrylic from polyacrylonitrile, rayon from regenerated cellulose, and nylon is a polyamide. Even within the broad generic classes of fibers, differences may be detected in their composition owing to variations in co-polymers. For example, there are at least nine varieties of acrylic fibers, each with different mixtures of co-polymers that can only be identified by FTIR.

4.1.5. Thermomicroscopy

Melting point can be used to distinguish between different types of nylon or olefin carpet fibers. Nylon 6 melts at about 213°C while nylon 6,6 melts at about 250°C; polyethylene olefin melts at 135°C while polypropylene melts at 170°C.

4.1.6. Comparison Microscopy

If all of the characteristics are still the same, the next step is to examine the fibers with a comparison microscope. Individual fibers are compared side by side; features, such as crimp, color, pigmentation, thickness, luster, and cross-sectional shape, are noted. This side-by-side and point-by-point examination is the best technique to discriminate between fibers from different sources.

4.1.7. Microspectrophotometry

MSP is the most useful way to distinguish fibers that are visually the same, but, in fact, differ only when seen in different light. As different wavelengths of light are passed through the fiber, MSP results in a graph of the color (absorbance vs wavelength of light) and the shape of the graph defines the color. Fibers from the same source will produce the same graphs.

4.1.8. Thin Layer Chromatography

The final step in most fiber comparisons is to extract the dyes from the fibers and compare the constituent dyes using thin layer chromatography. Extracts of the fiber dyes are spotted near the bottom of an absorbent plate, the bottom end of the plate is dipped in a suitable developing solvent, and, as the eluting solvent rises up, the absorbent it rises past the spots of dye, like when toilet paper is dipped in water. The individual dyes from the fiber are moved upwards at differing rates, separating the dyes into colored spots. Extracts from the questioned fibers and the known fibers are run side-by-side and the different dyes are compared with respect to color and position on the plate. Fibers from the same source will contain the same individual dyes. If, after all of these analyses, the questioned and known fibers are indistinguishable, it is likely they originated from the same source.

5. PAINT

In general, the purpose of the analysis and comparison of paint trace evidence is to determine whether two or more samples of paint are from the same source. Paint on a pry-bar used to break open a homeowner's window is a typical example. Traces of paint are recovered from the pry-bar and samples are collected from the window for comparison. The comparison is accomplished through microscopic and chemical analyses. If two samples cannot be distinguished, after completing all appropriate analyses, then a conclusion that they could have originated from the same source is possible.

In other cases, it is important to try to determine the source of the paint without the benefit of a comparison sample. For example, in order to search for a vehicle involved in a hit and run accident, the color, layer structure, and chemical composition of paint collected from the accident site are compared with databases of paint used on all the recently produced cars and trucks. Then the laboratory usually can tell the investigator the color, make, and model of the car they are looking for.

5.1. Collecting Paint

Loose paint chips on cars and window frames can be picked from the surface with tweezers. Intact paint films must be scraped with a strong sharp knife into folded paper packets. The entire paint layer, all the way down to the wood or metal, must be collected. In that way, all the layers will be present for analysis. If clothing is received, the clothing is placed on clean paper for inspection. First, the clothing is searched visually for evidence of a paint transfer. Next, debris is scraped with a clean spatula onto the paper and the debris is searched with a stereomicroscope for paint chips. Chips are examined with a stereomicroscope; the questioned and known samples are compared with respect to colors and layers. Samples are then isolated for PLM, FTIR, or SEM-EDS.

5.2. Paint Comparison

Paint is a protective film applied to a wide variety of products. After evaporation of the solvent vehicle used to spray or spread the coating, the dried paint layers consist of a polymeric binder film containing pigments and fillers (extender pigments). The binder provides a protective coat designed to meet the needs of its intended use. Therefore, the composition of the binder is specifically designed and will differ markedly between paints produced for different uses, such as the differences between exterior and interior house paints. The pigments are added to provide opacity and also to color the film. The number of possible colors is practically innumerable, as seen in a hardware store paint department. The color is caused by a nearly unlimited number of pigments, from the common titanium dioxide white to pearlescent-coated micas used on new cars. Therefore, the forensic paint comparison involves a detailed analysis of color, binder, and pigments for the usual purpose of determining whether two paints are similar.

Most surfaces are painted with multiple coats. For example, most cars are painted with a primer layer, a base coat, a pigmented layer, and a clear coat on the top. The colors, thicknesses, and sequence of the layers are compared. Paint on houses and a myriad of other structures is often applied repeatedly producing a random accumulation of many different layers of different paints of different colors. The number and sequence of the layers, their thickness, and their color, is often sufficient to prove that two multilayered chips of paint originated from the same source. The match is confirmed by aligning the layers under a comparison microscope.

Fracture matches of larger chips are always possible, but usually the paint chips are studied microscopically and analyzed using PLM, SEM-EDS, and FTIR. The comparison begins using a stereomicroscope with accessories for photography and continues using a polarizing microscope, fluorescence microscope and comparison microscope. SEM-EDS assists in identifying and comparing the pigments in each layer of the paint. FTIR is used to identify the binder. Finally, pyrolysis gas chromatography (PGC), a destructive technique that burns the paint and separates the components by gas chromatography, is used to identify the binder constituents and compare the questioned and known paints.

5.3. Quality Control

Complete written and photographic records are required for all trace evidence cases, but paint can be used to illustrate the types of information that are maintained with each case. For example, in addition to taking detailed written notes, during the initial inspection and subsequent analysis and comparison, the paint chips might be photographed. SEM-EDS, FTIR, and PGC results are recorded and maintained in the case file. All correspondence, chain of custody records, complete notes describing samples, testing, results of testing, and conclusions are kept in the project file. Additionally, all equipment used in the testing of samples is calibrated to insure proper performance. Most crime laboratories have approved written procedures that detail the proper calibration, maintenance, and operation of the instruments. Instruments not operating properly cannot be used.

6. GLASS

Glass is found in our kitchens and the restaurants we frequent, in our cars, in the stores where we shop, and in the windows of our houses and offices. The various types of glass are:

1. Flat glass used for windows, doors, display cases, and mirrors.
2. Container glass used for bottles and jars.
3. Tableware glass.
4. Optical glass used for eyewear.
5. Decorative glass, such as stained glass.
6. Specialty glass used for headlamps and cookware.

Fortunately for the forensic investigator, glass broken by impact can produce hundreds of small particles that can be used as trace evidence. Glass might be recovered at the scene of a hit and run accident or on the clothing of a burglar. In any of these cases, the first possibility is that pieces of glass can be physically matched back to the window or bottle from which they were broken.

6.1. Fracture Matching

To prove that two or more pieces definitely originated from the same object, they must be fracture matched. Fractured fragments are broken or torn objects split apart by force into separate pieces, e.g., a broken tool, paint chips, torn paper, or vehicle headlight lens. A fracture match is the re-assembly of two or more separated fragments that proves that the pieces were once one in the same.

Fracture matching in the crime laboratory, like all other analyses of associative evidence, always involves a comparison to determine whether the questioned evidence could have originated from the suspected source. Accidental (individual) characteristics in the fracture, such as imperfections or irregularities produced accidentally during manufacture, growth, or use, or those caused by abuse, corrosion, or damage when broken, are required to distinguish it from all others. As with all trace evidence, an absolute match cannot be made in the absence of individual characteristics. Although an arrangement in shape and printed design are sufficient to allow the putting together of a jigsaw puzzle, more seems to be required in the crime laboratory. Jigsaw puzzles are mass produced, so without the accidental markings caused by the tearing of the pieces, pieces of other puzzles might also match.

In the crime laboratory, the first of four criteria for a fracture match is that the objects must have been separated by either fracturing or tearing, not purposely cut like a puzzle. Second, the separated pieces must be realigned so that the object seems to fit together again. Third, the separated pieces must fit together like a lock and key in one or more of the following ways:

1. Along an irregular zig-zag-like edge.
2. Verified by surface markings like the puzzle picture.
3. Verified by a three-dimensional fit, so that all surfaces fit around the object including the upturned broken edges.

Finally, of course, the markings or broken edges must possess individual characteristics, such as growth rings in wood, machine marks on a tool, or the random marks on the edge of broken glass caused by the break. The match should be tested by moving the two fractured pieces back and forth, observing that they do not fit together in more than one way. There will be only one way in which they actually align in every detail. If they cannot be so aligned, the two pieces were never one and the same.

6.2. Collecting Glass

When looking for small fragments in clothing, the cuffs and pockets are turned out to free any glass that may be caught there. The item can then be tugged, shaken, or brushed over clean paper on the laboratory bench and the paper searched with a stereomicroscope for glass fragments. Shoe soles, weapons, and tools are examined directly with a stereomicroscope, looking for any damaged areas where glass might be embedded. Any cuts or holes in the soles of footwear are probed for glass.

A sharp conchoidal (shell-like) broken edge and transparency distinguishes freshly broken glass from plastic and sand grains. Glass is further distinguished from fragments of plastic and minerals by PLM. Glass is not birefringent like most minerals. Color can usually distinguish between sources of glass and the surface of some glass should fluoresce under short-wave ultraviolet light. Surface features formed during manufacture and a curved surface can help distinguish window glass from container, decorative, and eye glass. Finally, if both the inside and outside surfaces are still part of the glass fragment, the thickness can distinguish between different window glasses.

6.3. Comparison of Glass

If a physical match is not possible, physical and chemical properties of the glass are compared in order to determine whether two pieces could have originated from the same batch. There are two fundamental physical properties used by crime laboratories to compare glass. The first is density.

6.3.1. Density

The density of glass is measured by placing a glass fragment into a liquid, so it floats without sinking or rising to the surface. If the glass remains suspended, the glass and liquid have the same density. The density of the liquid is then either measured directly or the same liquid is used with another fragment of glass to determine whether they are of the same density. Density is very sensitive to small changes in composition. If two samples of glass differ in density, they could not have originated from the same source.

6.3.2. Refractive Index

The second fundamental physical property of glass is refractive index, which also depends on the chemical composition of the glass as well as its manufacturing history. The crime laboratory either uses a manual method or automated image analysis to microscopically measure the refractive index. Both methods are based on a double variation technique, developed by Richard Conrad Emmons at the University of Wisconsin circa 1928, and promoted to the forensic scientists during the second half of the 20th century by Walter C. McCrone. By the proper manipulation of both the temperature and wavelength of light, it is possible to obtain not only the refractive index of the glass, but also how the index varies with the wavelength of light used, called the dispersion curve of the glass. A hot stage is used on the microscope to control the temperature because the refractive index liquids used for these tests depend on the temperature. Color filters are used to control the wavelength of light. In both the manual and automated procedures, the match point of the refractive index is determined by observing the Becke line, like when measuring the refractive indices of fibers, and noting the point where the glass particle disappears (no Becke line), which is the point where the refractive index of the glass matches the refractive index of the liquid. With automated image analysis, the camera and computer detect the point where the glass disappears, records the temperature of the stage, and, thereby, the refractive index of the liquid and the glass. If two samples of glass can be differentiated by their refractive index, they could not have originated from the same source.

6.3.3. Elemental Analysis

The concentrations of most elements in glass are intentionally controlled by the manufacturers in order to make a particular glass product. However, all glass products display variations in the concentration of these elements and contain small concentrations of uncontrolled trace elements. Therefore, element concentrations may be used to differentiate among glasses made by different manufacturers and from different production lines. The methods for determining the elements in the glass include: SEM-EDS, X-ray fluorescence spectrometry (XRF), and inductively coupled plasma-atomic emission and mass spectrometry (ICP). ICP burns the sample up; therefore, all nondestructive examinations must be completed prior to any ICP.

SEM-EDS measurements are nondestructive, applicable to very small samples, and the most readily-available means for elemental analysis in most crime laboratories. The questioned and known glass samples are compared by measuring concentrations of the elements sodium (Na), aluminum (Al), magnesium (Mg), calcium (Ca), and potassium (K). The disadvantage is that SEM-EDS is not as sensitive for some elements as XRF and ICP. XRF requires a larger piece of glass than SEM-EDS, but the element detection for most elements are generally better for XRF than for SEM-EDS. Although destructive, ICP techniques are even more sensitive and measure lower concentrations of more elements, such as Al, barium (Ba), Ca, iron (Fe), Mg, manganese (Mn), Na, titanuium (Ti), strontium (Sr), and zirconium (Zr), providing more points of comparison and improving discrimination between glass sources.

Like all trace evidence comparisons, each of the observations and measured values must be consistent between questioned and known glass in order to prove that glass came from the same source. If any of the findings suggest that the glass differs, then the conclusion must be that the questioned glass sample cannot be associated with the suspected source.

7. SOIL

Mud and clods of dirt are sometimes found on vehicles, shovels, or suspects' shoes. Although soil differs greatly from other types of trace evidence, it serves the same purpose. The usual question is whether the soil came from the crime scene.

7.1. Collecting Soil

Although collecting the questioned sample from shoes, for example, is relatively straightforward, there is nothing else in criminalistics where the choice of a control sample is more difficult than with soil. The difficulty stems from the fact that soil is a dynamic accumulation of particles constantly changing—and usually changing over very short distances. Soil sometimes varies within inches across the landscape and within inches down into the ground. Primary known samples are chosen from the spot where it is suggested the questioned sample originated, such as the location of a shoe, tire print, or grave. Usually several known samples are required to be sure they adequately represent the site where the questioned soil could have originated. Alibi samples are collected from spots where the suspect says the soil is from, that is, the places used as an excuse for the mud on their shoes or their shovel. Alibi samples are of paramount importance. When the suspect's excuses are disproved, the soil evidence is strengthened.

7.2. Soil Comparison

The approach to a forensic soil comparison depends on the background and interests of the examiner. Some examiners have special skills in soil science or mineralogy, others have special skills in palynology (study of pollens and spores), whereas others might pay more attention to the building materials in the soil. Regardless of the emphasis, all approaches compare the microscopic constituents in the questioned soil sample with the microscopic constituents in samples collected from possible sources of the soil. In the end, irrespective of the approach, the conclusion whether the soil could have originated from a suspected source will be based on similarities between the questioned soil and one or more known samples.

The most common approach for comparing soil is to consider its:

- Color.
- Relative amounts of gravel, sand, silt, and clay.
- Mineral composition including the types of rock fragments, heavy minerals, and clay.
- Biological materials like pollen.
- The presence of man-made materials, such as shingle sand, mining and industrial contaminants, and, possibly in unusual circumstances, chemical traces of pesticides.

Color is the most useful of all the soil features for comparison.

More specifically, the color of each sample is noted and then the soil is passed through a set of soil sieves in order to determine the proportion of sand and silt. The color of the sand and silt is compared again. The coarse and medium sands are washed to remove coatings. Heavy minerals (those with specific gravity greater than the more common quartz and feldspars) are separated and the colors are compared again. The types of soil minerals are then identified using PLM and the number of each type counted. At any point where the samples can be distinguished, the process can end or more samples can be collected. When the samples remain indistinguishable throughout the whole process, the crime laboratory can conclude that the soil could have originated from the suspected source.

8. CONCLUSION

Trace evidence encompasses virtually anything that can be touched, broken, pulverized, transferred, shed, and left behind during a crime if a piece of it, no matter how small, can be found during the investigation. Trace evidence can originate from people and their clothing, from the products they make and use, and from the ecological environment. Therefore, it is impossible to describe every type of trace evidence. Furthermore, trace evidence can be used to investigate virtually every imaginable crime, from murder to the theft of Christmas trees. In the latter case, if the trees are taken from the ground and moved to another location, the soil in the ball can be compared with the holes left at the nursery. After recognizing the possibilities, the detective investigating the case must continue the investigation, following all the leads, so the appropriate samples can be obtained and compared in the crime laboratory. The value of trace evidence depends on what can be learned from its analysis and how it fits into the investigation. If the right evidence is brought to the crime laboratory, the crime laboratory has all the tools necessary to associate the trace evidence to the right culprits.

GLOSSARY

Absorbance:	The ratio of light (visible, ultraviolet or infrared) absorbed by a substance relative to the corresponding absorption of a blackbody or reference; when measured over a range of wavelengths, the resulting spectrum of absorbance is used to characterize materials.
Accidental or individual characteristics:	Characteristics of materials caused by unique growth patterns or by wear and tear, used to individualize evidence such as fingerprints or footwear impressions.
Alternate light source:	Usually hand-held crime scene investigation equipment used to produce visible and invisible light at various wavelengths to enhance or visualize potential items of trace evidence, such as body fluids, fingerprints, and clothing fibers.
Birefringence:	The numerical difference between the maximum and minimum refractive indices of anisotropic substances (minerals and fibers, for example); birefringence may also be determined with the aid of compensators, or estimated through use of the Michel-Lévy Interference Color Chart.
Comparison microscope:	Two matching compound microscopes joined together with an optical bridge that allows specimens on both microscopes to be viewed simultaneously, thereby

allowing a direct side-by-side comparison between the two specimens.

Compensator:
A birefringent section of optical quartz, gypsum, mica, or similar material that is positioned between the polarizer and analyzer in a polarizing microscope; the plate can sometimes be tilted and/or rotated to measure retardation.

Conchoidal:
The fracturing properties of certain kinds of stone, glass and ceramic; for example, in flint and glass, a fractured surface will exhibit roughly circular ridges radiating outwards from the point of impact, shaped like the exterior surface of a conch shell.

Condenser lens:
A lens mounted below the compound microscope stage whose purpose is to focus or condense the light onto the specimen; condenser lenses are not used on low-power stereomicroscopes.

Cuticle:
The outermost layer of the shaft of a hair, comprised of overlapping scales.

Density:
Density is the mass of a substance per unit volume, expressed, for example, as grams (g) per cubic centimeter (cc), pounds per square inch, etc.; specific gravity is the ratio of the density of a substance to the density of some standard substance, such as pure water with a density of 1 g/cc, usually taken as the standard.

Depth of field:
The distance between the nearest and farthest points that appear in acceptably sharp focus in the plane of the specimen; depth of focus is the distance between the nearest and farthest points that appear in acceptably sharp focus in the plane of the image; both vary with lens aperture, focal length, and lens-to-object distance.

Dispersion:
In optics, dispersion is a phenomenon that causes the separation of a light wave into spectral components with different wavelengths (colors of the rainbow); in microscopy it describes the variation of optical properties owing to the use of different wavelengths of light.

Energy Dispersive Spectrometer:
An instrument, usually attached to a scanning electron microscope, that collects X-rays produced by interaction of the electron beam of the microscope with the material analyzed and which have energies characteristic of the elements in the specimen; the abundance (concentration) of the elements can also be

	determined as a percentage of the total amount of sample analyzed.
Eyepiece:	Also called an ocular, the lens system closest to your eye when looking through a microscope; a small tube that contains the lenses needed to bring a microscope's focus to a final image in the eye; the magnifying power of the microscope is the magnification of the eyepiece times the magnification of the objective times any tube factor which may be present; a binocular or stereo microscope has two matching eyepieces, a monocular microscope has one eyepiece.
Fourier transform infrared spectrometry:	Infrared spectrophotometers record the interaction of IR radiation with substances which allows identification of the sample's functional groups in the chemical makeup; when the effects of all the different functional groups are taken together, the result is a unique molecular "fingerprint" that can be used to confirm the identity of a sample. A Fourier transform is a mathematical operation used to translate a complex curve into its component curves. In a Fourier transform infrared spectrometer, the complex curve is an interferogram, or the sum of the constructive and destructive interferences generated by overlapping light waves, and the component curves are the infrared spectrum. The standard infrared spectrum is calculated from the Fourier-transformed interferogram, giving a spectrum in percent transmittance (%T) vs. light frequency (cm-1).
Gas chromatography:	GC is a type of chromatography in which the sample, usually dissolved in a solvent, is vaporized and carried by an inert gas through a column packed with a sorbent to any of several types of detectors; each component of the sample, separated from the others by passage through the column, produces a separate peak in the detector. Pyrolysis gas chromatography is where the sample is made volatile by burning rather than by dissolving in a solvent.
Gunshot residue:	Gunshot residue (GSR) testing is used in the investigation of suspected use of firearms; the residues usually include gun powder particles and components from the primer, the bullet, the cartridge case and the firearm itself; some of the primer particles (containing lead, antimony and barium) in the residue are unique to GSR.

Heavy mineral:

Heavy minerals (e.g. rutile, zircon) have a specific gravity greater than 2.89; heavy mineral grains are often found as a minor but important component in soil; they are separated from the lighter minerals (quartz, feldspars) by flotation in a heavy liquid such as bromoform (tribromomethane) which has a density of 2.8899 g/cc; that is, the heavy minerals sink in the bromoform while the light minerals float.

Hot stage:

A platform that sits on a microscope stage under the objective lens and which holds the specimen slide and controls the temperature of the slide, refractive index liquid and sample; the sample can then be observed while the temperature of the specimen is raised and lowered in a controlled manner over a temperature range between room temperature usually to about a maximum of 300 degrees Celsius.

Image analysis:

Image analysis is the extraction from digital images of useful information such as sizes and shapes by means of computer processing techniques; image analysis tasks can be as simple as reading bar-coded tags or as sophisticated as identifying a person by his face.

Immersion liquid:

A liquid of known refractive index used to microscopically measure and compare the refractive index of small particles.

Inductively coupled plasma atomic emission:

A method for measurement of the concentration of elements in a substance; in ICP the plasma is generated from radio frequency magnetic fields in a torch resulting in extremely high temperatures; samples are injected into the center of the plasma where the sample molecules undergo instantaneous vaporization, dissociation, ionization and excitation. Atomic Emission Spectrometry is based on the principle that during reversion to the ground state an excited atom or ion releases absorbed energy as light (photons) with wavelengths that are characteristic of an element and intensities that can be measured to determine the concentration of the element.

Interference color:

In microscopy, these are the Newtonian series of colors seen when observing samples with more than one refractive index (anisotropic samples) between fully-crossed polarizers in non-extinction orientations; interference colors are illustrated in Michel-Lévy Interference Color Charts.

Luster:
: Brightness or reflectivity of fibers, yarns, carpets, or fabrics; synthetic fibers are produced in various luster classifications including bright, semi-bright, semi-dull, and dull; bright fibers usually are clear (have no white pigment) whereas the duller designations have small amounts of white pigments (delusterants) such as titanium dioxide.

Magnification:
: The magnification is simply the number of times the image of an object is enlarged when viewed through the microscope; the total magnification is the product of the eyepiece magnification, the objective magnification, and the variable tube factor if there is one.

Mass spectrometry:
: Instrumental method for identifying the chemical constitution of a substance by separating gaseous ions according to their differing mass and charge, often combined with other analytical techniques, such as gas chromatography (GC), liquid chromatography (LC) and inductively coupled plasma (ICP) mass spectrometry (MS).

Medulla:
: The central canal found in many human and animal hairs, usually visible with a microscope as a black line because the canal is filled with air.

Michel-Lévy birefringence chart:
: The Michel-Lévy Interference Color Chart, also known as the Michel-Lévy Table of Birefringence, graphically relates the thickness, retardation (optical path difference), and birefringence (numerical difference between the principal refractive indices) for transparent anisotropic substances viewed between the crossed polars of a polarizing microscope.

Microspectrophotometry:
: A technique for measuring the spectral absorption of light, usually in nanometers, by comparing the difference between the absorption of the sample and a reference sample.

Objective:
: The lens in a microscope closest to the specimen that first gathers light from the specimen and forms the first magnified image.

Ocular:
: The eyepiece of a microscope which serves to further magnify the image formed by the objec-

tive lens and focuses the image for viewing or photography.

Palynology: The branch of science dealing with microscopic, decay-resistant remains of certain plants and animals, particularly pollen and spores, both living and fossil.

Particle: A minute portion of matter; a very small piece or part of something bigger.

Polarizing microscope: A compound microscope employing polarized light to show changes in internal structure and composition of material not discernible with ordinary light.

Polymer: Any of numerous natural and synthetic compounds, usually of high molecular weight, consisting of up to millions of repeated linked units where each unit is a relatively light and simple molecule, usually formed into a plastic.

Refractive index: The ratio of the velocity of light in a vacuum to the velocity of light in a medium (solid, liquid, gas); expressed as n, the refractive index varies with wavelength and temperature.

Retardation: The number of wavelengths by which the polarized rays passing through a substance between crossed polars of the polarizing microscope fall behind each other; the amount of retardation increases with thickness and the birefringence of the crystal and is expressed in interference colors.

Scanning electron microscope: An electron microscope with a fine beam of electrons that systematically sweeps or scans (moves point-to-point) over the surface of a specimen, producing highly magnified, detailed images of the surface with excellent depth of field; most scanning electron microscopes are equipped with accessories for doing elemental analysis as well.

Sign of elongation: A term used to describe the location of the high and low refractive indices in an elongated, anisotropic substance; by convention, a specimen is described as positive (+) when the higher refractive index ("slow direction") is lengthwise ("length slow"), and negative (-) when the lower refractive index ("fast direction") is lengthwise ("length fast").

Thin layer chromatography: A procedure for separating compounds by spotting them on a glass or plastic plate coated with a thin layer of silica or alumina gel; a solvent is allowed to move up the plate by capillary action to separate components of the sample into visible spots; TLC is used for identifying and comparing materials which are highly colored or which fluoresce under ultraviolet light, such as fiber dyes.

Trace element:
An element making up only a very small portion of the substance, often in parts per million.

Trace evidence:
Trace evidence might be anything that can be described as small bits of solid material used in a forensic investigation, such as particles of dust creating a footwear impression, torn scraps of paper from a threatening note, gunshot residue particles, clothing fibers, paint chips, pubic hairs, or diatoms; trace evidence associates people with people, people with places, objects with people, objects with places and objects with objects; trace evidence, thereby, provides evidence to help understand the behavior of parties to accidents and crimes.

Wavelength:
The distance between two successive points of an electromagnetic waveform, such as light and X-rays, usually measured in nanometers (nm).

X-rays:
X-rays are a type of electromagnetic radiation between ultraviolet light and gamma rays in wavelength, frequency, and energy; X-rays have short wavelengths (and high frequency) as compared to visible light and therefore can pass through most solid objects.

REFERENCES

1. Schierenbeck KA. Forensic Biology. J Forensic Sci 2003;48:696.
2. Li ZR. Industrial Applications of Electron Microscopy. New York: Marcel Dekker, 2002.

SUGGESTED READING

Saferstein, R. Forensic Science Handbook, Volume I, Second Edition. Pearson Prentice Hall, Upper Saddle River, New Jersey, 2002; Volume II, Second Edition. Pearson Prentice Hall, Upper Saddle River, New Jersey, 2005; Volume III. Regents Prentice Hall, Englewood Cliffs, New Jersey, 1993.

Siegle, J. Saukko, PJ and Knupfer, GC. Encyclopedia of Forensic Sciences. Elsevier Academy Press, London, 2000.

Houck, M. Mute Witnesses: Trace Evidence Analysis. Elsevier Academy Press, London, 2001.

Houck, M. Mute Witnesses: More Cases in Trace Evidence Analysis. Elsevier Academic Press, London, 2004.

Murray, R. Evidence from the Earth: Forensic Geology and Criminal Investigation. Mountain Press Publishing Company, Missoula, MT, 2004.

Petraco N and Kubic T. Color Atlas and Manual of Microscopy for Criminalists, Chemists, and Conservators. Boca Raton, FL, CRC Press, 2002.

Index